Hoover Institution Publications 144

Radicals in the University

"The tension between self and community is inherent in our politics."

Barbara and Al Haber

" ... the movement has failed to make contact with the people who are in it, has failed to comprehend itself."

Paul Potter

"No one who believes that truth is on his side can honestly object to scholarly investigation, even of himself, his motives, and his actions."

Seymour Martin Lipset and
Gerald M. Schaflander

Radicals in the University

Edward E. Ericson, Jr.

Hoover Institution Press
Stanford University
Stanford, California

The Hoover Institution on War, Revolution and Peace, founded at Stanford University in 1919 by the late President Herbert Hoover, is a center for advanced study and research on public and international affairs in the twentieth century. The views expressed in its publications are entirely those of the authors and do not necessarily reflect the views of the staff, officers, or Board of Overseers of the Hoover Institution.

Hoover Institution Publications 144
International Standard Book Number 0–8179–6441–X
Library of Congress Catalog Card Number 75–27011
© 1975 by the Board of Trustees of the
    Leland Stanford Junior University
Printed in the United States of America

Contents

Acknowledgments

This book was written while I enjoyed a year of research as a National Fellow at the Hoover Institution on War, Revolution and Peace of Stanford University. I wish to express my sincere gratitude to Dr. Glenn Campbell, Director, and members of the Hoover staff for granting me this award and making my year at the Institution one of the most memorable of my life. In particular, I wish to acknowledge the invaluable help given me by the two Milorads of my acquaintance. Milorad Popov read the manuscript and offered incisive criticisms. Milorad Drachkovitch not only offered professional advice and assistance far beyond the call of duty, but has become a close friend and admired colleague. Few persons of my acquaintance have combined such high standards of scholarship in their own work with such breadth of learning and humane wisdom and such warmth and integrity of person. As a person much more than as a scholar, I am profoundly in his debt. Thanks also go to Kay Dull for indexing and proofreading this manuscript. Finally, I wish to acknowledge the patience and understanding of my wife and children in bearing with me as I have stolen time from them to do this project.

Introduction

The youth Movement of dissent in the 1960s which became known as the New Left has had a profound impact on the cultural topography of the United States. A veritable library of books produced on the subject is ample testimony to the extent and depth of the challenge posed by these new radicals. In some ways it is surprising that so much ink should have been spilled over a phenomenon which did not represent a cross-section of Americans, involved only a minuscule percentage of the population, lasted for only a few years, and destroyed itself without accomplishing its announced objectives.

The attention lavished on these young people by outsiders and their own confidence in their self-importance ironically undercut their egalitarian principles, but necessarily so: they were indeed an elite. Most of them attended prestige universities; thus, it was no accident that the new radicalism, while not strictly confined to such campuses, certainly showed far more strength there than anywhere else. After graduation, these students were expected to go on to positions of influence within institutions comprising the mainstream of American society, and to lead affluent private lives. That they rebelled against settling into the comfortable niches reserved for them made them newsworthy, and they received their due publicity. That this highly advantaged group of young people articulated the reasons for their refusal, and that these reasons were often intrinsically laudable, made them worthy of serious study.

Since most New Leftists were students, previous studies of the Movement have focused on its student component. Students do not remain students, however, and some New Leftists now have a decade or more of involvement behind them. The student Movement also attracted the adherence of some adults, generally young, who have had to face certain issues of maturation not yet confronted by students. A study of these issues reveals much about the basis for adult life which was afforded by the Movement. Many of these young adults—probably the most important adult exponents of the new radicalism—have found positions in the academy. Following the general collapse of an organized student New Left presence, radical caucuses formed by these adults within their several academic disciplines have been the most important remaining organizational manifestation of the Movement. It is these "aging" young radicals who will be the subject of this book.

Among the diverse pronouncements of the New Left, the determinative criterion for selection of those strains of thought which will be discussed is provided by such a focus. The New Left went through several phases in which conflicting ideas were promulgated. All of these phases and ideas had their impact on the academic radicals, but some have had greater influence than others. To be specific, it was the Students for a Democratic Society (SDS), the central organization of the white New Left, which served as the primary reference point for the radicals. So when the term *New Left* is invoked, it will generally refer to SDS. Moreover, the first generation of SDSers—later known as the old guard—provided a fairly coherent body of thought which can be fruitfully analyzed and which proved normative for the academic radicals. The major portion of SDS spokesmen will be from this group.

This inquiry had its genesis in an interest in the essays written by radicals in the literary profession. These faculty members expressed concerns which were not the general fare of literary scholarship: the relationship of literature to morals and to life in general, the nature of objectivity in literary studies, and a variety of questions about the very *raison d'être* and function of the teaching of literature in the university. Yet the political framework within which these issues were raised seemed altogether detachable from the important issues themselves, not at all intrinsic to them. To investigate these matters and, along with them, the total impact of the new radicalism on the literary profession was the initial design of this study.

That impact has been felt widely and deeply, beginning with what some radicals have labeled the "Little Bourgeois Cultural Revolution" at the 1968 convention of the Modern Language Association of America (MLA), the largest of the learned societies. Two of the last three presidents of MLA have been new radicals. Another edits *College English*, one of the most widely circulated journals in the literary profession and a house organ of the National Council of Teachers of English; a few issues of *College English* have been entirely devoted to essays by new radicals. Another is editor of *Victorian Studies*, a prestigious specialized journal. Since 1968 the literary profession's learned societies have devoted considerable time and energy grappling with political issues placed on the agenda by the radicals. No other points considered by these societies have generated as much interest and passion as those presented under radical auspices.

The number of new radicals in the literary profession has never been great. With one exception, they do not include the "big names" of the profession, although some have made a name for themselves through their recent activities. Their importance lies not in numerical strength, but in the intrinsic qualities of their opinions and in the dedicaton which has forced the profession to deal with their physical and intellectual presence.

Although the original subject of this study was intended to be the literary radicals, it was soon apparent that they were applying to the discipline of literature some of the broad challenges posed by radicals to the university as a whole. To place the literary radicals in proper perspective, it was thus necessary to consider the general claims of radicals against the university. It then developed that the proper context for understanding academic radicals was not the profession but the Movement. This was a point repeatedly proclaimed by the academic radicals themselves. The background for a proper understanding of the academic radicals thus required consideration of the Movement, particularly SDS, and most particularly the SDS old guard.

What emerges in this study is an organizational pattern of three concentric circles. SDS is first considered. In this section there is a persistent effort to follow the main lines of development of New Left thought and not to become sidetracked into discussions of the many fascinating but ultimately secondary matters which consumed much of the SDSers' energy. Many elements of the analysis of SDS contained in this section can be found elsewhere, but not in the same total configuration as herein presented.

The next circle is the New University Conference (NUC), the central organizational presence of the new academic radicalism that grew directly out of SDS. At point after point NUC replayed the same tensions and conflicts which attended the experience of SDS—another reason, of course, for analyzing SDS as background.

Finally, the literary radicals are considered, their present organizational form being the Radical Caucus in English and the Modern Languages. Again, one sees a playing out of those difficulties observable in both NUC and SDS. In each of the three concentric circles, the same basic issues underlie the discussion within the separate groups and hence in this study.

Because of these parallels, this study maintains a dual focus. The analysis of SDS casts a light forward on the academic radicals. But since the latter are direct products of the Movement of the 1960s, an analysis of them casts a retrospective light on the preceding New Left experience. By examining what they have come to be, to do, and to say, one can gain insight into the strengths and weaknesses of the Movement which nurtured them. The study of SDS, then, becomes something more than a piece of background for the study of academic radicalism. Interpretation of it becomes a goal in its own right.

Little attention is paid to the historical antecedents of the New Left. There are two reasons for this stratagem. One is simply limitation of space. But more important, the New Left was not established by conscious interaction with the thoughts of earlier radical movements and spokesmen. Theirs was a radicalism which issued from the gut, not from books. Cutting themselves off from the possibility of intellectual and political forebears, these new radicals sought to give birth to themselves. Thus, while interesting historical comparisons and contrasts could be made, they would not illuminate the unique character of the *New* Left.

The main thesis of this study is that the New Left was plagued with internal contradictions from which there was no escape short of abandonment of the original position which it had staked out for itself. The root conflict, out of which others grew, was the twin desire of the original New Leftists for personal and political liberation. These are not intrinsically incompatible, but articulation by the New Left made them so. All other contradictions—and the New Leftists themselves were keenly aware of them and tried valiantly to reconcile the disparate terms—grew out of this fundamental conflict. At point after point the New Left sought to achieve solidarity while seeking two goals. It could not do so, and it is therefore not by accident that these two poles—the personal and the political—have now split apart, many Movement people now openly pursuing one at the expense of the other. According to this analysis, such contradictions were inherent and inevitable, not tangential and accidental.

The New Left's longing to fuse the personal with the political affirmed a deep-felt need for unity, for a life in which thought and action, the private and the public roles, would be harmonious. The irony is that more than a decade of experimentation in this direction has ended in division and disarray. All of the primary organizations established during the 1960s have collapsed. The organizational death of the New Left makes this a propitious moment for an analysis of the phenomenon. A relatively stable point has been reached which allows a retrospective survey of recent history without too much fear of a shift during the process. Some individual radicals retain the primary allegiances which they developed during the 1960s. The dream dies hard, and for many it has not died at all. While a new phoenix could conceivably arise from the ashes of the Movement, the present moment would still represent a hiatus in the historical flux of this social phenomenon.

It is unlikely that the new radicals themselves will find this study to their liking; doubtless they would reject its central import. But it is often the case that self-interpretation is not always the most reliable; this seems especially applicable to the new radicalism. The very fact that they have so often shifted their ground and rejected central tenets of the position held a few years earlier is strong evidence that this is so. Gropings toward accurate self-definition continue. Such efforts—often highly articulate, revealing, and generally emanating from the old guard—are crucially helpful to an outside observer. Granting that participant status allows certain insights unlikely to be captured by an onlooker, the reverse is equally true: an outsider does not have the personal stake in the phenomenon which might readily and excusably cloud the participant's vision.

Because of the tremendous heterogeneity within the Movement, by citing fugitive references it is possible to make the phenomenon into anything one wishes. References included herein are intended to give a fair sampling of the main lines of the Movement's development. The heaviest reliance on quotations to carry the argument comes at those points where the interpretation offered seems to depart most radically from the received opinions.

Not only does this study describe the phenomenon under investigation, but it pays it the implicit compliment of taking it seriously enough to interact with it. While every attempt has been made to reflect the phenomenon accurately, this study is not intended to be a dispassionate, impersonal work of history. The radicals have urged that the scholarly profession reinsert into its dialogue the dimension of personal commitment. This study is premised on the belief that their urgings on this matter have a basic validity.

Regrettably, little help was received from the radicals in research for this book, though it was solicited. One correspondent suggested that the "finks" of literature should be examined and that he did not want to be studied. Others declared that they would not assist in a scholarly endeavor of writing on this subject unless the author was "a scholar of the left." Another justified the reluctance of his colleagues to be helpful on the grounds that the radicals were supremely concerned about the social uses to which scholarship was put; he suggested that this study, however fair-minded the intentions underlying it, would inevitably be used to weaken the radicals' position. Another radical made the same general point by saying that the book would be used by witch-hunters to ferret out communists from teaching positions. A few radicals were cooperative, and their help is gratefully acknowledged; for obvious reasons they shall remain nameless.

Part I

The Students for a Democratic Society and Radical Social-Political Criticism

The Early Phase of the New Left

A schema within which to understand the major movements of ideas during the history of the New Left's existence will not focus on such factors as organizations, personages, meetings, actions, and dates, but on those ideas which were the motive force underlying the external history of the New Left. Other elements will be introduced only as they are necessary to explicate those ideas. To determine what was new about the New Left is of major interest. Clearly, these young radicals inherited much from their parents and mentors, even when they consciously reacted against them, but there was a genuinely new element in their position.

Richard Flacks, an early member of SDS and an excellent analyst of the Movement, traced three phases in the history of the New Left. The first covered 1960–64 and was that of pacifism, protest, and reform. The second, spanning 1964–68, included confrontation, radicalization, and resistance. The third, from 1968 on, he entitled "Beyond Student Protest"— his euphemism, it seems, for violence.[1] While this division is helpful, it is tied too closely to important dates of recent American electoral politics and does not grow organically out of the internal dynamics of the New Left itself. Flacks was correct to discern three phases in the evolution of New Left thought, but the transitions were too blurred to make precise date-setting useful.

The first stage ran into 1965 and was a period of activist protest based on moral and personalist values. It was essentially non-ideological; the general tenor of its politics was more reformist than revolutionary. The second stage, roughly covering 1965 through 1967, grew out of disillusionment caused by lack of success in making significant changes in American society. There ensued a desperate search for an ideology to support the activism in which SDS was engaged and to provide it with an intellectual framework. In 1968 and 1969, the third stage saw a fragmentation of SDS into warring factions. Principal lines of opposition were a full acceptance of Marxism–Leninism and a reversion to the personalist and existentialist concerns of the early SDS. Each of these periods was of briefer duration than the previous one, as SDS hurtled toward its cataclysmic end in 1969.

These divisions are not rigid. While each introduced something new into the SDS position, it did not mark the end of preceding lines of thought. Many themes of the early SDS lasted into succeeding periods, often clashing with those being introduced. A number of the old guard retained their original sensitivities, though they were influenced to varying degrees by notions originating with their younger colleagues.

General Characteristics

Reform, Not Revolution

The early New Left was politically reformist, as was the parent organization of SDS—the League for Industrial Democracy. Flacks recalled, "In its beginning, the new left . . . hoped for an alliance for social reform that would combine elements of the labor movement, liberal political reformers, the civil rights movement, liberal churches and students and intellectuals— a movement that would use both direct action and the electoral process to build a political base for achieving racial equality, eliminating domestic poverty, ending the arms race and the cold war, and building a more democratically organized social order."[2] His call for "a restoration of democratic consciousness and democratic action"[3] reflected the moderate tone of the early SDS. As late as 1966, Todd Gitlin, president of SDS in 1963, stated the major guiding principle of early New Left politics and spelled out in some detail a program which would qualify as a successful implementation of that principle:

> *Power must be shared among those affected, and resources guaranteed to make this possible.* This formula is quite precise. It means, for example, that slums should be rebuilt according to plans adopted by the residents, with capital provided from public funds and labor from the neighborhood. Welfare programs should be supervised by recipients, until welfare becomes superfluous because a decent income is guaranteed for all who will not or cannot work. The mass media should be opened up to all comers, with no restrictions except a bias toward dissent. Political candidates should be publicly subsidized. The university's curricular and extracurricular decisions should be up

to students and faculty alone. The great corporations should, some-how, be made responsible to workers and consumers.... New political institutions are needed to localize and distribute as much power as possible.[4]

Antipathy toward Ideology

The early New Left felt that something was desperately wrong with American society, but it candidly admitted that it did not possess a set of programmatic answers. Gitlin's list, for instance, was intended to be only suggestive. Early New Leftists were consciously hostile to ideology *per se*,[5] and they viewed this hostility as a strength, not a weakness: "When you ask where SDS is going, if you mean ... 'what's the outline for the future society?' our answer is, 'we don't have one.' This is a virtue rather than a failing of SDS. In the course of action, the real action taken by SDS members, the answers will come. The future will emerge in the course of action."[6]

This hostility to ideology was, in large measure, what initially dis-tinguished the New Left from the Old Left. The New Left seems to have made an effort to be radical without reference to any previous tradition of radical political theory. Loren Baritz called it "an attempt to begin the world of radicalism anew, from scratch, in line with the self-consciousness of occupying a unique moment in time, a present presumably discontin-uous with the past."[7] It was not that most new radicals had studied Marxist or other revolutionary ideology carefully and then consciously rejected it; rather, they rejected it without careful study, because of what they per-ceived to be the sterility and failure of the Old Left since the 1930s.[8]

An index of the non-ideological character of the early New Left was the vague usage of terms which, in other hands, have been given precise definitions—terms such as *socialism, class, liberal, bourgeois,* and even *ideology*.[9] In a 1965 speech Paul Potter, then president of SDS, called for a naming of the system which the radicals opposed, but confessed his inability to do so.[10] Radicals liked to describe themselves as comprising a movement for social change, a phrase in which both terms, *movement* and *social change,* were deliberately vague. *Movement* conveyed a sense of motion but not direction; *change* expressed a process but not a goal, means but not ends. The imprecision of New Leftists caused one to remark, "In a sense we are lost, for we do drift about in rough and uncharted seas. We are fearful that if we do establish a steady course it may take us some-where we do not want to go."[11]

Negations

One need not have an ideological stance to be able to criticize the established order, and this the radicals did wholeheartedly. In Tom Hayden's words, "Thus far we have been quick to know what we oppose: racism, militarism, nationalism, oppression of mind and spirit, unrestrained capitalism, provincialism of various kinds, and the bombs. It has been an almost instinctive opposition. We have been hurt by what exists, and we have responded in outrage and compassion."[12] Greg Calvert and Carol Neiman were later to summarize the new radical consciousness of the early 1960s as " 'anti-system consciousness'—that is, as a non-historical, non-socialist rejection of the dominant social institutions."[13] Only so long as the radicals kept within the bounds of protest—that is, of negative politics—did their Movement cohere.

The Personal-Political Conflict

While SDS has generally been considered a political phenomenon, its earliest spokesmen gave equal emphasis to personal liberation. They saw integration of the personal and the political as the main distinction between themselves and radicals of preceding generations, who, they felt, countenanced a bifurcation between the spheres of public policy and private morality. Flacks summarized the early SDS thinking: "If I understand what we are trying to work on when we say we are building a 'movement,' I think it has to do with two types of goals. One, which we might call 'existential humanism,' is expressed by the desire to change the way we, as individuals, actually live and deal with other people. . . . Second, we say that we seek a radical transformation of the social order. In short, that we act politically because our values cannot be realized in any durable sense without a reconstruction of the political and social system."[14]

The Primacy of the Personal

In early New Left formulations, the personal always preceded the political. Problems always precede remedies; the problems were perceived as personal, while the remedies were perceived as political. The Port Huron Statement of 1962, the first SDS manifesto, stated clearly the desire for development of the individual: "Men have unrealized potential for self-cultivation, self-direction, self-understanding, and creativity. It is this potential that we regard as crucial and to which we appeal."[15] Reflecting on the experience of himself and other SDSers, Flacks summarized: "For many youths . . . the cultural crisis is experienced as a crisis of identity—an inability to define the meaning of one's life and to accept the meanings and models of adulthood offered by parents and other elders."[16] They were impelled to become radicals not by what they thought, but by what they felt. Thinking about society came afterwards and tried to mirror the feeling faithfully. As Keniston discovered, "Again and again, they [young radicals] stressed the personal origins of political beliefs, and the effects of political involvement in their personal lives."[17] This personalistic note ran like a thread throughout the history of the New Left. There were times when it was muted, but it never disappeared; it was central to the self-definition of New Leftists.

Rejection of the Apolitical Option

Despite the great importance which the New Left attached to the search for personal authenticity and coherence, the Movement did not pursue an apolitical development. It could have done so, as Flacks remarked: "it seems to me entirely possible for each of us to guide our own way of living according to such standards [those pertaining to existential humanism] and consequently strive to approach an ethical existence. And the achievement of some approximation of community for ourselves and those immediately near us seems plausibly independent of political change."[18]

There were two main reasons why the New Left did not drift into privatism. One was a strong sense of responsibility to be of use to others— what has been sarcastically labeled the "do-gooder" mentality of liberalism. Flacks's rejection of privatism was representative: "The danger here it seems to me is that of irresponsibility: of a search for personally satisfying modes of life while abandoning the possibility of helping others to change theirs."[19]

The second and more important reason why the New Leftists rejected the apolitical option was their belief that the causes of their personal anguish lay in the dislocations of the political order. Something was wrong with American life, and they could never achieve genuine wholeness as persons without having corrected those social ills. The Port Huron Statement articulated the New Left's mission as bringing people to "see the political, social, and economic sources of their private troubles and organize to change society."[20] Personal needs provided the motive power; politics provided a channel through which amelioration of those needs could flow.

The tension between the personal and the political is, by its nature, not an easy one to hold together. Flacks explained why: "The obvious difficulty

with trying to encompass both existential humanism and radical politics is
that they are not only plausibly independent, but sometimes incompatible.
Thus the effort to be politically effective can involve one in efforts at
manipulation and compromise. The effort to be morally consistent can
radically separate one from effective communication with others."[21] That
incompatibility which Flacks acknowledged was to become painfully
apparent by the late 1960s. Even early in the decade, SDS success in holding the two together was doubtful. While the political was certainly
present in the Port Huron Statement and other pronouncements by SDS
leaders, the personal seemed to command a much deeper allegiance.
Primacy of the personal over the political was not the relationship which
the SDS founders wanted to achieve between the two. But reality and
hope differ, and what they hoped for they did not realize.

The fundamental conflict between the personal and the political surfaced in several forms: for instance, the tension between seeking liberation
for oneself and seeking it for others, the tension between activism and
theory, and the tension between vision and organization. The point is not
that these tandem concepts are inherently contradictory, but that they
became so as defined by the New Left.

Liberation: for Self or Others?

The early New Leftists tried to encompass two goals: liberation for the
self and liberation for others. On the one hand, there was the early and
frequently reiterated New Left slogan, "A liberal wants to free others; a
radical wants to free himself."[22] On the other hand, the early SDS was
concerned with improving the lot of others whom it considered directly
oppressed by the American social structure. Calvert and Neiman reflected:
"The new left has consistently refused to fight its major battles on reformist
issues of immediate self-interest. . . . In the early years of the new left, the
new movement was involved principally in the liberal organizing programs
for civil rights and in protest against the war in Vietnam. In liberal fashion,
it fought 'other people's battles' as though the problems of America were
exterior to our lives."[23]

Keniston's essay, "You Have to Grow Up in Scarsdale," offered a schema
which illuminates this conflict. He spoke of two revolutions, each with a
different historical origin and both to be found in New Left rhetoric:

The first revolution is the now-traditional but once radical demand for
inclusion, citizenship, or "universalism"—the demand that all men be
granted the freedoms, goods, and privileges that were once the pre-

rogative of a tiny aristocracy or a small upper *bourgeoisie*. The second revolution is built upon the first: it is the revolution of those who take the freedoms, goods, and privileges of the first revolution for granted, seeing them largely as facts of life. Such people, mostly young, seek some new fulfillment beyond material abundance, some psychological liberation beyond political freedom.[24]

A call for societal change was inherent in any effort to effect the first revolution. Such was not necessarily the case regarding the second, the one which motivated affluent youths to join a movement for social change in the 1960s.

Activism and Theory

Just as liberation of self had primacy over liberation of others, so the early New Leftists gave activism primacy over theory. Carl Wittman and Tom Hayden wrote in 1963: "clearly it is not an ideology that will give us a legitimate and radical place; rather it is the role we play in the community."[25] The primacy of activism over theory did not mean that the activism was to be random; rather, general self-evident principles were to guide the action.[26] The Port Huron Statement, while eschewing closed theories, advocated an activism governed by basic principles of human and social values. It further contended that the actions designed to combat social ills made apparent by those basic principles would, in turn, yield an overarching theory about American society which would orient and shape further actions—a theory which grew organically out of an analysis of concrete social conditions and was not borrowed from some previous tradition of radical social theory.[27]

While the emphasis on activism left the radicals open to the charge of anti-intellectualism, the accusation only obliquely fitted the founders of SDS. They were "inevitably confronted with a conflict between acting in order to change things and reflecting in order to know what to change,"[28] but they did not opt for that "mindless activism" of which the New Left was later frequently accused. Rather did the early SDS set for itself a huge intellectual task: the construction of a new radical social theory that would be indigenous to America and that would fit with precision the contemporary American scene. Flacks spoke to this point: "Only a handful of people ever are eager to destroy the present without knowing something about what happens next—and these would be among the least wholesome persons to lead a movement."[29] That the New Leftists proved unable to invest a new comprehensive social theory convicts them of no more serious a fault than that of *hubris*—perhaps serious enough in itself.

The fact remains that the tension between activism and theory was never resolved and that activism prevailed over theory. This closely parallels the relationship of the personal and the political, the parent conflict which gave birth to that of activism vs. theory. In neither case were the two terms of the equation held in balance.

Ends and Means

Another tension growing out of the personal-political conflict was that between ends and means: the motivating vision and the day-to-day operations intended to move the radicals along toward fulfillment of that vision. During the early 1960s, the overarching vision remained a daydream for SDSers. They had not developed a radical social theory to provide an abstract model of their version of the good society. While they called for the development of such a vision, they were ambivalent about the possibility of working out even a hypothesis. The Port Huron Statement declared, "The decline of utopia and hope is in fact one of the defining features of social life today."[30] While it rejected the reassurance "that America will 'muddle through,' " a rejection which intimated the need for utopian thinking, it conceded "the pervading feeling that there simply are no alternatives, that our times have witnessed the exhaustion not only of Utopias, but of any new departures as well."[31]

The opposite of utopian thinking is apocalyptic thinking, and the New Left had more than its fair share of the latter. "Our work is guided by the sense that we may be the last generation in the experiment with living" was an early declaration of the Port Huron Statement.[32] This sense of the imminent end made even more difficult the dilemma that confronted the young radical when he faced the prospect of entering adulthood, and temporarily deflected some from facing that prospect. Flacks reflected:

> There is a timeless quality about the movement; it embodies an assumption that one always will be a student or an ex-student—leading the freelance, experimental, not-tied-down existence of youth. Such timelessness fits well with apocalyptic visions of the future: since nuclear war, fascism, or revolution are imminent (as many activists come to feel they are), one cannot plan one's future anyway. Nevertheless, if a part of you cannot accept the reality of the apocalypse, then the problems of the future become acute. One cannot go "back"

to societally programmed identities, but the movement offers little to help the process of going forward.[33]

An apocalyptic disposition is a weak foundation upon which to build a movement for social change. It requires projections to be limited to short-range goals.[34] This situational approach may seem an inadequate substitute for a utopian blueprint, as the New Left later came to feel, but it was all that was available to the early SDS.

There is nothing in the nature of short-term projections to preclude concrete positive alternatives. Some were offered by the early SDS, though they were presented tentatively and in most cases soon were recalled. Such erratic behavior is explained by the fear of co-optation. In 1968, Gitlin commented on this problem of ends and means encountered by the New Left: "[One] reason why we have generally refused to make concrete proposals is a fear of what in the left is called reformism. That is, as long as we break down our stance into concrete, manageable proportions, we fear that any one of those propositions, taken by itself, could be performed, could be implemented, and yet we wouldn't end up with what we really in our bones feel that we want and need. To put it another way, the whole of what we want is so far beyond the sum of its parts that the distance between the whole and the sum is stupefying, devastating."[35] The irony is that what Gitlin called the whole was itself never articulated. The New Left invented no new utopia. Whenever New Leftists engaged in some sort of program, such as their efforts to organize and radicalize ghetto-dwellers, they were caught in the dilemma which Gitlin outlined.

If the radicals could not articulate an alternative vision of society and if they could not implement short-range programs for fear of co-optation, the one innovative thing which they could offer was a new style in politics. After calling for a *"reflective commitment,* the combining of our passion and our critical talents into a provisional position," Tom Hayden asserted, in one of those rhetorical flourishes which saw the New Left temporarily over some rough intellectual spots: "Radical program is simply the radical style as it attempts to change the practical life."[36] Such vagueness would suffice for a while, but its inadequacy as a base for a political movement became more and more apparent. The conflicts traced here cry out for resolution. In the meantime, the New Left would try to live tentatively, trusting that the resolution would become apparent at a later date.

Corollaries of the Primacy of the Personal

The primacy of the personal over the political in the early SDS implied at least three corollaries: that the moral impulse was fundamental, that the

New Left was an indigenous American phenomenon, and that it shared large areas of commonality with the contemporary counter-culture.

The Moral Impulse

One index of the dominance of the personal was the degree to which the early New Left emphasized values and morality. Massimo Teodori, in his valuable book on the New Left, entitled a chapter "When Moral Revolt Takes on a Political Significance."[37] Precisely. The motive force was moral; the political stance grew out of it. Here is seen the SDS drawing inspiration from the commitment of the Student Non-Violent Coordinating Committee (SNCC) to action based on a moral rather than a political perspective. SDSers often viewed themselves as a Northern counterpart to SNCC.

Leaders of the Movement acknowledged the moral core of their efforts. Robert (Al) Haber, first president of SDS, commented on "the non-political nature of the movement" and the centrality of morality, even suggesting that focusing on morality limited the New Left to the status of "a protest, in contrast to a radical, movement."[38] Paul Potter and Hal Benenson concurred: "The moral protest of the early sixties represented in many ways a rather non-political set of acts of confrontation with injustice in this society."[39] An SDS pamphlet contended, "The vitality and idealism of the new movements are related in part to the directness of this relatively non-ideological moral position."[40] Even the idea of participatory democracy, the most original political concept of the early New Left, was admittedly a "basically moral proposition."[41]

The American Heritage

Many of the moral values of SDSers were simply those which have always characterized Americans and can be best explained in terms of inherited American tradition. The New Left was oriented toward action, toward doing. It was anti-intellectual in roughly the same way as were the American businessman and politician. It sought to make specific, concrete demands; it was present-minded, ahistorical; it even became violence-prone, a trait often attributed to Americans. Further, the focus of early SDS activity was almost exclusively limited to the American scene. SDS sought to change America, not the world. Those SDSers more inclined toward theory wanted to evolve a concept which would fit American society exactly, not one which would undergird an international revolution.

Radicals themselves recognized the strong component of traditional

American outlook embodied in the Movement. The Port Huron Statement announced: "Freedom and equality for each individual, government of, by, and for the people—these American values we found good, principles by which we could live as men."[42] Years later, Paul Lauter and Florence Howe, two SDSers, still contended that "the youth movement is peculiarly American in its eclectic mixture of Marx and utopianism, collective responsibility and individualistic assertion, political engagement and smoky escapism."[43] The American heritage of the New Left was explored in detail by Staughton Lynd.[44] If the New Left was new in comparison to the Old Left, which took its theory from Europeans, perhaps it was not so new when placed in the American historical context.[45]

The fact that New Leftists sometimes gave expression to a vitriolic anti-Americanism does not vitiate the American character of the Movement. Aronson illuminated this paradox: "Thus at one and the same time, the organizers violently reject American society—on a personal and moral level—and accept many of its theoretical underpinnings. As their society rejects Marx as irrelevant, so they reject Marx as irrelevant; as their society is anti-intellectual, anti-theoretical and pragmatic, so are they anti-intellectual, anti-theoretical and pragmatic; . . . as their society refuses to confront the roots of its problems, so do they refuse to examine structural causes; as their society proclaims the 'end of ideology,' so do they reject the term itself."[46] While Aronson in 1966 was criticizing the New Left's lack of interest in ideology, in later essays he reverted to something approximating early SDS emphasis on immediate moral and personal concerns. His case illustrates the fact that the essential conflict between the personal and the political was not represented by two factions within the New Left, but was a conflict lodged within the individual radical. It marked a divided person, not a divided group.

Commonality with the Counter-Culture

It has become the accepted practice to differentiate clearly between the New Left and the hippie counter-culture, the politicos and the privatists. While there was unquestionably a difference between the New Left and the hippies, the sharp line of distinction drawn by many writers does not stand up under close scrutiny.

Those traits which the New Left and the counter-culture had in common were many and were crucial to each of these two tributaries of the stream of youth culture. Both were experience-oriented; both emphasized liberation. Both supported the concept of community and berated the competitive élan. Both were alienated from the mainstream of American society; they were reacting to what they considered to be the failure of the American dream, and against centralizations of control wrought by liberalism. Both were anti-technological, anti-materialistic, and in certain ways anti-intellectual. Both expressed a negative attitude toward traditional Western civilization. Although drugs and matters of appearance—such as dress and hair style and length—were generally seen as counter-cultural manifestations, it was a rare radical who did not share them. Similarly, almost all of the habitués of that erstwhile San Francisco mecca of the counter-culture, Haight–Ashbury, were engaged in some form of political activity at one time or another.[47]

Some New Leftist commentators have seen the congruities between themselves and the counter-culture. Flacks set the radical student Movement against the context of the youth culture as a whole.[48] Lauter and Howe recognized that any sharp line distinguishing the radicals from the counter-culture must be blurred.[49] Perhaps the best examples of cross-fertilization between New Leftists and hippies were the Yippies, the best-known of whom were Jerry Rubin and Abbie Hoffman.

The radicals and the hippies shared personal alienation from the American consensus, but they diverged sharply in their views of how to resolve the malaise and achieve personal fulfillment. The usual description of this disparity is that the hippies were passive, while the radicals were active. Flacks saw the fundamental difference to be that the radical "intellectuals" who comprised the old guard of SDS had "some coherent value system . . . to sustain and orient them while in the pure case, the 'uncommitted' were more confused and adrift and, therefore, more passive and present-oriented."[50] Conventional wisdom gives the laurel to the New Leftists, because they realized that no escape was possible from "Babylon"; they carried America within them and thus would be corrupt even in attempted isolation. To the New Left, the hippies compromised with America by agreeing to live as parasites off its riches, confronting it with a minor nuisance rather than open opposition.

There is some truth in this analysis, but one could as easily reverse the case. The hippies considered their withdrawal from public life to be a positive act. It was a step which had to be taken consciously; not to have taken it would be passivity. From this viewpoint, it was the New Leftists who compromised with America. Paul Goodman wrote, "On their side, the hippies claim that the New Left has gotten neatly caught in the bag of the System. To make a frontal attack is to play according to the enemy's rules, where one doesn't have a chance; and victory would be a drag anyway. The thing is to use jujitsu, ridicule, Schweikism, nonviolent resistance, by-passing, infuriating, tripping up, seducing by offering happy alternatives. . . . A new politics demands a new style, a new personality and a new way of life. To form cadres and try to take power is the same old run-around."[51] The counter-culture faulted the radicals as seeking political redress for their personal alienation. They reasoned that if the present political order is corrupt, so are all political orders, and so will be any radical alternative. New men will make a new society, not *vice versa*.

Comparisons with Intellectual Traditions

The state of the early New Left can be illuminated by setting it against the context of existentialism, anarchism, and Marxism, the first two having much more in common with the early New Left than the third. Each of these three traditions encompasses great diversity within itself; yet the fact that these labels are used indicates that there is in each school of thought a core of ideas which provides a fundamental definition. At the expense of the subtleties which could be introduced into the discussion of each term, it is at this fundamental level that these designations will be used herein. These three terms describe identifiably distinct approaches to reality and therefore can serve as paradigms by which to gauge the tendencies of the early New Left.

Existentialism

The parallels between existentialism and the early New Left are especially illuminating. Both emphasized that man is not a machine nor an object to be manipulated, but a subject—a being with dignity and integrity which should not be violated. Both commenced their efforts from a feeling of alienation toward the general order (or chaos) which surrounded them and emphasized revolt against that unacceptable milieu. Both set freedom as the central goal. Both proclaimed the individual's responsibility for his own being; they emphasized action. Both desired the remaking of one's own essence. Both sought a revaluation of received values, to be effected by the individual's will. Both minimized the value of systematic ideological thinking.

Radical statements which coincide with the tenets of existentialism are so abundant that presenting a handful of quotations runs the risk of underplaying this strain in SDS thought. When Tom Hayden was asked, in 1961, to define the basis for a student movement, he replied, "I must value life and, ethically, we must have reverence for man. Reverence for man is to believe that if any man is not free then none of us is free."[52] Equally existentialist was his remark: *"Do not wish to be a student in contrast to being a man.* Do not study as a student, but as a man who is alive and who cares. Leave the isolated world of ideological fantasy, allow your ideas to become part of your living and your living to become part of your ideas. . . . the time has come for a re-assertion of the personal."[53]

Long stretches of the Port Huron Statement read like a manifesto of existentialism:

> *Human relationships* should involve fraternity and honesty. Human interdependence is contemporary fact; human brotherhood must be willed, however, as a condition of future survival and as the most appropriate form of social relations. Personal links between man and man are needed, especially to go beyond the partial and fragmentary bonds of function that bind men only as worker to worker, employer to employee, teacher to student, American to Russian.
>
> Loneliness, estrangement, isolation describe the vast distance between man and man today. . . . We would replace power rooted in possession, priviledged [*sic*], or circumstance by power and uniqueness rooted in love, reflectiveness, reason, and creativity.[54]

For radical Howard Zinn, this existentialism was the Movement's distinguishing trait: "There is an Existential quality to current radicalism that distinguishes it sharply from the style of the thirties."[55]

The early New Left was particularly attracted to Albert Camus. Of those SDSers interviewed by Jack Newfield for his book of 1966, almost all had read Camus, while only a few had read Marx and even fewer had read Lenin or Trotsky.[56] Leaders of the Free Speech Movement at Berkeley in 1964 proclaimed themselves disciples of Camus, though his prestige among radicals waned soon after.[57] Carl Oglesby devoted an article to interacting with Camus. While he consciously disagreed with the latter because of the radicals' growing interest in ideology by the time his essay was written in 1967, he knew that he had to nullify Camus's influence. Even in his disagreement, he demonstrated his profound indebtedness to the French writer, as when he asserted, *"The rebel is someone for whom injustice and society are only different words for the same thing,"* and when he drew "the rebel's picture of himself" as "a dead-earnest soldier for the humanity of man."[58]

Camus differed from the radicals, however, in one very important respect: he had a modesty which they lacked. He reached the painful conclusion that the total pattern of reality could not be grasped, but one could at least end the suffering immediately surrounding oneself. The New Leftists began with a similar motivation, but they soon found Camus's modesty cramping as they poured their frustrations into a political mold.

They succumbed to the altogether honorable desire to comprehend the whole of reality; with their political outlook, this led to pursuit of an ideology which would support the need for revolution. They thus turned away from being satisfied with partial answers and substituted the search for final, total ones. In the first stage of their development, they were at one with Camus in rebellion, but they were unable to maintain his distinction between rebellion and revolution.

Anarchism

Existentialism inherently does not contain a political component, but a political commitment was always maintained by SDS. Therefore, existentialism is not by itself an adequate paradigm with which to interpret that which was new in the New Left. There was a social-political perspective which had great areas of congruence with existentialism, however: anarchism. This tradition might be said to have provided a logical extension of existentialist concerns into the social sphere. The coupling of anarchism with existentialism *is* adequate to explain the new factor in the first stage of SDS.

In personal-political polarity, when Richard Flacks described the personal pole as existential humanism, the term seemed designed to avoid use of the naked word *existentialism* and to communicate the radicals' concern for others by including *humanism*. What the existentialist might seek for himself alone, the radical urgently desired to be the lot of all men. Here is where anarchism comes in. In oversimplified terms, it holds a social dimension that wants for all men what the existentialist seeks for the lone individual.

The two chief tenets of anarchism were decentralization and communitarianism, and these were leading motifs of the early SDS manifestoes. Rudolf Rocker's statement of what libertarianism means to an anarchist fits the early New Left: "For the Anarchist, freedom is not an abstract philosophical concept, but the vital concrete possibility for every human being to bring to full development all capacities and talents with which nature has endowed him, and turn them to social account."[59] Just as "most anarchists stress the role of the individual and individual action as the key to liberation and to the revolutionary transformation of society,"[60] so did the radicals. And just as "anarchism has always been anti-ideological: anarchists have always insisted on the priority of life and action to theory and system"[61]—so have the new radicals.

Anarchism is a term which has a bad ring to most American ears; it is generally equated with nihilism—the urge to destroy—and is therefore a revolutionary theory with little credibility in the modern world. As Todd Gitlin noted, "*anarchism* is easily discredited because it never had in the United States, either intellectual roots or a tradition as a movement, and so it's simply an idea hanging in space, with neither interesting nor respectable intellectual credentials, nor a movement propounding it."[62] Even most New Leftists shared the popular misconceptions of anarchism, though some recognized their common ground with that tradition.

Anarchists did not, in fact, prefer disorder to order: "anarchism is anything but antisocial."[63] Anarchists claimed to offer something other than a theory advocating the commonly understood meaning of anarchy. They believed that "a society ruled by government can not be orderly, that government creates and perpetuates both disorder and violence."[64] They therefore urged the abolition of government. But there was also a positive side of anarchism. "The basic anarchist vision is one of a society where all relationships are those of social and economic equals who act together in voluntary cooperation for mutual benefits."[65]

While most analyses of the New Left have not emphasized its connections with anarchism, some commentators have treated it, most notably two self-confessed anarchists, Murray Bookchin and Paul Goodman. It may be objected that they have a vested interest in wanting to claim the Movement for their point of view and that their analysis of the New Left should be trusted no more than the self-analysis of the new radicals themselves. Nevertheless, the content of their analyses has intrinsic cogency, and it is significant that both of them have had a warm reception in certain sectors of the Movement. *Post-Scarcity Anarchism*, by Bookchin, has been reviewed favorably by radicals,[66] and Paul Goodman was an early SDS hero. When the Free Speech Movement was allowed to invite one outsider to speak in its behalf at Berkeley in 1964, it selected Goodman. That he praised the young radicals in the early 1960s and criticized them later is evidence both that their early mood coincided in substantial aspects with his own anarchism and that they turned away from anarchism as the decade progressed. If the radicals had an anarchistic streak greater than they themselves were willing to admit, it might well be that anarchists would be able to articulate those feelings of the radicals better than they themselves had done.

Bookchin argued that "anarchists have probably given more attention to the subjective problems of revolution than any other revolutionary movement."[67] His description of the concerns of anarchism could as easily have been a description of the concerns of the New Left: "Its commitment to doctrinal shibboleths is minimal. In its active concern with the issues of everyday life, anarchism has always been preoccupied with lifestyle, sexuality, community, women's liberation and human relationships. Its

restructurings of our society so that human needs take priority over all others. In a deeper sense we mean vast changes in human nature, changes in the way we relate to each other, to our work, and to society. . . . The condition of freeing ourselves from the bonds capitalist society has created—material, cultural and psychological—is 'socialism,' which is in fact the very changes in human personality, relations, and daily life that we have talked about."[81] There are many terms which would seem more accurate than socialism to summarize the description in this reference. As Goodman remarked, "American students today are provokingly uninterested in economics, even—or especially—when they talk socialism."[82]

The element in Marx most appealing to the early New Left was his concept of alienation. While "alienation, for Marx, is an objective, not a subjective condition,"[83] it was the reverse for the new radicals. They felt that alienation rooted in feelings of loneliness and personal despair to which existentialism had given normative expression. Feuer's comment on the contemporary intellectual's use of the term applies equally well to the new radicals: "The fondness of the contemporary intellectual for the concept 'alienation' has little to do with the modes of alienation associated with mass, class, competitive, and industrial societies."[84]

The Fascination with Politics

If those rebellious youths who formed SDS were more existential than ideological, why did they insist on pursuing politics? On one level, the radicals began from the assumption that the personal alienation which they experienced, and which they believed that other Americans—especially those whom they viewed as oppressed—experienced, was based outside the self. On a more elemental level, the political orientation of the New Left grew from the assumption that everything is political. Thus, Paul Breines could analyze: "For the meaning of the Movement's 'politics of the unpolitical' lay in its recognition that nothing in modern society is unpolitical; that every detail of daily life is saturated with and reproduces the hegemony of the ruling system; that the object of critical thought and action is 'the system' as a totality."[85]

If this statement means that life cannot be segmented into mutually exclusive areas and that all details are connected to all others, then it is defensible. But it seems to say more than this: namely, that politics takes priority over all else. It expresses a world view that places a political perspective around all reality, and declares politics to be the principal category by which to analyze all human experience.

Other perspectives place something else at the center. One such view—

and one with a long history in Western tradition—sees religion as that integrating element by which to approach reality. Indeed, it could be said that the role which religion once played in the life of Western man is today played by politics. Having largely turned away from the transcendental realm for finding ultimate meaning in life, modern men have substituted a concern with the quality of this life, and the form which that concern takes is often political. It need not have been so. Some men in the nineteenth and twentieth century sought a secular substitute for traditional religion and found it in art; Matthew Arnold was one such. But that is not now as widely followed an approach as is the substitution of politics.

Disillusionment with Liberalism

In practice, if not always in theory, modern political liberals begin with the assumption that politics is the supreme category. Here is the clue to the insistence of young radicals that in the political sphere lay solutions to problems which they felt existentially: they were disillusioned liberals. At the 1965 rally in Washington to protest the Vietnam war, Carl Oglesby explained that those who directed the war effort were all liberals. He added, "But so, I'm sure are many of us who are here today in protest. . . . Maybe we have here two quite different liberalisms: one authentically humanist; the other not so human at all. Not long ago, I considered myself a liberal."[86]

Many early SDSers were not ready to eliminate liberals from their number. Clark Kissinger urged, "A new left must be broad enough to admit both liberals and socialists, no single political grouping having a monopoly on truth, experience and talent."[87] The New Left's liberal roots also showed in the name of a research group which preceded the Radical Education Project and published papers of several SDSers: the Liberal Study Group.

Nevertheless, the New Left soon saw itself in reaction against the liberal consensus. Calvert and Neiman envisaged the New Left as "the rejection of all forms of bourgeois liberalism."[88] This new radical attitude toward liberalism was distinctly different from that of the Old Left, who saw the enemy as fascism and the liberals as possible allies. Lynd remarked, "The sentimentalizing of FDR, the New Deal, the Democratic Party, and the CIO bureaucracy by the Communist Party in the Thirties and Forties helps to explain the rage with which New Leftists attacked liberals and sought to unmask liberalism as an ideology."[89] Some of the new radicals themselves recognized both the strength of this reactionary rage and its unhealthy impact on the Movement: "Unfortunately, when the movement began to break away from its liberal pacifist leadership, it felt the necessity to repudiate everything that had gone with that period of its development. . . . Since the liberals had preached nonviolence, then the radicals must preach violence. And so on."[90]

It is not coincidental that Flacks outlined the phases of the Movement's history to coincide with the dates of presidential elections—1960, 1964, 1968. His point was that the direction of the Movement would have had a positive input into the normal process of electoral politics if the Democratic Party had been responsive to the needs being expressed by the protesting young. Lack of such response caused the SDS to settle for the negativism of protest. Flacks's divisions are an index of the extent to which the young radicals were liberals, albeit disillusioned ones.

Acknowledged Indebtedness to Liberalism

Some SDSers recognized that their group was significantly influenced by its heritage of liberalism and incorporated much of it into their politics in the process of consciously rejecting liberalism and developing a new political style. James O'Brien, an SDSer writing a history of the New Left in an SDS publication, offered this explanation of early SDS politics: "This threat was not, at first, unambiguously radical: it was liberal in the nature of its surface demands (such as racial integration, an end to nuclear testing, and free speech) but radical in its distrust of compromise and in its proclivity for direct action."[91]

The most important manifestation of vestigial liberalism in SDS was the Economic Research and Action Project (ERAP), established in 1963 as an attempt to implement the principles expressed in the second major SDS position paper, "America and the New Era."[92] Rich Rothstein has written, "SDS still believed in the possibility of change within the framework of the formally representative institutions of American government. ERAP's goal was to goose those institutions a bit."[93] He added that "speaking truth to liberals remained a key part of ERAP organizers' program."[94]

ERAP sought to organize the ghetto poor of Newark, Chicago, Cleveland, and other Northern cities. Far from ruling out aid from establishment sources, ERAP actively sought it. In discussing the SDS effort to organize the unemployed, Flacks advocated seeking support from the widest possible constituency, including labor unions and social service agencies, and making demands on the government which could reasonably be fulfilled.[95] Wittman and Hayden urged that SDS develop "proposals for broad new government economic policies" and declared that "ultimately . . . the national level is where political pressures must be directed."[96] Gitlin concurred in planning to help the poor: "Here again, any proposed solution must be *national*—a constitutional amendment providing for guaranteed income and guaranteed education, a national planning structure—and will require Federal action."[97] He left open the possibility that a third party might be the best way to achieve these and related ends.[98] Rennie Davis went "part of the way with LBJ" (an SDS slogan in 1964): "A 'strategy of insurgent response' begins by asking what is most worthwhile about Johnson's War on Poverty and in what ways we can encourage its better tendencies."[99]

While ERAP's prescriptions were inevitably liberal, its underlying impulse was not. Kirkpatrick Sale was correct in explaining that ERAP was rooted in the concept of participatory democracy and sought the creation of " 'counter-communities,' anarchistic units where participatory democracy could be tried out firsthand."[100] While genuinely concerned for the poor, ERAP also sought personal satisfaction through direct identification with them—a fact which caused Al Haber to scorn "the romantic, almost apolitical, elements which prevailed among ERAP people from its inception."[101]

ERAP lasted from 1963 to 1965. Its organizational collapse did not end the thinking on which it was based, but it did nurture a sense of despair about activating American society. The old guard of SDS thus was susceptible to influence by the revolutionary rhetoric introduced shortly thereafter by a younger generation of SDS leaders. ERAP's failure was the most significant episode contributing to a total break between SDS and liberalism.

Unacknowledged Indebtedness to Liberalism

The relationship between the New Left and liberalism was a complex one. If SDSers became disillusioned with liberalism, their taste for politics was formed when they were still under its influence through the lessons absorbed from their liberal professors and parents. To the extent that the radicals insisted on working with political categories, they inherited liberalism. Their refusal to embrace Marxism was a manifestation of the end-of-ideology line prominent in liberal circles. But their conscious rejection of liberalism, while retaining the liberal assumption that amelioration of human problems is to be sought in politics, compelled them to take a political stance apart from both liberalism and Marxism. Since these two were the only well-articulated positions on the left, the SDS was forced into an inarticulate and overwhelmingly negative posture. Some common ground was shared with conservatives, such as rejection of the liberal hegemony, preference for decentralization and localism, and—to some extent—libertarian personalism. Conservatism was so *déclassé*, however, that it did not appear to be a serious alternative to these disillusioned young liberals. This explains, then, why the young radicals were (a) negative and protesting in their politics, (b) in need of developing a brand new social theory, and (c) attracted, often unconsciously, to anarchist notions.

The 1960s witnessed the breakup of the old liberal hegemony which had dominated politics and the academy in America for three decades. People were flaking off to both sides, and the radicals were those who went further toward the left. Ironically, they were ultimately less radical in their rejection of liberalism than were those who dropped out or moved to the right, since they retained liberalism's devotion to viewing all reality through political lenses. Those college youths who retained their liberal identification were, of course, the best and most dedicated students of their liberal mentors. But second to them as faithful disciples of those old liberals were the new radicals.

The liberal inheritance of the new radicals explains their reformist suggestions in roughly the same way that their unacknowledged anarchism explains their stance of negative protest. Liberalism accounts not for what was new about the New Left, but precisely what was not new about it. What was new came from existentialism combined with anarchism. The break between SDS and its parent organization, the social democratic League for Industrial Democracy, happened only gradually. As SDS evolved and eventually embraced Marxism-Leninism, it was its liberal component which was most thoroughly eradicated. The existentialist and anarchist elements persevered, though their expression was muted in the process of developing ideologies. The inherited liberalism of the early SDS did not survive at all.

— 2 —

The Middle Phase of the New Left

The second phase of the New Left covered roughly 1965 through 1967 and ran into 1968. It was essentially a transitional period when many early SDS ideas were being modified or rejected and those characteristic of the late 1960s were beginning to be articulated. The boundaries of this segment are thus blurred, especially the one which separated it from what followed.[1] If 1965, as Oglesby has said, was the year when the Movement "explicitly abandoned reformism,"[2] it took a couple of years for an alternative to emerge clearly.

This middle phase saw a marked shift away from the initial non-ideological stance toward a concerted search for an ideology to satisfy the visceral responses felt by the young radicals. There was a growing sense that "without revolutionary theory there can be no revolutionary practice."[3] One SDSer, attacking anarchist and liberal tendencies in the Movement, complained, "There is very little ideological thinking in SDS."[4] Another bemoaned the fact that "many direct action advocates still fail to balance personal morality and outrage with reasoned political analysis," though he added that "this need does not mean that action should be postponed until someone comes up with an ideology for social change."[5] It was already becoming difficult "to believe, as so many of us used to, that 'the movement' was born under a lucky star which would make all its experiments cumulatively fruitful and extract from its experience just the kind and amount of theory and leadership that it required."[6] Lynd's comment, "I don't see what sense it makes to talk about resisting capitalism without affirming an alternative,"[7] summarized the growing mood. If the early New Left sought a tension between the personal and the political but was dominated by the personal, in this second phase the New Left still sought equal balance but began to shift toward the political.

At this time the newly-elected Johnson administration bitterly disappointed its liberal supporters by substantially increasing the size of the American armed force in South Vietnam and commencing to bomb North Vietnam. Continuing support for the Johnson administration by the labor movement, organized liberals, and social democrats "sealed the already apparent cleavage between the New Left and the liberal coalition with which it felt at one time a critical identification."[8] This situation caused Michael Miles to assert that the success of the Movement "was largely guaranteed by the facts of social oppression themselves and by the unnatural absence of an organized left."[9]

The success was dramatic. Richard Flacks estimated that in 1963 SDS had perhaps one thousand members and no more than twenty functioning chapters, while by the summer of 1965 it was ten times larger and had become the recognized center for student protest.[10] When SDS called for a national student march on Washington in April 1965 to protest the war, "much to the surprise of the organizers, some 25,000 students participated—by far, the largest national student protest activity in the United States since the 1930s."[11] Lee Baxandall cited the speech by Carl Oglesby at that anti-war rally as one that "guided as well as marked the change" from reformism to revolutionary socialism.[12] The numerical successes of SDS in the mid-1960s caused "something which the New Left until that time had not really contemplated—that a mass student movement was emerging, capable of acting independently on its initiative and in behalf of its own felt interest."[13]

The sudden increase in SDS membership also underlined a pivotal deficiency: "the sorry intellectual shape of the anti-war movement. For a movement based primarily on intellectuals, its sophistication and level of understanding of society and its politics are shockingly low."[14] While the Vietnam war revealed the strength of the latent radicalism among the young and brought much of it to the surface, it also exposed the need for an ideology to explain both the war and the society which played what the radicals considered such a despicable role in it.

SDS grew beyond the wildest expectations of its founders, but in retrospect one wonders if this was not a disadvantage. A relatively small group of SDS leaders was forced to assume responsibilities which would have staggered the most seasoned political veterans. With only a few years of Movement history behind them, they were thrust into the national spotlight; it might be said that they were pushed into the big leagues before they were ready. Events cascaded around them with such speed and intensity that they did not have sufficient time to work out either theories or strategies capable of moving SDS from one success to the next. They were forced out of their relatively safe positions as critics of the established order and summoned to produce some sort of positive alternative. Instead of being on the outside looking in, they held a position of power within a significant cultural-political force and were more exposed than they could have imagined they would be.

The Search for Ideology

Growing uneasiness over the lack in SDS of positive alternatives and ideological foundations was greatly strengthened by the chorus of criticism on these points from persons outside the Movement—both Old Leftists and liberals. Jacobs and Landau, writing in 1966, declared, "What is required of The Movement today is an organized search to develop an ideology for the purpose of gaining political power, to replace both its own righteous moral posture and the traditional politics of compromise."[15] Eugene Genovese commented that "the New Left may know that American society is unjust and sick, but it hardly knows why. It has no theory of society, no theory of social change, and no understanding of the nature and promise of socialism."[16]

Radical Education Project

To meet the need for analysis and theory, in 1966 SDS set up the Radical Education Project (REP), largely controlled by the old guard, its central function being "to provide internal education for SDS and other groups in the movement."[17] REP agreed with SDS's critics that "the movement tends to be negative in its approach to the present and vague in its description of the better future in whose service it seeks to enlist support," and it concurred that "we must also begin to develop and debate concrete models of the structure of institutions and social relations that derive from our shared ideals."[18]

Nevertheless, REP was rooted in early SDS thinking and signaled only the transition from the first phase of SDS history, not the development of the second phase. In announcing the search for ideology, REP underlined the existentialism of the early SDS. "Man is the end and man is the measure. The rock bottom foundation of radical ideology is a view of man— human nature and human possibility. Is man creative or ordinary? Is his goodness simply thwarted by oppressive social institutions, ready to come forth once the social oppression is removed? (Or does a deformed society deeply deform men, so that human change is needed as well as social change?)"[19]

Not only was this way of talking about human nature far removed from Marxism, but REP's proposed route to ideology specifically eliminated adoption of classical Marxism. "The unifying thread in its work will be the insistence that conclusions stem either from experience or research (or both) and not simply be extrapolated from a dogmatic framework. . . . The project is not a substitute for political action or organization. It seeks to complement the action thrust of the movement by insuring that the necessary intellectual and educational resources are available."[20] The aim, then, was to retain the activism of SDS while supplementing it with theory, not to substitute theory for action. Further, the ideology was to grow organically out of experience. Finally, the ideology was to be new, not borrowed from past traditions of radicalism. REP anticipated continual revision of its social analysis, reassessment of its formulation of values, and reconsideration of its vision of the good society. It believed that "it is out of this on-going interaction between exposure and reformulation that radical ideology comes into being."[21] REP was the effort of a non-ideological organization to add the ingredient of ideology without sacrificing any of its original spontaneity.

Rhetoric of Revolution

At the time that the search for ideology commenced in earnest, there was a dramatic rise in the rhetoric of revolution, with a concomitant diminution in popularity of the slogan, "participatory democracy." Now began the following kind of elocution—this example by Todd Gitlin: "nothing substantial in this country can change without a revolution, by which I mean a tumultuous and total change in the power relations of the society. And . . . without such a change, without such an underplowing of the society . . . nothing that we might propose will take root. So what we really want, it turns out, is the dismantling of the entire institutional apparatus of the society. Nothing we propose can come into being without being absorbed and transformed into something that we didn't intend or discarded."[22]

Greg Calvert and Carl Davidson, chief spokesmen for SDS in 1966 and 1967, regularly and almost casually invoked the rhetoric of revolution. A *National Guardian* reporter quoted Calvert as saying, "The crucial ingredient . . . is a socialist analysis of capitalism to reinforce and give revolutionary substance to SDS's existing libertarian rejection of a manipulative and exploitative American social system."[23] This had little in common with the tone of the Port Huron Statement.

It is doubtful that certain implications carried by revolutionary rhetoric were recognized by its initial purveyors. For one thing, it evidences the deepening alienation which cultivates a sharp cleavage between "us" and "them." Self-declared revolutionaries thus take upon themselves total responsibility for changing society. The responsibility they accept is total also in the sense of the need to change everything. According to the definition that the New Left gave it, revolution cannot settle for changing things piecemeal. So, coupled with the apocalyptic mentality of the New Left, this entailed hardening into an all-or-nothing attitude. "Either engage in something that will bring revolution and transformation all at one blow, or do nothing, it seems to say."[24] Revolutionary rhetoric also implies the need to develop a strategy for gaining power.

Not all SDSers capitulated readily to the new revolutionary rhetoric. Potter and Benenson, advocating an ideology which would grow organically from experience and cautioning against a facile adoption of Marxism, wrote in 1967: *"despite radical rhetoric there is very little comprehension of what the words we sling around mean either as descriptions of the society or as prescriptions for action."*[25] Eric Mann complained, "The frequent and facile use of the word 'revolution' reflects the fact that few of us have any idea of how a revolution in America would come about, and more importantly, don't really believe we'll ever have to participate in one."[26]

Growing Appeal of Marxism

The need being sensed for a revolutionary theory led straight in the direction of Marxism. Once the rhetoric of revolution was called upon, the New Left cut itself off from the anarchist tradition because of what the word *revolution* meant to the New Left: "In Anarchist theory, 'revolution' means the moment when the structure of authority is loosed, so that free functioning can occur. The aim is to open areas of freedom and defend them. In complicated modern societies it is probably safest to work at this piecemeal. . . . Marxists insist that piecemeal change is mere reformism, and one has to seize power and have a strong administration in order to prevent reaction."[27] What *revolution* meant to the New Leftists had little in common with what Goodman attributed to anarchism and much in common with what he attributed to Marxism. The use of revolutionary rhetoric thus cut the Movement off from its original political impulses and drastically foreshortened its range of theory and action. It forced the New Left into channels different from those which it had initially marked out for itself. Its relationship with Marxism in modern America was summarized crisply by Aronson: "a theory without a movement, a movement without a theory."[28] It was inevitable that the two would come together.

In this second phase, attention turned from concrete activism oriented toward single issues to the abstract appeal of a coherent socialist movement. Loren Baritz saw a 1966 article entitled "Socialism and the New Left" as "a pivotal argument in the development of a new Left."[29] Declaring that "*activity*, although essential within a worked-out political perspective, leads nowhere by itself," it offered a remedy: "The first step is for new Leftists to examine the content of their radicalism and determine if they are committed to a transformation of American capitalism into that higher form of society envisaged by Marx."[30] Commenting retrospectively on the mid-1960s, George Graham said, "The spontaneity of the movement was gradually modified by intense strategic and tactical thought. . . . The relevance of Marxism, which is the summary of revolutionary experience, to our society became increasingly apparent. The system knew we were communists before we did."[31]

Some of the new radicals tried to make the case that the New Left had been Marxist all along and that there was continuity rather than discontinuity between the early and middle 1960s. For example, in Lynd's opinion, "SDS always accepted an essentially Marxist analysis of American society, even if the 'ruling class' was termed the 'power elite' and 'monopoly capitalism' was termed 'corporate liberalism.' "[32]

In the mid-1960s, SDS merely exhibited an openness to the influence of Marxism and began to mouth its more popular nostrums, without committing itself to a thorough study of Marx's writings and a concerted effort to demonstrate their contemporary relevance. The search for ideology only began during the second phase, and while it was eventually to culminate in an adoption of Marxism, the Marxist element was still embryonic at this time. There was an effort on the part of some SDS spokesmen to avoid joining forces with the Old—and still widely discredited—Left, and to warn their fellow new radicals against an easy submission to Marxian categories. To the extent that the New Left did look to Marxism at this point, the desire was to rework it so that the New Left could retain its separate identity from the Old Left. But, as Miles pointed out, "left politics abhors an ideological vacuum, and direct action requires guidance on how to proceed. As the best-articulated systematic alternative to liberal social analysis, the Marxist tradition increasingly supplied the analysis necessary for strategic decision."[33]

Imprecision of SDS Marxism

The appeal of Marxism was rooted in negative, not positive, factors. Nothing inherent in Marxism lured New Leftists toward it. Rather was something lacking in themselves and their position that they hoped Marxism might supply. It is therefore not surprising that their declarations in the name of Marx were generally vague and inexact echoes of the original.

The imprecision of SDS Marxism in the mid-1960s was demonstrated by its attraction toward revolutionary movements in the Third World, rather than to those who explicated the intellectual tradition.[34] As a result, the New Left actually underlined its distance from Marxism, as Miles remarked.[35] "The whole New Left commitment to Third World revolution is a sentimental, largely unreciprocated love affair,"[36] as was its commitment to fight the battles of the poor and oppressed in America.

The need for an ideology, coupled with the presence of Marxism as the only credible body of revolutionary ideology, was the main reason for SDS infatuation with Marxism. But it was not the only reason. In 1966, the Progressive Labor Party decided to infiltrate SDS; other SDSers, who desired a consensus fostered by the notion of participatory democracy, sought to accommodate these new members with their variant of Marxist ideology.

Another reason was that Marxist clichés showed the deep hostility of the new radicals toward the established order. Marxism was a scare-word for most Americans, as the young radicals knew. Their use of the term separated them more firmly from popular anti-communism than could anything else. Megill admitted that "in the beginning they were perhaps only rejecting the anticommunism which has been an important part of the liberal theory."[37] Gabriel Kolko distinguished between Marxism functioning as "an inspiration of radical faith and commitment," and as "an intellectual system capable of being applied in an elucidating manner to social reality."[38] Julius Lester made a similar distinction between enthusiasm for revolution and revolutionary enthusiasm.[39] The New Left had the former, not the latter.

A third reason for turning toward Marxism was incipient despair about the future of the Movement. Flacks charted the New Left's passage "through a period of optimistic reformism toward increasing disillusionment," and he remarked, "Despair generates the urgency of revolution as necessity."[40] Although Flacks was talking primarily about the later period of the New Left, the despair which reached its zenith at the end of the decade was already present. Originally disillusioned with liberalism, by the mid-1960s the radicals had lost faith in their negative stance of protest.

Not all New Leftists were satisfied with the sole use of Marxist phraseology. If the Movement was turning to Marx for intellectual sustenance, some members felt it their duty to develop a flexible Marxist critique which would correspond to the social ills which it was intended to diagnose. David Horowitz warned against a "Marxism of the hand-me-down variety, where an ideological perspective and vocabulary developed in a different epoch or a different political-cultural environment is transposed whole and adopted as an all-embracing wisdom."[41] Rather than such an unreflective invocation of Marx, Horowitz recognized the need for fresh thought by New Leftists.

Howard Zinn also appealed for a flexible adaptation of Marxism.[42] Such flexibility, however, was actually selective borrowing. Zinn expressed his distrust of the state and the untenability of the "traditional Marxian idea of a revolution taking place because of a breakdown in the capitalist mechanism and an organized, class-conscious proletariat taking over."[43] His alignment of Marxism and the New Left was skewed:

> From all this it is quite clear what Marx's values were; the free man, in his individuality, in his sociality, in his oneness with nature. The New Left is in accord here. Where it parts, I think, is in Marx's claim— although some attribute this to Engels . . . that this vision of unalienated man springs not from a wish, but from an observation—from a scientific plotting of a historical curve which moves inevitably in the direction of man's freedom.
>
> Surely we don't have such confidence in inevitabilities these days— we've had too many surprises in this century.[44]

From a wish or an observation? Here was the conflict between the determinism of Marxism and the indeterminacy of existentialism. Zinn came down on the side of existentialism—in the very essay in which he was trying to conjoin Marxism and his New Left stance.

The Search for a Revolutionary Agent

The major difficulty confronting the New Left in its efforts to develop a revolutionary ideology was the question of who would make the revolution. As Flacks said, "The central issue for the New Left has always been the problem of *agency*—that is, which classes and strata in the society are more disposed toward active opposition to the status quo, what means of power can they exercise, and with what effect? . . . Since about 1965 the question of agency has been endlessly perplexing, and has not yet been answered with anything like the coherence found in the early sixties."[45] Tom Hayden, writing in the mid-1960s, conceded candidly, "There simply is no active agency of radical change—no race, class or nation—in which radicals can invest high hopes as they have in previous times."[46] So the search was on to find an agent capable of making a new American revolution.

The classic Marxist answer was that the working class would be that agent, but the workers were distinctly hostile to the new radicals—a prob-

lem interfering with their assignment of a role in the revolution. Herbert
Marcuse, who pioneered the explanation that the workers had been
co-opted by an affluent society, observed, "The prevalence of a non-
revolutionary—nay, antirevolutionary—consciousness among the majority
of the working class is conspicuous."[47] If not the working class, some new
radicals suggested that perhaps blacks would be the agents of revolution.[48]

By far the most popular view among SDSers in this middle period was
that they themselves, the young intelligentsia, would serve as agents of
the new revolution. Assigning agency to any other group was to consign
themselves to merely catalytic and supportive roles, and not too many
found such subordinate roles self-fulfilling even in theory. Furthermore,
they themselves made up that segment of the population which evidenced
the greatest alienation and the greatest interest in revolution. As Baxandall
warned, "We cannot look for a constituency to those who still experience
fundamental insecurity about their material well-being. . . . At a certain
point the belly question will poison their consciousness. . . . We cannot
squander our limited energies on constituencies that are sooner or later
the affluent Establishment's."[49]

Only those who had tried affluence and found it wanting were ready
for a new American revolution. It was C. Wright Mills who first saw in the
students and young intellectuals the most likely repository of revolutionary
potential, and this was his major contribution to the emergence of the
New Left.[50] To call youth and/or students a class was to deviate from
classical Marxist doctrine, but it was also the New Left's effort to adapt a
Marxian category (class, in this case) to the realities of modern life (student
rebellion). The tension is apparent between needing Marxism and not
knowing what to do with it when it was available.

Out of this concern to see students as the agents of revolution, com-
bined with a desire to employ the Marxian categorical term, grew the idea
of a new working class. It was the most original theory developed by the
New Left in seeking an ideology. First delineated by Bob Gottlieb, Gerry
Tenney, and Dave Gilbert in a paper called wryly the "Port Authority
Statement,"[51] it was effectively publicized by Greg Calvert in a speech at
Princeton in 1967, elaborated by such SDS leaders as Carl Davidson and
Richard Flacks, and widely adopted by New Leftists. Calvert's speech
read in part: "What we have come to understand is that the great American middle class is not middle class at all. None of the 19th Century
definitions of the bourgeoisie apply. . . . The vast majority of those whom
we called the middle class must properly be understood as members of the
'new working class': That is, as those workers who fill the jobs created by
a new level of technological development within the same exploitive
system."[52]

This new theory was heralded by New Leftists as one of the most important distinctions between Old Leftists and themselves.[53] It was derived from Marx, but not orthodox Marxism. The new working class "had the potential in both radicalism and in leverage to be a major force for social transformation. These new workers—in human services, education, science, technology, mass communications—along with the youth who were preparing to enter this class, represented a significant sector numerically, and were showing many signs of unrest and ferment."[54] These were what Flacks called "educated labor"[55] and even *a mass intelligentsia . . .* those engaged vocationally in the production, distribution, interpretation, criticism, and inculcation of cultural values."[56]

The apparent advantage of the new working class theory was that it brought into phase two elements which must coincide in any realistic revolutionary theory: the abstract conception of agency and the concrete source of deepest discontent. At the same time, the theory betrayed the crucial weakness of the New Left throughout its history. Revolution, which must always be made in the name of the people, was now placed in the hands of an elite, unrepresentative segment of the populace. The popular revolutionary battle cry, "Power to the people!", had to be employed with great selectivity.[57] Not only did New Left ideology remain limited primarily to the academic world, but its greatest success among students was to be found at elite universities. Further, the new theory inevitably subordinated economics, since material deprivation was not a characteristic of this suggested agent of revolution.

This adaptation of Marxism remained faithful in large part to the initial New Left instinct for personal fulfillment. That it soon became discredited for most SDSers, who moved on to a more classic Marxist-Leninist line, marked a major step toward the demise of the New Left as a theoretical entity which was genuinely new, and eventually as an organized presence. By 1968 and 1969, SDS had to agree with Stanley Aronowitz's view: "The central constituency for any Left is the working class and the oppressed minorities. . . . When the Left has hegemony over significant sections of the working-class and people's movements, then the talk of revolution will ring true."[58]

Classical Marxism vs. the New Working Class Theory

The conflict between classical Marxism and the new working class theory engendered a number of subsidiary conflicts in regard to New Left praxis in this period—conflicts which continued to sharpen until they tore SDS apart. Should the New Left be a mass organization or a vanguard?

Should its membership be exclusionist or not? Should radicals seek national power? How can participatory democracy be made harmonious with the effort to acquire power? Should revolution be made for oneself or for others? These were issues about which there was a good deal of wrangling in this second phase, but no general resolution. Because they were rooted in a fundamental theoretical conflict, they remained divisive issues within the Movement.

Mass Organization vs. Vanguard

The New Left never reached a consensus on the subject of building a mass organization or establishing a vanguard party of cadres. Bob Pardun wrote an article about cadres, but he could not resolve the conflict, as shown in his concluding sentences: "The contradiction between mass organization and cadre will not be made to disappear by ignoring it. Rather it must be resolved in a way which will further the struggle."[59] Miles took note of the fact that "the drift to Marxism-Leninism has been undeniable," but concluded that "the New Left has failed to develop the characteristic Marxist-Leninist organization, the vanguard party, and thus continues to operate as an amorphous movement."[60] However, the Leninist concept of a vanguard party did appeal to some New Leftists.[61] Others confessed fascination with the vanguard idea, but were ambivalent for the obvious reason that the idea was Old Leftist; most New Leftists were not yet ready to capitulate to Old Left patterns of organization any more than to those of ideology. "No one wants to give their lives to another sect; they want to win."[62]

Perhaps the reason for the growing appeal in the concept of the vanguard party was that new radicalism was limited mainly to students; there was no apparent ground swell of radicalism through all sectors of the population. Almost by default, therefore, the new radicals were impelled in the direction of preferring vanguardism to mass organization. Noam Chomsky, who hoped—as did many radicals—for a mass movement, said, "A serious mass movement of the left should involve all . . . segments of American society. Its politics and understanding must grow out of their combined efforts to build a new world."[63] When such a prospect was not forthcoming and seemed unlikely, the idea had to be scratched and an alternative sought. The appeal of the Leninist formula grew.[64]

Exclusionism vs. Nonexclusionism

In the context of the SDS in the mid-1960s, exclusionism continued to limit the Movement to New Left radicals. Nonexclusionism indicated the desire to forge a merger between the New Left and the Old, thus breaking down some of the antipathy of the new radicals toward the doctrinaire purists. The issue split the editorial board of the radical journal, *Studies on the Left*. While Tom Hayden and some others thought that "the editors should focus on exploring dilemmas instead of proposing organizational formulas," most board members "favored an organizational call of some sort: a unification of the new movements; a coalition of the old and new left; a new Socialist Party; or at least a common and guiding radical ideology."[65]

The irony in this controversy was that Hayden, who was closer than the opposition to the early SDS stand of non-ideological protest and sought to avoid the factionalism endemic to highly-developed ideologies, ended as an exclusionist. That his position lost was important to New Left history in showing the extent to which ideology and revolution had replaced participatory democracy and protest as the leading motifs of the New Left. It was even more ironic that exclusionism was again to become an issue in the third phase of SDS, but this time in reverse. The doctrinaire ideologists sought to make SDS into their own image, and those who remained faithful to early SDS impulses found themselves unwelcome in the house they themselves had built.

Participatory Democracy vs. the Gaining of Power

Another conflict which wracked SDS in its middle period was that of participatory democracy opposed to the assumption of power. Calvert saw this problem as especially crucial: "The primary contradiction of SDS involves the conflict between the notion of participatory democracy as a vision of the good society and its ineffectiveness as a style and structure for serious radical work."[66] While the idea of participatory democracy seemed less satisfactory in the mid-1960s than it had when first enunciated, it continued to have its champions. Flacks advocated it, saying it was "silly to talk about taking power" because of the Left's small size and because "more fundamentally, it is not power which we, as committed democrats, ought to be after."[67] Gitlin agreed: "We simply haven't the power."[68] But successful actions, such as the strike at Columbia, had a way of drowning out realism. Hayden could thus effuse, "What is certain is that we are moving toward power—the power to stop the machine if it cannot be made to serve human ends."[69]

The conflict between participatory democracy and the quest for power was never resolved. Calvert suggested, "We need to go beyond the rhetoric of participatory democracy without losing the visionary power which it embodies"[70]—whatever that means. One sees here the dynamics which caused Lynd to lament that "the movement vacillates between extremes of anarchism and Bolshevik centralization."[71]

In the place of the ideal of participatory democracy came the reality of elitist manipulation. Rich Rothstein conceded that elitism and unrepresentative manipulation increased after 1963. For instance, rotating all the offices merely resulted in a hegemony of the permanent staff in the SDS headquarters.[72] Here was bureaucracy on the lowest level; the effort to institute participatory democracy could not control even this, much less the federal bureaucracy. Garson concurred that phrases like "participatory democracy" and "let the people decide" had "degenerated into pure demagogy."[73]

When SDS entered its second phase and revolution became the watchword, the idea of participatory democracy, with its bias against centralization, was hopelessly irrelevant. Revolution demands centralization, a coordinated effort. It is not surprising that even democratic centralism began to look good to some of the young radicals.

In addition to the manipulation going on within SDS and other Movement organizations, the radicals were forced by the realities of personal and group relations into manipulative tactics toward those outside the Movement. Lynd attempted to articulate the radical position on seeking recruits: "We are not planning a conspiracy and we should not hide as if we were. It is not our intention to manipulate people, to put something over on them through an innocent guise. We need to feel about ourselves and act consistently with the belief that we are trying to give substance to those aspirations toward a better life which people know they are being denied."[74]

There is the question of whether those other people knew what Lynd knew they were being denied. Some radicals reluctantly admitted that they did not, leaving the radical organizers in the awkward position of trying to convert persons who did not know that they were lacking what the organizers claimed. Given New Left faith in the individual's ability to guide his own destiny, the organizers were placed in a dilemma perceived by Aronson: "Here is where the political goal of developing a radical movement falls into contradiction with the utopian demands almost inevitably placed upon that movement. The role of organizer as educator requires that he be more advanced than those he would organize. He has greater knowledge, his capacities are generally more developed.... But the personal stake in organizing as a new life, freed from such things as inequality and manipulation, makes it difficult to admit this. One of the consequences may be a neurotic organizing manner, which continually seeks to deny this fact."[75]

Revolution for Self vs. Revolution for Others

Intimately related to the tension between participatory democracy and the drive for power was the tension of the subject of revolution. This tension was present from the beginning of SDS, but was heightened by the search for ideology. Marcuse emphasized revolution for the self. Explaining why radicals could not be content to say, "What is necessary is to destroy [*sic*]; afterwards we will see what comes," he counseled: "our goals, our values, our own and new morality, our OWN morality, must be visible already in our actions. The new human beings who we want to help to create—we must already strive to be these human beings here and now."[76]

Spokesmen for a revolutionary analysis often couched their appeal in personalistic terms, while emphasizing the need to free others—typical of the SDS desire to fuse the two revolutions. Calvert wanted others to feel what SDSers felt for themselves: "we must involve them on the basic level of their own lives, on the gut level. We have to build a movement out of people's guts, out of their so-far internalized rejection of American society, and present people with a revolutionary alternative to the American way of life."[77]

By 1968 there was a strong reaction against the perennial SDS emphasis on the personal. Les Coleman, then an SDS leader, voiced it: "The cult of personal liberation leads to a no struggle ethic. The substitution of the beautiful community for collective struggle often finds its theoretical underpinning in Marcuse with an assist from Calvert. . . . I am not part of any faction which condones privileged individualism and the no struggle line."[78] So strong was this reaction against the personal that by then SDS had relegated its immediate constituency, students, to the status of the tail to be wagged by the working-class dog. Revolution for the sake of others was paramount. Mike Klonsky, SDS national secretary, offered the membership a resolution from the National Council which read in part: "At this point in history, SDS is faced with its most crucial ideological decision, that of determining its direction with regards to the working class. . . . students alone cannot and will not be able to bring about the downfall of capitalism. . . . This means that our struggles must be integrated into the struggles of working people."[79]

Unrealistic Self-Assessment

Flacks has said that SDS knew what it was doing in the early 1960s, but that later it lost its way. There is some truth to that. In the second period, radicals were thrashing about desperately in various directions, searching for coherence and not finding it. Internal squabbling became vicious. If the radicals were correct in perceiving that the non-ideological route of the early SDS was a dead end and that a clearly articulated ideology of revolution was needed, they still proved themselves unable to handle ideology; that route also reached a dead end. Not only did a coherent overall position never develop, but what formulations did appear only fragmented the Movement and impaired its effectiveness. It is possible that the very call for a revolutionary ideology was misguided; radicals may have been asking themselves for the impossible. A coherent revolutionary ideology would have been possible only if the radicals were correct in what they assumed to be the nature of the reality of America. It was an article of faith among them that their assumptions were accurate, but that is precisely the point: it was a matter of faith—a faith not shared by the overwhelming majority of Americans.

What was perhaps most striking about the New Left's continuing search for ideology was the unrealistic judgment which accompanied it. For example, Sidney Lens offered this scenario:

It is impossible to chart the specific road to power by the New Left and the mass of Americans whose interests it represents, but one can outline its directions. As a catalyst the New Left will mount one campaign after another against the manifestations of imperialism and racism, splitting away one segment of the population after another which currently identifies strongly with the establishment. As it wins over these segments from the middle classes, labor, the military, it will use its countervailing power to whittle away the present institutions, the profit motive, the competitive elan, until finally it can reconstruct a new society based on popular participative power.[80]

It is obvious why radicals had to maintain this optimistic pose. To quote Chomsky, "For a person to commit himself to a movement for radical social change, with all of the uncertainty and hazard that this entails, he must have a strong reason to believe that there is some likelihood of success in bringing about a new social order."[81] But was there a strong reason to believe in this revolutionary venture? A number of radicals doubted it. Lynd confessed, "In our hearts, most of us most of the time don't believe it [a transition to socialism] can happen."[82] Oglesby agreed: "We are not now free to fight The Revolution except in fantasy."[83] And again: "If you are trying to tell me you know already what The Revolution Itself will look like, you are either a charlatan or a fool. We have no scenario."[84]

In retrospect, the air of unreality in New Left rhetoric about revolution and socialist ideology was inevitable. Not only did the ideological search betray a lack of understanding of the American people, but it did not even fulfill the deepest impulses which originally propelled the New Left into being. The hopeless incoherence in ideological posturing assumed by the New Left is everywhere apparent. The original New Left was primarily a humanistic groping for personal liberation; so it is apparent why the narrowing of its focus to politics distorted the members' mission and resulted in an intolerable degree of self-delusion. This process had already become clear during the mid-1960s. The later period would make it even more obvious.

— 3 —

The Late Phase of the New Left

In the late 1960s the New Left moved into a third distinct phase. Contradictions which were present from the beginning of SDS grew into open factionalism. Ideological formulas and revolutionary rhetoric, which began to surface in the second period, now gained ascendancy, and spokesmen competed with one another for the hardest line and the most strident tone. The earlier history of SDS was viewed as something which had to be (or had been) transcended, and the defining characteristic of the New Left— the indivisibility of personal and political liberation—was abandoned in the confusion. Calvert asserted: "The Port Huron Statement has been transcended in our experience: it is high time that it was replaced by a new document which would correspond to the new understanding which we have developed."[1] Even old guard Clark Kissinger dismissed the Port Huron Statement as "quaint" and "interesting."[2] No new manifesto was forthcoming, however—for the simple reason that SDS could achieve no consensus.

Most radicals clearly magnified the political at the expense of the personal; some, in reaction, did the opposite. If the first phase saw a leaning in the direction of the personal and the second saw the start of a tilt toward the political, at least the Movement maintained the fiction of natural unity through both stages. That unity was now a shambles. And with the abandonment of the chief principle which made the New Left unique came the demise of SDS and related organizational presences of the new radicalism. What survived could no longer lay legitimate claim to being a *new* Left. Incoherence had now grown into something approximating schizophrenia.

The death of the New Left as a unified movement was not due to a lessening of the sense of alienation among the young. The widespread student unrest of 1969 and 1970 demonstrated that never had radical consciousness been stronger.[3] Rather, it died from exhaustion and despair.

Various strategies and theories had been proposed, but none of them affected the established order. Nothing had worked. Whatever could be called an accomplishment was piecemeal and reformist, and the rhetoric of revolution dismissed it as inconsequential.

By 1968, Marxism had "come to occupy a central position in the theoretical development of the new left."[4] Carl Davidson announced, "It should be clear that the aim of the resistance strategy is to transform itself into a class-conscious revolutionary socialist movement."[5] At the 1968 SDS convention, candidate Bernardine Dohrn was asked if she was a socialist. She replied, "I consider myself a revolutionary communist"—and was promptly elected to high office.[6]

That the New Left seemed to have forgotten that it was supposed to reject the Old Left as well as liberalism was a frequently noted irony. David Horowitz warned, "The self-styled Marxist-Leninist-Maoists of SDS would do well to remember that the New Left grew out of two bankruptcies—not just liberalism, but old-line Marxism as well."[7] In the opinion of Greg Calvert and Carol Neiman, the New Left's romantic identification with the Third World liberation movements was mainly responsible for the factionalism.[8]

Even the new ideologues feared the debilitating effects of factionalism. Les Coleman warned: "As the ideological struggle in the organization sharpens, as we move to self-consciously define our work and struggles as part of a working class struggle, there is a great danger that the resulting factionalism will obscure rather than clarify the ideological questions we must face."[9] But this fear was not strong enough to suppress ideological struggle; only "false factionalism" was to be shunned.[10]

Michael Miles has observed, "The history of the 'Movement' is a history of movement leftward. . . . By the late 1960s, the momentum of the New Left had carried it to the end of the political spectrum: left-wing communism."[11] To trace the history of the New Left according to such categories, its reformism might place it somewhere between liberalism and the Old Left in the early 1960s. In mid-decade, its location on the spectrum became fuzzy and unclear. When clarity re-emerged in the late 1960s, it was further left than the Old Left—at least, its dominant voice (not always its best) placed it there.

The Triumph of Sectarianism

Factional disputes within SDS became so byzantine in 1968 and 1969 that they defy brief summary. By the 1969 convention, all major factions could at least agree that they were Marxist-Leninist and pro-Maoist communists. One unused to the ways of Marxist ideologues might suppose such agreement to preclude deep divisions and to establish a basis for community. Such was not the case. The sense of community was much stronger before ideological purity became a desideratum. Now it was a matter of each sect seeking to interpret the holy writings of Marx in the purest fashion. Before the Movement went Marxist-Leninist, its differences of opinion were not couched in an appeal to authority. SDS factionalism caused Staughton Lynd to lament: "present SDS practice appears to me indistinguishable from that of the Old Left sects in the days of my youth. Caucuses form, meet secretly, and circulate position papers. Finally, amidst much mutual denunciation, there is a vote. Whatever factional position gets most votes becomes 'the correct political perspective for the coming period.' "[12]

Progressive Labor Party

Perhaps the most dramatic episode of sectarianism in SDS was that which centered around the role of the Progressive Labor Party (PLP) after it infiltrated SDS in 1966. Its members were quiescent for a while after joining SDS, but by 1968 and 1969 their effect was seriously fracturing. Progressive Labor sought the establishment of a Worker–Student Alliance which would allow the students only an auxiliary role, the real revolutionary agent to be the working class—and rather narrowly defined at that. In the eyes of other SDSers, PLP was guilty of a number of erroneous views, among them opposition to all nationalistic movements of liberation— including the National Liberation Front in South Vietnam—and rejection of independent movements for liberation of blacks and women. But the main fault of PLP—which led to its expulsion from SDS in 1969—was that it envisioned itself as the vanguard of the revolution and therefore sought to take over and run SDS.[13] PLP's contribution to SDS theory was to make class analysis central; even the factions that united to expel PLP accepted the necessity of class analysis, rejecting only PLP's particular variant of it.

Perhaps the most significant aspect of the PLP episode is that it had such a substantial appeal within SDS. Its Marxism was wooden and unsophisticated, and its sectarian spirit clashed with the earlier free-wheeling temper of SDS. But it had a logical consistency about its ideology which was attractive, and to many SDSers floundering about in a miasma of abortive theoretical discussions, even PLP looked like a port in the storm.

Revolutionary Youth Movement

The two principal factions to emerge from the battle over PLP were the Revolutionary Youth Movement II and Weatherman, both initially belonging to an SDS group called the Revolutionary Youth Movement (RYM). They joined forces to eliminate the competition of PLP, but it soon became apparent that their reasons for doing so were different. No sooner was PLP out of the way than ideological squabbling increased between the two former collaborator–groups.

In 1968 SDS passed a resolution entitled "Toward a Revolutionary Youth Movement" which called for the transformation of SDS from a protesting *student* movement into a *revolutionary youth* movement and which invoked Marxian categories as a matter of course. It recommended "the transcendance [*sic*] of SDS from a radical student organization to a class conscious movement of the youth of the entire working class."[14] Further, the task of a revolutionary youth movement was "*to develop a force which can help to seed an anti-imperialist movement among the mass of people and especially among the mass of working people who must lead that movement. Where possible this force must aid in the building of the communist party that can guide this movement to victory and to socialism.*"[15]

Weatherman.   Weatherman was the faction of the Revolutionary Youth Movement which successfully elected its slate to national offices in SDS at the 1969 convention. It is difficult to explicate the Weatherman line. Carl Oglesby said, "Any close reading of the RYM's Weatherman statement will drive you blind."[16] It spoke of such divergent matters as "the vanguard nature of the black struggle in this country," "the self-conscious organizing of women" as "a primary responsibility" of SDS women, a "neighborhood-based city-wide youth movement," and a "mutual aid anti-pig self-defense network."[17] It saw revolutionary efforts in the United States as following the lead of more advanced liberation movements abroad and as part of an international movement.[18]

While other factions of SDS were equally ideological—and even more so—none was as militant as Weatherman. Weatherman sought to move beyond ideological formulas and actually to begin a revolution. If its suggestions were as crude as was its theoretical discussion, at least there was a genuine effort to link theory with practice:

A revolution is a war; when the movement in this country can defend itself militarily against total repression it will be part of the revolutionary war.

This will require a cadre organization, effective secrecy, self-reliance among the cadres, and an integrated relationship with the active mass-based movement. To win a war with an enemy as highly organized and centralized as the imperialists will require a (clandestine) organization of revolutionaries, having also a unified "general staff"; that is, combined at some point with discipline under one centralized leadership. Because war is political, political tasks—the international communist revolution—must guide it. Therefore the centralized organization of revolutionaries must be a political organization as well as military, what is generally called a "Marxist-Leninist" party. ... The strategy of the RYM for developing an active mass base, tying the city-wide fights to community and city-wide anti-pig movement, and for building a party eventually out of this motion, fits with the world strategy for winning the revolution, builds a movement oriented toward power, and will become one division of the International Liberation Army ... Long Live the Victory of People's War![19]

Revolutionary Youth Movement II.   Those members of the RYM who disagreed with the Weatherman line called themselves the Revolutionary Youth Movement II (RYM II). Their principal position paper concurred in Weatherman's view that the chief enemy of the worldwide proletariat was U. S. imperalism, and in the concept of the vanguard party. But they disavowed Weatherman's infatuation with the model of national liberation struggles abroad, preferring to emphasize the possibilities of their own native Movement: "THE YOUTH MOVEMENT IS NOT A STAGE, OR A TEMPORARY REBELLION. IT WILL FIGHT THROUGH TO THE END."[20] RYM II was not yet ready for Weatherman's declaration of war and what that entailed.

The attack on Weatherman, curiously, tried to link it with positions mutually rejected by Weatherman and RYM II. One detractor found Weatherman in several instances "in company with PLP," considered that "the *Weatherman* viewpoint represents a restatement of the now discredited 'new working class' argument," and asserted that "*Weatherman* does not believe in the class struggle."[21] His conclusion followed logically: this most militant wing of SDS was really just bourgeois.

In Praise of Factionalism

While the main criticism of SDS by outsiders during the mid-1960s was that it did not have enough ideology, now SDS was to be faulted for having too much. In their own defense SDS members actually took to praising factionalism. The REP collective, those in charge of bringing ideology to SDS, spoke of "the anti-communism implicit in ultra-democratic objections (over-adherence to the surface forms of democracy, with no consideration of the need for discipline) to disciplined factions."[22]

As an indication of how far SDS had moved in a few years, an essay written in 1965 by Al Haber treated the question of whether the New Left should be open to Marxist-Leninists and to others who were leftist but not part of the anti-communist left. His answer was affirmative.[23] In just three years the issue was the opposite. Those who were not Marxist-Leninist were now the ones likely to feel excluded. Exclusionism won out within SDS, though not the type against which Haber had warned. One either toed the line or dropped out.

In the final analysis, it seems that Progressive Labor had the last laugh. SDS collapsed after it expelled PLP. Weatherman went underground, and RYM II faded away. PLP was one faction which survived the death of SDS in 1969. The group which went by the name of Students for a Democratic Society after 1969 belonged to PLP as its front organization on campus.

Effect of New Factions on Old Guard

By the late 1960s the old guard was conspicuously absent from leadership roles in SDS. Still, they retained primary loyalties to SDS and considered themselves Movement people. Where else could they turn for sustenance for their radicalism? They were, therefore, influenced by the tergiversations of SDS, although sometimes reluctantly.

The capitulation of those with old-guard tendencies who had formerly rejected Old Leftism was reflected by Carl Oglesby, when he conceded, "*There was—and is—no other coherent, integrative, and explicit philosophy of revolution* [than Marxism–Leninism]."[24] Yet in the same article he testified to the personal dislocation experienced at this time by older SDSers: "For a long time I was baffled. Last fall [1968] the word began to reach me: It was being said that I had 'bad politics.' How could that be, I wondered, since I thought I had no politics at all. But by winter I conceded the point: no politics is the same as bad politics. So there followed a time in which I experimented with only the 'mass line.' Could Klonsky and Coleman be right? It didn't come to much. My mind and my instincts only became adversaries. By spring I had to deactivate, couldn't function, had to float. What I know now is that this did not happen to me alone."[25]

Tom Hayden's case offers a clear example of the extent and direction of the influence by the last generation of SDS leaders on members of the old guard. Hayden—the chief architect of the existentialist, reformist Port Huron Statement—now openly referred to himself as a revolutionary. His analysis of America had shifted from seeing it as under the hegemony of liberalism which sought to co-opt dissent to finding it a fascist state that sought to repress dissent.[26] He praised "the seriousness of the Weathermen, for here at last was a group willing to go beyond the pseudo-radicalism of the white left into a head-on showdown with the system."[27]

Hayden was quite explicit about the need to adapt to new moods of the constituency in which he had played a leadership role:

> In a white movement that arose from the nothingness of the fifties, it was no accident that leadership went to articulate, aggressive males, and no doubt this pattern will continue for some time. But forms die, or at least change, and the test of a revolutionary may be how well he or she adapts to new possibilities. . . . From the younger revolutionaries in general comes the insight that our pressure politics, our peace mobilizations, and our theatrics, though legitimate in raising issues in the sixties, are inadequate to the task of surviving and making revolutionary change in the seventies.[28]

In the penultimate chapter of his 1970 book, *Trial*, Hayden reached his concluding peroration: *"We are living in a time of universal desire for a new social order, a time when total revolution is on the agenda."*[29] It is a long way from the Port Huron Statement to this, but Hayden-the-leader had followed dutifully the changing New Left line.

Whether they stayed in or dropped out, many of the old guard acknowledged the failure of the original Movement. Richard Flacks said, "The New Left which emerged in this country during the sixties had disintegrated."[30] Rothstein elaborated: "The regular appearance of new radical books and journals, rather than new projects and organizations, describes our situation. This book is an example. We are a cultural phenomenon, not a political threat."[31]

Predictably, those who retained elements of the original SDS vision saw the doctrinaire ideologues as the villains. Gitlin accused: "in the name of Marxism, or loyalty to the world proletariat (and specifically to Vietnam), the movement proceeded to drown its novelty and to deny its right to exist for itself. In the process, of course, it became rather useless to others, since it could do little for others unless it were first organized for itself."[32] In the view of Calvert and Neiman, when SDS careened into the thicket of ideological squabbling, it left behind its earlier confidence in the rightness of its basic instincts, and this proved fatal.

> Because people felt weak and vulnerable, they began to use rhetoric which seemed strong and courageous. It was like a revival meeting with the old tune "I am weak but Thou art strong, Jesus save me from all wrong." But in this case, the Lord had become Marx or Lenin or Mao. . . . Reuniting the personal and the political was the New Left's

attempt at transcending the dichotomy of history and the novel by making *history* and *my story* come back together in a politics of experience. . . . The New Left tried to overcome that split in people's lives by re-establishing the unity of the self. When it failed, the schizoid language of Marxism and Leninism was used to fill a gap which experience had been unable, or only partially able to fill.[33]

Backlash: Renewal of Personalistic Motives

If the main organizational drift of SDS was toward an ideological hardening, that process also set in motion a backlash in the form of a reversion of many New Leftists to what are properly considered extensions of the early SDS passion for personal liberation. While the dogmatists were divided among themselves over jots and tittles and hence responsible for the demise of the SDS organization, there arose a division of thought which was deeper and of greater significance. Many radicals caught up in the search for ideology eventually realized, much as did John Stuart Mill in his autobiography, that if everything that they advocated in the public sphere came true, they still would not be personally happy. Just as Mill turned to the development of himself (in his case, through the reading of poetry and a liaison with a married woman), so did some of the radicals. This conflict is seen in Todd Gitlin's important essay, "The Politics and Vision of the New Left," in which he declared himself afraid to state what he really wanted, since—if each item were effected—it would not be enough and the anger and pain would remain.[34] Coupled with the reluctant conclusion that there would be no overall socialist revolution in the America of their generation and perhaps never in the foreseeable future, such abiding radical discontent drove many radicals back to the early New Left concern with personal liberation. They thought that social changes could be effected to ease their existential anguish, even if "revolution now" was impossible.

Radical Feminism

The most important of these separatistic endeavors in the late 1960s was the radical wing of the women's liberation movement. There is an analogy between the radical women's liberation movement and that for black liberation, which had always been personal and therefore had never fitted smoothly into the development of primarily white radical groups like SDS. Radical blacks had not always explicitly rejected making common cause with radical whites, but they intuitively reached for the more immediate goal of personal liberation of themselves and their brothers and sisters.[35]

The fact that many radical women turned their attention from making a socialist revolution to liberating themselves from the social structures that kept them from full self-expression had a deleterious effect on radical organizations. In some cases it was a major cause of their total collapse. The best indicator of the primacy which they gave to personal liberation is that these women would allow such a fate to befall organizations to which they had deeply committed themselves. Radical feminists still recited the slogans of socialist revolution, but they did not shrink from undermining organizations trying to bring about that revolution in order to seek their own liberation.

An indication of the return to the early style of the New Left was the appearance of autobiographical essays such as that by Roberta Salper in the book she edited.[36] It included only minimal generalizations and was clear evidence of the existential focus which was primary in radical feminism. Another indication of the primacy of the personal among these radical women was their elevation of sexism over imperialism.[37]

The indictment of male supremacy did not exclude radical males. The radical feminists came to "the realization that as women radicals we are not radical women . . . We realize that women are organized into the Movement by men and continue to relate to it through men."[38] In the words of a group called the New York Radical Women, "We ask not if something is 'reformist,' 'radical,' 'revolutionary,' or 'normal.' We ask: is it good for women or bad for women?"[39]

The 1968 SDS convention marked a turning-point for radical women. They presented a demand that SDS take a strong affirmative stand on women's liberation, but it was rejected. That action cleared the way for a separatist movement among radical women and made it inevitable. The radical feminists, therefore, rejected the idea of restricting their movement to a caucus within SDS, and declared that it "should have its own structure and program, although it should work closely with SDS, and most of its members would probably be active in SDS (or other Movement projects and organizations) as individuals."[40] Some radicals recognized that while "the quest for personal self-liberation, the New Left's keynote, was now most of all exemplified in the lives of politically active women," the rise of the women's movement nevertheless was one indication of the end of the New Left with its defining goal of combining the personal and the political.[41]

To say that the radical feminists gave primacy to the personal is not to say that they ignored the political; rather, they claimed that "the feminist movement is the first to combine effectively the 'personal' with the 'political' "[42]—exactly the claim made by the early SDS about itself. One of them testified: "After years of fragmented university existence, split between my love of literature and interest in education on one hand, and commitment to political activism on the other, I finally feel coherent and whole, thanks to the Women's Movement."[43]

An indication of this need to combine the personal and the political was the frequent use of political imagery for issues of sex, for example: "Our bodies are free territory to other male colonizers when not 'protected' by an individual male colonist. What is rape but an imperialist act upon the territory of our bodies."[44] Lillian Robinson analogized between husband/wife and bourgeoisie/proletariat.[45]

The effort to link their personal concerns with Marxian categories popular in the late 1960s posed endless problems. Typical of the efforts to fuse analysis of both sex and class was the "National Resolution on Women" presented to the National Council of SDS in 1968:

> Women are not oppressed as a class but they are oppressed as women within each class. . . . the fact that male supremacy persists in the movement today, raises the issue that although no people's liberation can happen without a socialist revolution in this country, a socialist revolution could take place which maintains the secondary position of women in society. Therefore the liberation of women must become a conscious part of our struggle for people's liberation.[46]

Another stratagem for uniting feminism and Marxism was the call for working-class women to lead the women's liberation movement, since they were "super-oppressed and super-exploited" by virtue of both sex and class.[47] But in their struggle with Marxism, radical feminists usually ended up modifying it significantly before pledging their allegiance to its theories.[48]

Some women recognized that the effect of their feminism was a dilution of their involvement in radical politics. Kathy McAfee and Myrna Wood reflected the disillusionment that many Movement women experienced with women's liberation groups: "More often than not these groups never get beyond the level of therapy sessions; . . . they often encourage escape from political struggle."[49] Some radical feminists called others back from self-indulgence to the task of making a socialist revolution, though without giving up their feminism. Roberta Salper, with a straight face, warned: "A theory and practice that involves a long-term rejection of men as a class is unworkable because men comprise nearly 50 percent of the population. If we are ever to redistribute the power in this country, we cannot ignore one-half of the population. We need a class analysis that is bisexual, not unisexual."[50]

The call for radical feminists to reassert their leftist politics in many cases has been ignored; in at least one important case it was directly countered. In a fascinating open letter printed in *Ms.* magazine, Jane Alpert, a fugitive from the law who was convicted because of her Weatherman-style revolutionary violence, announced "my conversion from the left to radical feminism."[51] She addressed her open letter to her "Sisters in the Weather Underground" and wrote to "persuade you to leave the dying left in which you are floundering and begin to put your immense courage and unique skills to work for women—for yourselves."[52] Insisting that "the politico-feminist split is a real one," she advised, "let your own self-interest be your highest priority."[53] It is too early to determine whether most radical feminists will follow the advice of Alpert or Salper. But Alpert's position has a logical consistency and single-mindedness which avoids the inevitable personal-political dichotomy shown by Salper.

The Case of Paul Potter

While radical feminists were the major illustration of the renewed interest in personal liberation among radicals of the late 1960s, many male radicals felt the same appeal. Perhaps the clearest example was Paul Potter, who served as President of SDS in 1965 and whom Todd Gitlin recently called "a personification of SDS."[54]

His deeply perceptive book, *A Name for Ourselves,* was a memorial of the existentialist orientation of the Movement. Like the early SDS, the crucial problem facing the young radicals is pinpointed as that of the relationship between autobiography and politics.[55] Like the early SDS, it was anti-ideological and in that sense anti-intellectual. Potter confessed, "when I was frank, I admitted that I didn't put all that much stock in writing. It wasn't as if I'd picked up Marx or Mao or Jefferson or anyone else and had the world change in front of my eyes. If anything, it was the other way around. It was only when my world had begun to change that some writers I considered important began to come into focus, make sense, and help to articulate what I already felt."[56] He understood from experience why the Movement turned toward ideology: "one day we reach the point of political frustration where suddenly the idea of a rigid (well-worked-out), closed (self-confident), religious (authoritative), sectarian (distinguishing us once and for all from all of them) system becomes terribly appealing."[57] But even Lenin's writings did not suffice. "What upsets me is the assumption that those musty books, even if they are correct in every didactic thing they say, can ever substitute for the creation of an ideology out of our own, immediate, verifiable experience."[58] Ideology blotted out experience. "It is incredible that we could create a political ideology and not give ourselves even superficial examination, but that is exactly what we did."[59]

In retrospect, Potter saw the need for "a movement that told people the revolution was inside them, inside their real and potential breakaway experience."[60] But what could provide the basis for such an experience? Potter was astonishingly simple: it is love. In an important passage which outlined as clearly as anything written the radicals' sense of alienation, he commented:

> The experience of growing up is the experience of having the society plant something deep down inside of you, almost at the very bottom, that is not your own.... What is ours is the sense of emptiness—a sense that we have been torn away from ourselves, lost track of who we are, and in so doing, lost track of the capacity to touch the other people around us. What is very much ours is a terrible need to fill that emptiness.
> Let me call that need the need to love.[61]

Potter was well aware that his assertion that "what most Americans want more than any other thing is love . . . is not what a radical is supposed to say."[62] But when he explained why he needed love, he did associate with his fellows' writings: "when I say that what we want most from life is love, I mean that what we want is to be whole and free."[63] Other radicals spoke frequently about their personal need for wholeness and freedom, particularly in the early days of the New Left.

His touting of love did not compel Potter to go apolitical, because he placed the reason for his lack of love not in himself, but in society.[64] He made the move from recognition of the existential need for love to a political resolution as follows: "Love *is* real. But love is not possible. To understand that love is impossible but real is to formulate a revolutionary proposition about the society that made love impossible."[65] By not connecting love with politics, radicals have made politics alien, in Potter's opinion, because they "have not been able to draw clear, straight, sharp lines between our need and political goals."[66] Potter praised the radical feminists for having begun to make such connections.[67]

In 1965 Potter called upon SDS to "name the system" against which it was revolting. In response, Carl Oglesby offered the name "corporate liberalism." While the Movement developed further ideologies which later changed that name to imperialism, Oglesby's label did not satisfy Potter.

His disappointment with Oglesby's speech was in its precision at the point where Potter felt ambiguity to be essential: new hope for radical change must include a rejection of the old terminology of leftism.[68] When he finally offered a name for the system which he was rejecting, Potter certainly could not be faulted for undue precision:

> If I was forced to give the system a name now, I would not call it capitalism. I would perhaps say that it was hate and we are love. . . . What we experience is depersonalization through bureaucracy, standardization of human beings to meet bureaucratic and technological demands, the destruction of the family and the primary community, the impossibility of love—and all of those things are rooted in a deeper essence than is described by the term capitalism.
>
> We are not middle-class. We are love; we are courage; we are community. They are hate, fear and isolation. That is the beginning of a better understanding.[69]

Later he described himself and his fellow-radicals as "fucked up" and expressed thoughts of suicide. If "we are love," "we" are not health.

Potter's break from activism was complete: "The old focus, the old politics ('new politics') that carried me from fall 1957 through the first three months of 1970 is gone."[70] And what was left for Paul Potter? "In its place, there are only impressions and fragments—except there is a relationship with Leni—focal and primary—a place where sometimes I can relax and share and reach out and find good things."[71] The long years of seeking personal fulfillment through political activism ended in the love of a girl. Potter's privatism outstripped that of the early SDS, and it did so for the obvious reason that his many and sustained efforts at public redress proved ultimately to be failures. He was a person of boundless energy, but the shipwreck of the Movement left him foundered.

Other Cases of the Revival of Personalism

While Potter's book was the fullest and most articulate expression of the personalism which resurfaced during the third stage of the New Left's history, it was not an isolated case. Calvert and Neiman sounded the same note: "If you want to know what we mean by the good society, it is this. We would like to live in a world in which each person in the community of humankind would have the deep and powerful experience of being in touch with his feelings and with himself, a community in which each individual could say: '*I am a lover in a society of friends.*'"[72]

Ronald Aronson, who in 1966 voiced the need for developing an ideology,[73] in 1970 urged "spending as much time looking inward as looking out, as much time locating and breaking free of hangups as in locating and attacking the enemy."[74] He eulogized the good old days, before ideology swept in. "The early New Left had its finger on something more vital. But it failed to follow through its anarchism and rejection of ideology and demand for a new life."[75] This renewed personalism led Aronson to turn on his old mentor, Herbert Marcuse, whom he had grown to see as an example of the retreat into radical thought divorced from action:

> revolutionaries had to begin by feeling in their gut the need for liberation. Feeling it in my gut, however, drew me away from your writings. Even mastering all your ideas has not been enough. Two themes which I didn't find there helped me to get clear on what liberation means: being whole and being myself. . . . Being whole means . . . having ideas about life which correspond to my needs, political reactions which flow from my pain and urge for happiness, analyses which are drawn from my experience, actions which come from my sense of what is appropriate. Being whole means above all trusting myself and not forces outside me, putting myself at the center of everything I do. Being whole *is* being myself.[76]

It is no accident that the revival of personalism was manifested particularly by those SDS leaders who were active in the early days. While some of them occasionally made Marxist noises, they seem to have recognized—at least intuitively and often even intellectually—that doctrinaire Marxism was not a medium through which they could express their true selves. The leading SDS spokesmen in its ideological phase came into the Movement at a later date and helped to divert it from its original course.

Marcuse's Advice to the Polarized Radicals

Among those who recognized the developing polarization between the personal and the political in the New Left of the late 1960s was Herbert Marcuse. His paternal instincts toward the young radicals were evident in his latest book, *Counterrevolution and Revolt,* published in 1972, a substantial part of which was devoted to attempting to head off this split and to remeld the two in viable and creative tension. He scored "the anti-intellectualism rampant in the New Left"[77] and cautioned against what he called "the new individualism," reminding the Movement, "To be sure, no revolution without individual liberation, but also no individual liberation without the liberation of society."[78] With an eye toward the feminists, he said in particular that sexual liberation will not suffice to roll back the counter-revolutionary forces.[79]

Marcuse was aware that New Left hopes for a quick revolution had been dashed, and he called on the young radicals to show the steadfastness required for long-term fulfillment of their goals. In the closing sentences of his book, he finally reached the point which had motivated his writing it: "Strategies must be developed which are adapted to combat the counter-revolution. The outcome depends, to a great extent, on the ability of the young generation—not to drop out and not to accommodate, but to learn how to regroup after defeat, how to develop, with the new sensibility a new rationality, to sustain the long process of education . . . For the next revolution will be the concern of generations, and 'the final crisis of capitalism' may take all but a century."[80] It was the turn toward privatism which would undercut this "long-march" revolution. But the new individualists have wearied of waiting for the revolutionary Godot who never comes, and Marcuse has good reason to be worried.

The Continuing Radical Impulse

The New American Movement

Although the organizations of the New Left were mostly in a state of ruins by 1970, the radical impulse was very much alive. It was therefore inevitable that some radicals would attempt to revive an organizational presence, the most noteworthy being the New American Movement (NAM), founded in 1971. It was an effort to establish a national organization which would provide "a place for the masses of Americans who have become radicalized in the past few years," rather than a cadre organization.[81] As the founders of NAM saw it, Americans were ready for leftism in the early 1970s as never before, but the left itself was the major impediment to establishing a mass base of radicalism—a base which NAM leaders estimated could run as high as twenty percent of the population if properly cultivated.[82] NAM thought of itself not as "the final vehicle for working people to take state power, but as an interim institution, built for the next several years, that can move to consolidate and provide leadership for the marked trend to the left of recent years."[83] If a revolutionary vanguard party was eventually to prove necessary, NAM would then have served the role of helping "to create the preconditions for such a party."[84]

NAM's attempt to dissociate itself from the failures of SDS and other New Left groups of the 1960s was evident by its use of such terms for the New Left as "the established movement," "the organized left," and "the old New Left."[85] While the authors of the original NAM document were

New Left veterans, they prided themselves on correctly identifying the errors of SDS. These were, in their view, an anarchist rejection of all leadership, an over-reliance on Third World struggles and examples, and short-range, romantic attitudes toward social change processes.[86] NAM also reacted sharply against the anti-intellectualism of the New Left, complaining, "There is almost no serious study of American life in the movement. Feeling replaces thinking."[87] Finally, NAM faulted the Movement for its personalism, its existential concern with the quality of the lives of the persons in the Movement.[88]

While NAM sought to offer something new in the way of a radical organization, it did not offer a new ideology. In criticizing some of the Movement's earlier ideas, it continued in fact to reiterate them. When it tried to elaborate its definition of socialism, it did so in the same kind of vaguely anarchist language which it found in error in SDS:

> Socialism is frightening to many—they think it means that government would rule our lives even more than now. That is not what we mean. . . . We believe in a vision of a nation transformed, a society in which the very ways people relate to each other can change. . . . We share the faith of our ancestors in the ability of ordinary people to decide their own future in decentralized, democratic communities. . . . We can build a society where both human equality and the uniqueness of each individual are recognized, in which we understand the dignity and worth of all people out of an appreciation of our own humanity.[89]

This is the language of participatory democracy without the label. It is in no way an advance over the thinking which governed the earlier SDS. Furthermore, while NAM advocated decentralization, the new organization's very existence represented its antithesis: it called for nationally coordinated efforts by radicals.

The fact is that NAM had nothing new to offer except an external form. And it has had very little impact. Most Americans have never heard of it, and it certainly has not resuscitated the moribund radical Movement. What it signaled particularly was that the radical impulse lived on and that some radicals would continue to search for new ways to make their radicalism an effective influence on American society.

Keeping the Faith

The New American Movement was not the only evidence that the dream dies hard. Young adult radicals entering professional fields, primarily but not exclusively college teaching, have formed and continue to operate radical caucuses. For the most part, these groupings have been inspired and led by members of the SDS old guard and colleagues who share their outlook and intellectual history.

Richard Flacks is an old-guard stalwart who lived through all the phases of the New Left and still kept his radical faith intact. While acknowledging that the early 1970s have seen "a noticeable withdrawal of many from active political participation, a decline in dramatic protest activity, and a shift away from action to introspection, self-expression and privatism,"[90] he nevertheless contends that "the purposeful effort of the New Left to revive American radicalism ... succeeded."[91] His prognosis was that "the radicalization process is likely to intensify, not only among youth but in a number of other sectors as well."[92] He explained ingeniously that the death of the New Left was really a sign of its success, since its real task was not revolutionary overthrow of the government but something preliminary to that. "It had hoped to generate independent radical consciousness; this has happened on a mass scale. It had hoped to organize a mass student movement; it never imagined how extensive such a movement was to become, nor that large numbers of non-student youth would also be deeply affected."[93] If "the era of *campus* confrontation and *student* revolutionism has ended not because it failed, but because it reached the limit of its possibilities,"[94] it set the stage for a revolutionary movement of larger dimensions in the future.

Flacks's optimistic reading of history was not shared by many of his old guard colleagues, and to date there has been little if any evidence that his optimism was well placed. If the radical impulse still lives, there is no consensus about either the meaning of the 1960s or the future direction which the new radicalism should take. And if it still lives, it does so mostly among young adults who have passed beyond their undergraduate days. The student base is gone, apparently beyond recall.

*   *   *

Through an historical overview we have see that it was internal contradictions which pulled apart both SDS and the Movement as a whole, not simply mistakes in strategy or timing. These contradictions are no closer to being resolved today than they were before. Nor is there any reason, on the basis of past performance, to believe that the conflicts will ever resolve themselves in such a way that a united revolutionary movement will arise from the ashes of the Movement of the 1960s.

Part II

The New University Conference and
Radical Criticism of the University

— 4 —

Radical Organizing of Academicians

For proponents of collectivism, organizing is as much an ideological principle as a practical necessity. An initial focus on the organizational efforts
and patterns of faculty radicals calls for wider discussion of the issues
underlying their activities.

The Background:
Radical Student Criticisms of the University

Since the new radicalism originated among university students, it was
natural that they would turn a considerable portion of their critical attention to their immediate environs. The attitude of the early New Left
toward the university was ambivalent. On one hand, in their desire to find
an agent for social change, radical students could locate no such institutional agent outside the university and thus hoped to see the university
itself galvanized into that role.[1]

On the other hand, the university seemed to be so largely a reflection
of the society as a whole that radicals despaired of transforming it into an
agent of change; it was part of the problem, not part of the solution. Tom
Hayden captured this early SDS ambiguity by writing "that the university
situation in America is more a symptom than a basic cause of our problems. But a college is one place to embark on a movement of reform, a
place with intellectual equipment and a reservoir of unused creativity, a
place from which reason might make a last attempt to intervene in human
affairs."[2] The pessimistic side of the equation was generally the more convincing of the two, and it became more pronounced as the 1960s wore on.

One of the most influential SDS papers on the university was Carl
Davidson's "Toward a Student Syndicalist Movement" of 1966. Declaring

that "the issue for us is student control,"[3] he signaled the rise of a nation-wide student power movement. Davidson suggested that radical students make *"the abolition of the grade system"* their "primary and central issue," since "grading is a *common condition* of the total student and faculty community" and its abolition is "a demand that cannot be met by the administration without radically altering the shape and purpose of the educational system."[4] That the radical students were unsure of themselves is startlingly clear from the fact that only six months after this essay appeared, Davidson wrote another which asserted that "any attempt to build a student movement based on 'on-campus' issues only is inherently conservative and ultimately reactionary."[5]

Conflicting Visions of the Role of the University

While specific details of university life did not escape the critical eye of student radicals, they directed most of their attention toward substantive theoretical matters concerning the university's role. One such issue was the alleged irrelevance of the subjects being studied to the students' actual existence. The strong research orientation was perceived as the major villain. The issue was brought up as early as the Port Huron Statement of 1962: "academia includes a radical separation of the student from the material of study. That which is studied, the social reality, is 'objectivized' to sterility, dividing the student from life. . . . The specialization of function and knowledge, admittedly necessary to our complex technological and social structure, has produced an exaggerated compartmentalization of study and understanding."[6]

Another aspect of the student radicals' critique of the university was that its structure and functioning provided an example of the liberal bureaucracy which dominated all of the nation's major institutions.

That most dramatic of all radical attacks on the university, the Berkeley Free Speech Movement of 1964, while ostensibly concerned with freedom of speech on campus, was actually, as its leaders explained, "a revolt against a liberal bureaucracy."[7] Paul Potter remarked that, for most students, their university experience was "the first encounter with the full inflexibility of mass bureaucratic organization."[8] Not only did the university illustrate American bureaucracy, but it prepared persons to become cogs in the national bureaucratic machine. Far from being autonomous, universities existed for the express purpose of channeling personnel.[9]

Running as an undercurrent through most radical critiques of the university was an implicit ideal of what the university should be, and it was consonant with the general vision of what the early SDSers wanted from life itself: the development of the individual in all of his fullness. In Tom Hayden's words, "The main and transcending concern of the university must be the unfolding and refinement of the moral, aesthetic, and logical capacities of man in a manner that creates genuine independence."[10] He advocated an education "which transmits human culture from generation to generation and place to place, transforming some parts, modifying others, concurring with still others, yet expressing reverence for the whole."[11]

If student radicals faulted the university for not pursuing truth, what they wanted the university to do was certainly not that. They wanted to make it the institutional agent for social change: "The ideal academy would recognize that criticism of social institutions can not be separated from action in behalf of their modification."[12] Their quarrel was not with giving the university a practical social function to perform which would be at odds with the ideal of the disinterested search for truth, but with which practical social function it was to be given. This was a crucial issue and one about which the radicals seldom spoke with clarity. Hayden and his fellow radicals apparently sensed no conflict between their appeal to the traditional ideals of a liberal education (grounded in their existential need for personal fulfillment) and their advocacy of transforming the university into a vehicle to change society (grounded in their political concerns). Both themes appeared in the early 1960s. But as the decade proceeded, the liberal arts rhetoric was heard less and less, while the call for politicization of the university became more and more pronounced.

The Academic Aim of the Radical Education Project

When SDS established the Radical Education Project in 1966 to develop a theoretical foundation for New Leftism, REP members also assumed the task of developing the radical critique of the university. Their motivation for doing so was one of self-interest, because they foresaw that "many, if not most of the present campus radicals will, in a few years, themselves hold positions in the professions."[13] In their relations with the university, they recognized that they would face the same existential dilemma which they already faced in their relations with American society in general: the difficulty of finding self-fulfillment in an alien environment.[14]

Consequently, REP set for itself the huge project of beginning a "reconstruction of intellectual theory and teaching" through the formation of task forces in key disciplines, whose initial task would be "to develop radical educational materials for students in introductory liberal arts courses."[15] REP saw clearly what was needed, but it accomplished very little. Radicals in the professions today are not much closer to this goal than they were when REP first enunciated it. Nearly all their energy was spent in a negative critique of the evils of the university; almost none of it has gone into the positive formulations which REP envisioned as the main task.

The Target: Society or the University?

One of the central tensions in the New Left's attitude toward work in the university was whether changing the institution itself or changing society as a whole should motivate its efforts toward university reform. Since the university was a central institution in contemporary society, the Berkeley Free Speech Movement seemed to indicate that by confronting the university one confronted the basic problems of society.[16] So SDS could call for "a free university in a free society" (a call later revised to "a socialist university in a socialist society") without fear that efforts at university reform might deflect them from the larger task.

As time passed, however, radicals sharpened their perceptions of the tension between working to change the university and working to change society. If society shaped the university and determined its character, the radicals had to conclude that "we cannot liberate the university without radically changing the rest of society."[17] Carl Davidson argued that "the student power movement" should set, as its "single over-all purpose," "the development of a radical political consciousness among those students who will later hold jobs in strategic sectors of the political economy."[18] This objective implied radicalizing vocationally oriented students, which in turn suggested focusing efforts on non-elite campuses.[19] But elite campuses always remained the center of SDS activity.

As the Free Speech Movement of 1964 signified the focusing on university issues, so the 1968 uprising at Columbia University was the most dramatic moment signaling the shift away from that approach. "The Columbia militants proclaimed revolutionary objectives (rather than university reform or student power) as their real intentions."[20] An SDS leader at Columbia reportedly said, "As much as we would like to, we are not strong enough as yet to destroy the United States. But we are strong enough to destroy Columbia!"[21] The university-oriented issues, then, became mere pretexts.

Faculty Radicalism as an Outgrowth of the Student Movement

While students first formulated the radical critique of the university, it was radical professors who articulated it most fully. Their criticisms were generally elaborations of criticisms made originally by student radicals. The radical professor was often the same person as the radical student, now a few years older. Even those faculty radicals who were not former members of SDS or some other radical student group had been radicalized, for the most part, through their sympathies with the causes espoused by radical students. As one source said, "In our opinion, it's now a matter of picking sides. It is bluntly: Are you for the students or against them?"[22] In this case is seen the unusual phenomenon of students influencing professors rather than the reverse.

Faculty radicalization was generally more visceral than intellectual: "The student revolt is forcing all of us to act long before we can think out the pros and cons of our action."[23] It was not that these radicals searched for a place in which to express their radicalism most effectively and then consciously chose the professions. Most of them drifted into the professions naturally, because of their academic orientation and ability; only afterwards did they seek a rationale to sustain their drive for personal wholeness in an essentially alienating situation.[24] The new radicals planned their strategy for "the long march through the institutions"[25] only after they were on the road.

The Socialist Scholars Conference

The desire for collectivity led to the formation of organizations for radicals in college teaching such as the Socialist Scholars Conference (SSC), founded in 1965. Because it started with the assumption that "American Capitalism had entered a period of long-run stability, eliminating the possibility of any mass socialist opposition," its focus was on furthering socialist scholarship: "Thus, socialist scholars should devote themselves to the serious intellectual work necessary for the development of a socialist intellectual tradition, which hopefully could be drawn upon at some propitious time in the future."[26] The success of the Movement later motivated SSC to shift its focus toward a more aggressively activist stance. A 1970 SSC statement saw "the opportunity for socialist attack" and the possibility for SSC "to play a more direct role: to support and influence the growth of an American Socialist Movement."[27] Despite this turn toward greater activism, SSC expressed the hope that "the commitment to serious scholarship—objective socialist scholarship, will not be lost."[28]

Most of the young radical professors were not attracted to SSC; for them this group—with its roots in an older radical tradition—made too many compromises with the scholarly establishment, and was not sufficiently activist. One new radical, after visiting an SSC meeting, offered this analysis:

> It [SSC] is specifically non-political, that is, it seeks to create a climate in which socialist scholars holding different political views can come together to carry on a productive exchange of ideas. "It is the job of the Socialist Intellectual," ran this year's announcement, "to do what he best knows how to do: provide a body of theory and scholarship. Only when this is done will we be able to create institutions capable of sustaining mass Socialist consciousness."
>
> Take comfort, all ye who long for a Socialist America. No one knows how large a body of theory and scholarship must be before a mass Socialist consciousness can be erected on top of it. In the meantime, write on, brother, write on![29]

The irony of SSC is that shortly after its decision to become more activist, the collapse of the student Movement resulted in activist radical academics seeking refuge in Marxism so that they could successfully navigate the transition from an aggressive radicalism to a more intellectual radicalism which would sustain them over the long haul. Caught in this cross-current, SSC folded.

The New University Conference

NUC's Relationship to SDS

The organization to which the new radical academics flocked was the New University Conference (NUC). Envisioning itself as "the first national post-student radical organization of the sixties"[30] and as "one of the first solid adult organizations from the New Left of the '60's,"[31] NUC acknowledged that it shared "the basic goals and commitments of the student movement."[32] In fact, NUC grew directly out of the student Movement itself. Many of its members were former SDSers: Richard Flacks, Staughton Lynd, Paul Lauter, Florence Howe, Rich Rothstein, Bob Ross, Al Haber, Tom Hayden, and others. It was the "graduation" from SDS and its student-oriented interests which prompted the establishment of NUC.

Nevertheless, these SDS graduates did not create NUC in the image of the original SDS. Too much had happened to them since the days of the Port Huron Statement. By the time of NUC's founding in 1968, SDS was already in decline. NUC spokesmen recognized the difficulties which accompanied this timing:

NUC has been caught in the trap of its own origins. . . . We were formed at the end of the beginning—before anyone began to seriously question the political flaws of a movement grounded almost entirely in a disaffected middle class. Our movement was and is without roots in basic institutions or sustained contact with non-radical elements of the American society. . . . NUC began more as a general "movement" organization for graduate students and faculty who had outgrown their roles in SDS rather than as an organization committed to struggle against educational institutions.[33]

The NUC statement of purpose manifested that same curious amalgam of early SDS ideals and later SDS revolutionism which generally characterized those old guard SDSers who tried to adapt to the changing SDS line: "The New University Conference is a national organization of radicals who work in, around, and in spite of institutions of higher education. We are committed to struggle politically to create a new, American form of socialism and to replace an educational and social system that is an instrument of class, sexual, and racial oppression with one that belongs to the people."[34] That the statement called for a new, American form of socialism was an indication of the New Left's concern with developing its own native ideology, not simply borrowing a ready-made one. To name socialism as its goal demonstrated a shift from the early, non-socialist days of SDS, and the reference to class oppression also indicated a heightened ideological tendency in the New Left. The forceful presence of radical feminists within NUC from its very beginning instigated the reference to sexual oppression. Calling for replacement of "an educational and social system" suggested continuing uncertainty about the main object of the radical attack, whether it should be the university or society as a whole. The same indecision showed in the vague phrasing "in, around, and in spite of institutions of higher education."

Historical Overview of NUC

NUC's first years witnessed a healthy expansion in the number of affiliated chapters and individual memberships. By early 1970 the membership was around 500. This figure crested in early 1971 at about 675, in approximately forty-five chapters. By early 1972 the number of members had dwindled to around 375 and the number of chapters to fifteen, some of them alive only on paper.

The early 1971 *NUC Newsletter* expressed an expansive, satisfied tone with the feeling that better things were yet in store for NUC. It was the only time in the publication's history when such optimism was shown. Later issues of the *Newsletter* were almost totally devoted to introspection about troublesome questions concerning NUC's *raison d'être,* strategy, and future.

NUC's dues were two and one-half percent of the member's income, a solid indicator of the serious purpose of the members. At the same time, the high price of membership meant that NUC had to deliver satisfactory results or the members would not keep on paying that much money toward its support. Women who shifted their primary loyalties to feminist activities were likely to drop out of NUC rather than to be so highly taxed for membership in an organization now holding only second place in their interests. In the summer of 1971, a proposal was offered to set a flat ten dollar fee and add compulsory graduated assessments from a quarter of one percent for those earning less than $3,000 to ten percent for those with incomes over $20,000. The most ingenious proposal for meeting NUC's financial crunch was that NUC members marry each other and file joint income tax returns, the amount saved from filing individual returns being paid into the organization. The marriage was not intended to be consummated, so it could be annulled whenever one party wished to do so. With a conservative savings estimate of $250 per year, two hundred such marriages would net NUC $50,000 annually. "Rather than trash an obsolete capitalist institution, this proposal recommends that we rip it off. And $50,000 is a considerable rip off."[35] At its peak, NUC had an annual budget of $60,000. By early 1972 the monthly revenue was only $2,750 as compared with the monthly $5,000 of a year earlier. The last national convention, in the summer of 1972, was poorly attended. Toward the end of that meeting only forty persons remained.

NUC had a stormy history. Acrimonious debates filled the *Newsletter.* Ideological quarrels predominated. Reflecting on the 1969 convention, one member commented, "The NUC national convention raises a number of question [*sic*], the most important of which is, ought NUC to have an ideology? And, if it ought to have one, how ought it to go about getting one?"[36] This was a bizarre way to discuss a group and its ideology, but it was accurate. NUC did not start with an ideology, but with shared criticisms and general perspectives. It then went in search of an ideology. None developed organically from within the group. In this respect, it repeated the history of SDS. The same commentator clarified NUC's difficulty:

An ideology is some schema capable of explaining and predicting historical and political phenomena. The first thing that one must note about NUC is that its members do not share any common ideology. At the NUC convention I met delegates who identified themselves as Anarchists, Communists, Resisters, ex-SDSers, PLPers, assorted non-denominational Marxists, not to mention left-liberals, a Wobbly or two, Satyagrahaists, Christian Pacifists, Catholic Radicals, and one gentleman who claimed to be a graduate of the Up-Against-The-Wall-Mother-Fuckers. Thus, no ideology, or ideologically impregnated position paper, is likely to become the official policy of NUC without alienating a large group of its members.[37]

Another member pleaded for ideological flexibility by holding up the recent history of SDS as an example for NUC to avoid. He added, "It is important that a man or woman coming to the radical persuasion be able in NUC to find himself or herself aided and put at liberty; and not intimidated and accused by various and obscure versions of radical purity."[38] But a different member, noting the ideological splits in SDS, advised NUC not to try to avoid these issues but to plunge into the ideological maelstrom or run the risk of losing touch with the rest of the Movement. However ugly and tedious ideological debates might be, they nevertheless dealt with real and important issues.[39] This advice was in fact followed, with the same disastrous consequences for NUC that battles over ideologies had for SDS.

At the organizing session of NUC in 1968, the early SDS personalistic note was heard from some speakers. A line which appeared repeatedly in NUC material, starting with the organizing meeting, was that "We are committed to the struggle for a democratic university[,] one within which we may freely express the radical content of our lives."[40] A report on the founding session was so candid about the personal motivation behind the founding of NUC that it opened the possibility for liberals as well as radicals to join. It recounted the defense of these personalistic motives: "it was argued that the groups should be explicitly personal and should allow group members to dig deeply into their own real concerns and try to understand those of other members; in this way a gradual alteration of self conception might occur. Others argued that a group which sees itself as primarily a mutually supportive community was in danger of ending in contemplating navels instead of acting politically. At this the supporters of primary groups answered that the members were already active radicals, and that—schmuck—it was a question of emphasis. Of course these should be politically engaged groups."[41] By late 1971 NUC saw itself as attempting to "make the transition from 'New Left' ramblings to serious socialist politics."[42] Once again, as in SDS, the personal dimension became subordinated to the political. The vision of the early New Left was dismissed with a set of quotation marks.

The issue of whether to focus on the university or on society was also an open question from the beginning. One editorial contended: "For many of us, the question of whether or not the university ought to be destroyed is not a real one. . . . Many of us, as individuals, are interested in being scholars. . . . We don't want to drop out."[43] Another view expressed "great skepticism about the logic of professionalism" and urged an alternative self-concept:

> In this perspective we start, not from institutional affiliation (the university) but from shared values and political perspective (broadly conceived). We start, metaphorically, not as colleagues but as comrades. In this view, our place of work in higher education is a matter of convenience in uniting us. Our comrades may be from diverse walks of live [sic]; therefore we see attacks on the university not as a challenge to our personal integrity but as political attacks on an institution we know full well to be politically aligned with those who oppose us in general.[44]

It was the radicals favoring a university orientation for NUC who felt clearly on the defensive.[45]

The Drift toward Militancy

In general, the drift of NUC throughout its history was toward greater militancy and stridency. Activism and ideological purity were emphasized at the expense of scholarship and diversity.[46] While the first NUC brochure referred to the university that radicals were pledged to build as "an institution which plays a creative and exemplary role in American society . . . which *exports* radical graduates, radical opinion, and the radical example of its internal democracy," three years later the NUC line advocated the destruction of the university as "an instrument of class, sexual and racial oppression": "Being a radical intellectual in this context [following the seizure of Columbia University] meant being committed to destroying the higher educational system not on the basis of its excesses, but for its efficiency."[47] Three specific issues illustrate NUC's increasing militancy: its view of the concept of cadre, its attitude toward the establishment of a revolutionary party, and its attitude toward violence and terror.

John McDermott wrote an article calling for NUC to become a cadre organization, albeit one which would "incorporate the advantages of cadre-type organizations while avoiding their disadvantages."[48] One corollary was that "membership in NUC should be by election only"; another was that members would have to agree "to develop primary organizational loyalty to NUC."[49] The cadre concept implied doctrinal purity, and it ruled out the concept of a mass membership organization. Some NUCers disliked the cadre concept,[50] but its very introduction into the discussion illustrated the increasing rigidity of the organization.

The main significance of the concept was that it demonstrated that NUC was evolving in the same direction as had SDS. While SDS began with quite other intentions than becoming a socialist or revolutionary political party, by the time NUC was founded such ideas were in the air among SDSers, and they affected NUC from the outset. In 1968 Bob Ross urged that "we see NUC as the university section of a not-yet-existing revolutionary party."[51] McDermott's concept of cadre included each member's "committment [*sic*] to build a revolutionary socialist party."[52] And— such was the lesson of the Old Left which the New Left had earlier shunned but now embraced—this implied a democratic centralist form of organization. Mel Rothenberg specified, "a revolutionary communist organization which intends to seriously contend for state power must have a democratic centralist form of organization."[53] He blamed SDS's collapse on its unwillingness to follow revolutionary rhetoric to this logical organizational end.

The concept of democratic centralism appalled some NUC members; it was over this issue that Rosario Levins, formerly a Communist Party member, left NUC. Her parting shot dealt with "whether NUC should form itself in a Party, a Leninist Party. Every minor decision became one more irrevocable step along (or occasionally off) the road to that unspoken goal.

"This accounts for the most flagrant obnoxiousness of our meetings: the maneuvering and the manipulating. We were in the process of becoming the future Central Committee of the future Communist Party—the first in history to be almost totally academic."[54]

The willingness of NUC members to denominate themselves as communists indicated both a shift from the New Left's rejection of the Old Left and a growing enchantment with international Communism—especially the Third World varieties. One *NUC Newsletter* carried a quotation from Che Guevara on its front cover: "I envy you. You North Americans are very lucky. You are fighting the most important fight of all—you live in the heart of the beast."[55] In 1969 fifteen NUC members went to Cuba. One reaction, that of Elizabeth Diggs, was typical: "The most difficult thing about describing a trip to Cuba is to restrain one's enthusiasm enough so that people will accept one's account as reasonably balanced and objective. But it is difficult to restrain one's enthusiasm for Cuba."[56]

Terrorism posed a profound problem for NUC members. As academic types, they shrank almost reflexively from violence. Some of them, how-

ever, saw it as the litmus test which separated the dedicated revolutionaries from merely disaffected critics of the established order. Whether to
approve and practice violence and terror forced the radicals to face the
question of just how much they meant by their use of revolutionary rhetoric. Michele Russell urged her fellow NUCers "to behave not simply as
'cultural workers' (although that is important) but also as political and
technological saboteurs," a role which, of course, would have to be "clandestine."[57] The Ann Arbor chapter of NUC tendered a proposal for "Terrorism Now."[58]

NUC's position on terrorism still vacillated. Using the Angela Davis
case as a hypothetical example, it chided those liberal professors who
defended her academic freedom but not her possibly criminal acts because
they distinguished between advocating illegal activities and engaging in
them, thus separating thought and practice. Yet while the radicals found
this distinction intolerable, they admitted "that by our actions (or inaction)
'radical' academics appear to hold the 'distinction' between rhetoric and
deed almost as sacred [as liberals do]."[59] This same article in the NUC
Newsletter went on to glorify the "revolutionary violence" of Angela Davis
the professor and Jonathan Jackson the dropout.[60] Such glorification of
violence was rare for NUC, but it again indicated that militancy was gaining ascendancy in the organization. Ambivalent members of NUC refused
to criticize those who committed terroristic acts in the name of revolution:
"We cannot make the struggle against comrades with whom we have
tactical differences take precedence over the struggle against American
power. However we may disagree, those who petition and those who
sabotage are our brothers and sisters in the ultimate struggle against
American repression in Cambodia, Kent and New Haven."[61]

Furthermore, it was not easy to draw a precise line between what was
violence and what was not. While sit-ins and related actions were non-
violent and therefore readily sanctioned, destruction of property was a
more difficult matter to decide and harm or death to individuals even
more so:

> It is difficult to decide if destruction of property is "violent" or if the
> term would be most useful if only applied to the injury of persons.
> Whatever the use of the term, the destruction of property is on a con-
> tinuum with other tactics. . . . There is some property which should
> not exist and whose use might at times be prevented by forceful
> means if necessary. . . . Injury to persons, even further on this con-
> tinuum of tactics, must be considered gravely by any movement com-
> mitted to life, liberty and happiness for all. But the struggle . . . may
> demand action not only against institutions but also against people

carrying out politics of war and repression. . . . If those with repressive power do not listen to reasonable argument and massive protest, and continue to slaughter innocent human beings, their forceful restraint would seem to be entirely appropriate.[62]

This passage shows that the search for the line between violence and non-violence was academic in the worst sense of the word. For the logic of the rhetoric of revolution is that any action, no matter how violent, must be sanctioned if it serves the cause. The position enunciated in this NUC pamphlet might be shocking to non-radicals, but it was a consistent extension of the attitude which radicals propounded quite openly in regard to work within an academic discipline or within the university. The only surprise about this particular pamphlet is that NUC was willing to declare itself so openly. It is quite proper to use this issue of terrorism as a test case by which to gauge the legitimacy of the radical position, as both insiders and outsiders have done. The pamphlet doubtless caused some radicals to feel twinges of uneasiness. It is unlikely that any beliefs were reversed by seeing, as the logical outcome of their position, the approval of violence perpetrated upon another human being. But they demonstrated their inconsistency to the extent that they held mental reservations about the issue. The matter of terrorism stands in a long line of issues on which most radicals had no choice but to hold divided opinions.

As contradictions within NUC surfaced, the organization searched for programs which would unite the membership in common action. Staughton Lynd suggested, in late 1969, that NUC devote its energies in the following spring to exposing and fighting those "international corporations whose third world investments and control over the federal defense budget generate imperialist foreign policy."[63] The *Newsletter* published the locations of stockholders meetings in a list of these corporations; it urged NUC members to try to get their universities to use their stock portfolios as a lever, to coordinate mass meetings outside and agitation inside the stockholders' meetings, and to start boycotting products of those corporations. Economics had not played a major role in the New Left critique in the early 1960s, but hardening of the ideological line in its later days led the Movement in that direction. Another frequently voiced proposal was the possibility of cooperating with labor unions and working with them in order to demonstrate solidarity with the workers.[64] These and similar suggestions reflected the drift of NUC away from university (and, for radical professors, personal) concerns toward a more doctrinaire Marxist position.

As interest in NUC ebbed, other proposals were forthcoming based on a realistic assessment of NUC's limited capacities. Tom Hecht advised consolidating NUC's position on campus: "NUC, at this stage, cannot and probably should not organize beyond its immediate base. To do so would be to deflect political energy at a time when such energy is generally low. ... It is not a popular position. The aura of 'community organizer' is strong stuff. And many people still feel a nagging guilt about their presence on campus. The result of this, however, is that neither campus nor surrounding communities have been organized."[65] Six months before NUC folded, Hecht suggested publishing radical teaching material and circulating it widely outside the NUC membership in an effort to "begin to build bridges back to a constituency from which we have drifted." This would mean lessening efforts to build a tight cadre, if only temporarily; but some clear project had to be forthcoming "if we are not to rot in our own inconsequence."[66] Hecht's proposal was voted down by the NUC Executive Committee: three for, three against, four abstaining.

The Causes of NUC's Demise

When NUC was established, representing only a small minority of professors, there was general optimism that the issues were so compelling that a serious effort in recruiting and organizing would give it profound influence. That never happened. In 1972 NUC collapsed. Explaining why it did so is a complicated matter, because responsibility for NUC's demise cannot be placed on any one of the many currents of thought within the organization. At least seven reasons can be distinguished.

The first and most important is that NUC never articulated clearly what function it would serve and what role it would play. Because of competing self-concepts of its members, no clear-cut identity or image of the radical professor was ever established. The same applies to the organizational form of NUC: mass organization, or a cadre "organized around Marxist-Leninist principals [sic]"?[67] Underlying these confusions was the lack of a unifying ideology around which all NUCers could rally. NUC always wavered between the two worlds of the university and the youth revolt; never did a clear consensus emerge on the method to relieve this tension and those attendant upon it. Nor was the tension creative; it was the opposite. Whatever agreements were reached cost the loss of dissenting members.[68]

A second reason why NUC folded—one closely related to the first—was simply that it tried to do too much. Barbara Andrews noted that "the executive committee, because of lack of definition of what it has to do, has often tried to do a little of everything."[69] What was true of the Executive Committee was true of the organization as a whole. Some members admitted that a major problem was "our inability to realistically gauge our capabilities and assess how much we can carry out in any given national program in an organization of autonomous chapters."[70] A group planning to "Smash the Hegemony of Bourgeois Ideology" (an NUC slogan) and to usher in the revolutionary state sets itself goals which insure failure. Everything needs to be done at once. Had NUC chosen only a select area for its work, such as radical criticism within the academic disciplines, it might have reached some significant measure of success. But its revolutionary ideology forbade such modest, concrete goals.

Within its membership, the division between sexes was a third cause of the group's death, according to many NUC women. Internal debates about program and strategy were exceeded only by wranglings about sexism. From the beginning there was a Women's Caucus in NUC, but its divisive impact grew only gradually. In early *Newsletters* the chief enemies were racism and imperialism; sexism was later elevated to complete the "anti"-trinity. Len Radinsky stated the problem in practical terms: "I think sexism (rather than other political differences) is the primary contradiction within NUC and one which is crucial now. . . . In the older chapters there is a tendency for men, especially the most active ones, to remain in the chapter while women, including many of the most experienced ones, leave. . . . I think this will mean an end to NUC."[71] NUC women expressed the problem for themselves: "Women are hesitant to join NUC where chapters are male-dominated. . . . I think we are now feeling angry about the unchecked chauvinism we find all around us and are ready to stop being liberal with our brothers on this issue."[72] In the thinking of NUC women, the problem finally involved deciding whether sexism or other political issues were primary.

There were attempts to claim indivisibility of the issues, which argued for radical feminists to stay in a mixed organization like NUC: "one might ask why the Woman's [*sic*] Caucus remain [*sic*] in NUC. . . . The answer is that the Women's Caucus does not see the liberation of women as an isolated issue. NUC women are committed to fighting racism and imperialism, to building socialism and creating a liberated educational system as well as to eliminating male supremacy; the Caucus sees all these issues as inseparable."[73] Indivisibility of the issues was, of course, what had led to the problem of trying to do everything at once, of assuming more responsibility than NUC could handle. But women did leave NUC over the issue of sexism and over their desire to devote their energies directly to the struggle for female liberation.[74] Working directly for female liberation also reflected personalistic needs which, in general, were uppermost in the radical feminist activities. They experienced sexual oppression more personally than class oppression. So while NUC women tried for a while to retain a vision of the indivisibility of the issues, when a choice had to be made, they opted for the personal issues rather than those ideologically defined.

Four lesser factors also contributed to NUC's collapse. There was the conflict between local interests and national scope. The concerns of national officers sometimes seemed grandiose to NUC members whose main sphere of interest was their own campus. Less than a year before NUC folded, national spokesman Tom Hecht acknowledged that the organization had dwindled to the point where its focus, of necessity, should be restricted to local issues.[75]

Another liability was lack of adequate leadership to carry out the free-flowing ideas of the brainstormers. Noting that "chapters have demised and the national organization suffered because of a failure to generate leadership," Barbara Andrews called for the establishment of regional networks to link local cells with the national organization.[76] In the same essay, she indicated the real problem behind the lack of leadership. "The structure of the organization implies people serious about developing chapters, caucuses, regional networks, programs and projects, etc. That often has not correlated with the reality of the organization."[77] There was something about NUC which did not elicit the complete participation demanded by its vision of itself. NUC was not composed of inept persons lacking in leadership ability; rather, it was unable to marshal that leadership for use in its activities.

The transiency of its membership was also a problem. Andrews, noting that more than thirty percent of the mailing list changed addresses every fall, commented: "If the organization is to predicate its nature on the chapter structure, it must be with the axioms that those chapters will have to be rebuilt nearly annually and that some person or group of persons with the energy to rebuild those chapters will have to be in those places."[78]

A final reason for the end of NUC was the loss of the base upon which it was predicated. One long-time NUC member explained, "Once we had no radical student movement to go along with—following the breakup of SDS in 1969—we tried to retrench into radical teaching and union work within the university. But we finally had to face up to the reality of objective conditions."[79]

These reasons suggest that NUC folded because, as it had constituted itself, it had nowhere to go. The critique that it was capable of making had been made. Like SDS, NUC forced its discontents into a mold which did not conform to their natural shape. Basic contradictions were never resolved: rather, they engendered even more severe dislocations.

— 5 —

The Riddle of Academic Radical
Self-Definition

No subject vexed the academic radicals as much as that of self-definition. The following cry of anguish is typical: "I wish someone *would* write a serious defense of the radical intellectual—probably starting with the possibility of inherent contradictions in the term itself, let alone the role."[1] Scholar vs. propagandist, intellectual vs. activist, professional vs. partisan—is it possible to combine these polarities within a single individual?

Some radicals who did not enter the professions saw their academic compatriots as "armchair revolutionaries"[2] and "second-class radicals,"[3] as compromisers who might even have mercenary motivations.[4] Carl Davidson spoke for these non-academic radicals when he declared, "The idea of a radical professional is an implicit contradiction, because the teacher is revolutionary when he obstructs the system and gets fired."[5]

The Crisis of Serving Two Masters

Such criticism from full-time Movement activists clearly stung the professionally-inclined radicals, and they were unsure how to parry these thrusts, even to their own satisfaction. While they retained primary loyalty to the Movement, the fact of their presence within academic institutions forced upon them another, and often competing, loyalty. They had to face the problem of serving both the institution and the Movement.

The Radicals in the Professions Conference

Such was the sense of conflict engendered by this dilemma that in 1967 a Radicals in the Professions Conference was convened to try to resolve it. The session "was a response to an essentially personal crisis of remaining radical beyond the college or graduate school years, or beyond the two year initiation period into the movement."[6] The conferees recognized that their existential dilemma stemmed from the fact that the ethos of the Movement called for a certain style of life which was contrary to professional work—and, for that matter, to adulthood: "The problem with the current notion of ideal political man is that althrough [sic] it seems to work as a means of unifying personal rebellion and political opposition for young people just entering the movement, it creates dysfunction among the older people in the movement. After the initial conversion period the myth ceases to correspond to the experience of the people. . . . The movement has no language to give legitimacy to the problems of people preparing realistically for the long haul."[7] These radical professionals were committed to trying to fuse the two terms, *radical* and *professional;* but they admitted frankly that "the experiment may prove that being a professional makes no sense for a radical."[8]

The Movement for a Democratic Society

An example of the crisis was the Movement for a Democratic Society (MDS). Formed in the late 1960s by a group of young adults who had "graduated" from SDS, they, too, struggled to find roles for adults who still were loyal to the Movement: "The basically religious stipulation to leave all and cleave only unto us will produce a hard core devoted cadre of the pure, but will not organize enough people to change one stop sign. And it will not speak, except on the level of daydream, to the man who has kids to support. We must develop a radical community of young adults both working in the Movement and working in the establishment institutions. We must do this in spite of obvious conflicts of economic levels and life styles between MDS people and younger, full-time Movement people."[9]

Implications of Dual Loyalty

Serving two masters gave rise to a number of specific conflicts. One was the sense of losing touch with the Movement that had sustained the radical faith within individuals. Barbara and Al Haber, reporting on the Radicals in the Professions Conference, stated: "The most pervasive problem expressed was the feeling of isolation from the mainstream of the movement. Many people described difficulty in finding emotional sustenance for political activism. They felt they were going dry, losing perspective."[10] To meet this need, the Habers suggested the creation of "a network of comradeship that can serve as a reference group outside of the professions for radicals working within established institutions."[11] This was the role which the Movement for a Democratic Society had been designed to serve, but it was short-lived. More effective was the formation of radical caucuses within the separate professional fields, such as the Medical Committee for Human Rights, the Social Welfare Workers Movement, and a string of radical caucuses within the various academic disciplines. To be associated with like-minded colleagues would, of course, be a comfort; but it obviously does not begin to resolve the conflict which brought them together.

Another problem was what the Habers called the "time bind": "when practical demands of the profession come first, the political work is shoved onto a sideline and often it drifts out of the picture altogether."[12] Radicals in the professions "were not merely looking for ways to be radical in their spare time; they did not want to support the status quo in their work and life style, reserving their spare time for politics."[13]

Apart from the allocation of time, what happens when the two masters that one serves place conflicting demands upon the servant? Here the full-time activists and the professionals agreed. In Davidson's words, "The question is not one of working 'inside' or 'outside' the system. Rather, the question is do we pay [*sic:* play] by the established rules? Here, the answer is an emphatic no."[14] Ted Steege conceded that "the radical usually violates many assumptions that professional people hold about the nature of their duties."[15] The lines were drawn most starkly by the Habers:

A radical cannot see his loyalty as being to the profession, or institution in which he works. Our loyalty is to our political comrades and to
the political aims for which we are organizing. Obviously this pre-
sents a moral difficulty because others will assume we have traditional
loyalties; and we will, in fact, be playing a two faced game, knowing
that we ill [*sic:* will] "betray" them when difficult issues arise. But,
then, that is what being a radical is about and the question is whether
you betray your professional colleagues or your political comrades.

A corollary of political loyalty is that we can criticize movement
policy and actions among "the brothers and the sisters," but not to
outsiders. We are not intellectuals above it all who say the truth to
whomever [*sic*] will listen or asks: we are partisans who support the
movement against the outside world, whatever our private criticisms
might be.[16]

The Habers appended a line which appears over and over like a litany in the writings of the radicals in the professions: "the basic point is: which side are we on?"[17]

This passage reveals a curious admixture of candor and deviousness which characterized many of the new radicals. That is, they were candid with one another about the need to be devious with outsiders. Did they think that no non-radical would read what they wrote? As they told each other, the claims of truth would have to be subordinated to the dictates of propaganda whenever these two might conflict.

Those attending the 1967 Radicals in the Professions Conference discussed "four kinds of strategic emphases which work in the professions could serve" in furthering the cause of the Movement:

1. to organize political struggle against the power structure of the profession or institution in which we work.

2. to try to transform the way in which the profession is practiced and the content that it contains.

3. to fight the social control functions of the profession or institution.

4. to recruit more people into the movement.[18]

It would be possible for a radical professional to do more than one of these, and various radical individuals could devote themselves to different strategies. But the multiplicity of options also illustrated the uncertainty strongly felt by the radicals concerning the role appropriate to them as professional persons.

The cause of this incertitude was that the New Left's general analysis of revolution remained unclear. Was the new working class theory correct? In that case, perhaps the radical professionals were destined to form the basis of a revolutionary party. Would the revolution occur because of a breakdown in the national economy? Would it be a pluralistic revolution based on issues of life style and occurring only very gradually because of the stability of the present economic system? The Habers could not decide, and they suggested that radicals engage in experiments based on all three views. The theory of revolution logically precedes the decision about the proper role for radicals in the professions, but this issue was never resolved.

Of one thing the Habers were sure: " 'Self-fulfillment' of individual radicals is not the goal the movement must strive for: finding ways to use people to create a movement of radical social change is. That will mean, inevitably, that as radicals we will often have to do things we are not good at, and do not enjoy. It means that we ourselves cannot be our final worry."[19] Yet these were the same commentators who reported that the 1967 conference grew out of the personal needs of radicals in the professions. The radicals did not resolve the conflict between the personal and the political. As always, this was the basic problem.

The Radical Professor as Organizer

There was general consent that the radical in the university was strategically located to be a recruiter and organizer; his task was to radicalize others, presumably mostly students.[20] The New University Conference called itself an organization of organizers. Even organizing, which would seem to be a positive activity, was defined primarily in negative terms. Tom Hecht, an officer in NUC, said, "One of the key justifications for placing organizers in an education system is to interrupt the transmission of bourgeois values and perspectives."[21] This was the role of "the radical as subversive."[22]

But subversive teaching is not enough for the radical professor–organizer. Radicalism must permeate every aspect of his work. Robert Meredith gave some sense of the magnitude of the task:

No radical in a university context can reasonably limit himself to the special kind of subversion teaching involves. He tries to radicalize faculty politics (e.g., he relates discontent to the hierarchical way decisions are made, promotes democratization of the curriculum, urges abolition of grading "systems," supports courses and programs with radical content). He organizes teachers and graduate students (into NUC chapters if possible), janitorial and maintenance workers (into unions), the community (into women's liberation groups and cooperatives). His research and writing progressively become less professional in the old sense and more intimately part of his work and reflection as a radical. In short, radicals more consciously than most men struggle to be whole people (wholeness is part of their ideology), their life combining and not dividing action and thought, work and play, research and teaching, politics and love.[23]

The riddle of self-definition was posed implicitly by Meredith in terms of specialization *versus* generalism. He opted for generalism. In his view, a radical must embody the whole gamut of radical interests. Some academic radicals advocated the legitimacy of specialization, but their viewpoint never gained ascendancy. And if there was consensus that the radical professor should be an organizer, there was equal consensus that he could not limit his role to that task.

The Founding Session of NUC

The same issue of radical self-definition which motivated the 1967
Radicals in the Professions Conference and the founding of the Movement
for a Democratic Society held center stage at the initial convention of the
New University Conference. Papers by Staughton Lynd, Richard Flacks,
and Jesse Lemisch presented three different models for the radical professor: that he should be, respectively, an off-campus activist, a university
activist, a truth-seeker. As summarized in an *NUC Newsletter,*

> Lynd's thesis . . . was that the trivia and institutional conservatism of
> the universities make them difficult places to center ones [*sic*] work
> and identity, while the new movements against war and racism pro-
> vide more relevant personal and political contexts. . . .
>   Flacks's presentation emphasized the strategic role of the univer-
> sity in training and servicing the corporate, military, and technological
> elites of Imperial America. The university's strategic importance in
> training and legitimizing this elite[,] he argued, provides the justifica-
> tion for working against its current orientation, for subverting its
> ability to play this role. And within the university lies the potential
> for creating a political and cultural atmosphere of dissent and experi-
> ment, a counter-culture of humane concern. . . .
>   Lemisch . . . argued for still a third perspective: the radical scholar
> *as* a radical scholar. Lemisch held that although the radical interpre-
> tation of our past and present is not always of obvious utility to
> current movement needs, there is no guarantee that our current inter-
> pretation of what we need is correct, and the result of scholarly work
> may change our perspective.[24]

While NUC tried to coalesce all three views into one, they proved in
practice to be incompatible. Of the three, Lynd's view seems to have
found the greatest resonance, even at the start of NUC.[25]

The Contradictions of the Radical Professor

Conflicting Attitudes toward Scholarship

Professors are, by definition, interested in scholarship. Radicals are, by
choice, in reaction against academic business-as-usual. Radical professors,
therefore, had a problem in relating to the world of scholarship, a problem
illuminated by elaborating Jesse Lemisch's defense of the ideal of the

radical scholar, summarized above—an ideal which was rejected by an overwhelming majority of his peers.

Lemisch agreed that "the structure of the profession is an obstacle to honest scholarship," but he insisted that "the radical defers to no authority but that of evidence and proof."[26] Since "the Left can afford to face truth" and "cannot be content with self-congratulation, for it must know how things work," he argued: " 'What is your evidence?' can be a very radical question. As we challenge existing institutions, we should challenge existing ideas, demanding to know whether evidence demonstrates their necessity and validity, or whether they rest on authority alone."[27]

While Lemisch was highly critical of the partisanship already present in the non-radicalized profession, he admitted that partisanship could have deleterious effects among radicals as well. "If our research should not be tyrannized by existing action, neither should it be tyrannized by existing theory. Thus, to take one example, the history of women *might* fit into a class analysis, but the requirement that it *must* might distort the truth, impede the liberation of women and the development of theory not only about sex differences but also about such other natural differences as race, beauty, and what is called intelligence."[28] This example was especially apt. Radical feminists who did not want to sever ties with the Movement spoke as if a sex analysis automatically would be consonant with a class analysis. The fact that many radical feminists have turned away from Movement pursuits to a direct concern with female liberation implicitly bespeaks the validity of Lemisch's cavil; class analysis has not satisfied them.

Lemisch acknowledged the radicals' prevailing disdain for scholarship, and his rebuke of it was quite specific:

> Louis Kampf tells me that a man doing research on 12th century trade patterns would better use his time in contemporary activism. . . . We have been told that where it's at, baby, is not in the ivory tower but in slashing professors' tires, which seems to include all professors who do not adjust their research to the needs of the movement. Now I have plenty of reason myself to dislike professors, and I think that most of the work that they are currently doing in all fields is trivial. But I do not dislike scholarship. . . . I do not share Staughton [Lynd]'s disdain for truth-seeking. . . . What if the movement is wrong? As Staughton pointed out . . . , it has been wrong many times . . . . And what kind of an enduring Left will we have in this country if Left intellectuals feel that they have to apologize for leaving the picket line to go back to the ivory tower to write a Marxist history of art?[29]

Lemisch's viewpoint is more palatable to non-radicals than is that against which he argued, but he was not necessarily more consistent with basic radical principles. He left room for the radical intellectual to play a somewhat specialized role within the Movement. On this point he was out of step with most other radical academicians. At the NUC meeting where he delivered his opinions, the general mood differed sharply from his outlook: "The radical teacher ought to be concerned with projecting a radical 'lifestyle'. He must be model as well as mentor. . . . The point that the radical teacher must be committed to the whole spectrum of radical activity is one that we returned to often. The serious radical will not be seriously upset at the idea that the gap between his professional activities and his radical activities must be closed."[30]

Another radical for scholarship was Noam Chomsky. He expressed the issue in terms of the competing demands of truth and power,[31] and he chose truth over power in determining the proper role for the radical intellectual.[32] He felt that power inevitably corrupts the intellectual. Further, he saw the likelihood that objective scholarship could be ultimately useful to the radical cause, and he refused to join those young radicals who dismissed it out of hand. "The left badly needs understanding of present society, its long-range tendencies, the possibilities for alternative forms of social organization, and a reasoned analysis of how social change can come about. Objective scholarship can contribute to this understanding."[33]

But Chomsky's urgings also fell on deaf ears. He and Lemisch belonged to a beleaguered minority among the radicals. If the full-time Movement activists had accused the academic radicals of being compromisers, scholars like Chomsky and Lemisch gave academic radicals who had an anti-scholarship bias someone at whom to point an accusing finger.

Libraries: To Burn or Not To Burn?

The extent of this rejection of scholarship comes into clear relief over the question of whether or not to burn libraries. Although the very issue may strike many as too bizarre to discuss seriously, the radicals not only treated it seriously but were divided on which position to take.

Chandler Davis acknowledged that most radicals seemed sympathetic to activists who destroyed university property, including library holdings. "All right, granted, we 'fight' to demystify them [dominant views in the academy], to redress the enormous imbalance in access to media, to get our messages to people as they get theirs. That's a matter of power. But we don't really 'fight' their ideas. We answer them. . . . Battles of words are not really battles. Struggles against confusing ideology must be ideological struggle. Burning libraries, or even offices, is not that."[34] Davis's defense of libraries took the form of an interesting analogy between books and guns. Both are weapons, and both are to be put into the service of the revolution. "Granted, books can be instruments of oppression, but that doesn't prove any case for book-burning. After all, guns are instruments of oppression too, and yet revolutionaries mostly don't reject guns which are offered for their use.

"We have to tell them...that THE TRUTH WILL MAKE YOU FREE. We have to tell them, THIS LIBRARY IS AN ARSENAL. SAVE THESE WEAPONS—PUT THEM IN THE SERVICE OF REVOLU-TION."[35]

Davis's case was built on the premise that a division of labor within the Movement is legitimate, that the academic leftists "should be that portion of the movement that knows and explains the value of learning."[36] But he knew what would be the response of the militant activists: "Can we really say it to the Crazies: As they advance on the Stanford Behavioral Center with their gasoline cans, and we stand in their way holding whatever signs, won't they ask us which side we're on anyway?"[37] Even his equivocal concluding slogan, "BOOKS—SI! BULLSHIT—NO! THEORY FOR THE PEOPLE!"[38] would not convince them.

Nor would it convince many of his fellow academic radicals, one of whom responded to Davis as follows:

My gut reaction, like yours, is to shiver a bit at the thought of a library in flames. But I think that book burning should be criticized as part of a coherent tactical view of what makes an appropriate target. All activity and institutions are obviously bound up with an exploitative system and in one degree or another contribute to that system. But we distinguish between the bad and the intolerable.... The educational task of the movement is to make the bad intolerable and some day any collaboration with the U.S. government may make a target legitimate. At any rate, for today the library is not an appropriate target in most cases, but not only because of a sanctity of knowledge.[39]

The logic here is fascinating. Only the gut feeling of a person who had spent much time in libraries stood between books and their burners. Let us call that sentimentalism. The actual argument, even in a statement calling for temporarily sparing the books, was on the other side. The only reason offered was that the tactically right moment for burning books had not been reached. But if the author had his way, the time would come when the bad (in this case, libraries) would become intolerable, and then the tactics would demand destruction. The worse, the better. The one theoretical basis suggested for not burning books—the sanctity of knowledge—was explicitly rejected as inadequate. Here is a classic example of the conflict between the gut reaction of an intellectual and the ideology which he has adopted. The result is a divided person.

Professionalism and Partisanship

While many radicals recognized the tension between scholarship and propaganda, few have dealt with it in any constructive manner. One who has is Richard Flacks. He wrote a book about the youthful protest Movement in which he had played a leading part, and he acknowledged that "my commitment surely biases my interpretation of the youth revolt as positive, as historically decisive (rather than as marginal), and as socially necessary."[40] As a professional sociologist, however, he developed professional commitments along with his partisan commitments. He freely admitted the resulting tensions between the two and attempted to fuse them within one person:

> Unquestionably, there is some tension between professional and partisan commitments. Commitment to partisan goals implies a dedication to the triumph in society of particular cherished values, while commitment to professional ends connotes a dedication to the use of rational and objective methods in pursuit of truth, regardless of the consequences.
>
> Without arguing the point, I contend that partisanship and professionalism can be mutually supportive. The professional–partisan who maintains both commitments may be in a position to probe more deeply, scrutinize more carefully, and be more sensitive to certain ranges of experience than the professional who has tried to remain aloof from political engagement is able to be. Furthermore, the aloof stance may be an unconscious (or conscious) cover for concealed allegiances to the status quo. On the other hand, the rational, objective, truth-telling stance of the ideal professional is a spirit that, in my opinion, ought to be alive in any social movement that has humanistic goals. The fusion of these stances is what I try for here; nevertheless you should be alert to the ways in which this fusion fails.[41]

Flacks's forthrightness in admitting his bias and in cautioning his readers to make allowances for it is wholly admirable, as is his desire to maintain both poles of commitment in his book, a goal rare among radical writers. However, one wishes that he had taken the time—here or elsewhere—to argue for what he said he would merely assert without supporting argument. All of the specifics of the above quotation referred to his individual case. Would he be as quick to grant the legitimacy of partisan commitments to those who support opposing political viewpoints? Can an engaged non-radical scholar, who, like Flacks, eschews aloofness, be granted the same right which Flacks claimed for himself? He admitted that his biases might distort interpretation and create blind spots. This does not invalidate the insights which can come from a person with his point of view. But it at least suggests that one with another point of view may be in a position to cast a different and equally valuable light which Flacks cannot offer. If the professional–partisan is a legitimate academic commentator, he is so regardless of his unique vantage point.

It is significant that Flacks saw the tension in terms of professionalism and partisanship, not in terms of scholarship and propaganda. There is a crucial, if fine, distinction between being a partisan and being a propagandist. The partisan is one with a point of view, but there is no necessary corollary that other points of view must be eliminated. The propagandist sacrifices all other values, including those of the scholar, for the furtherance of his cause. It is the difference between a man who has beliefs and a man who is a "true believer" (to borrow a term from Eric Hoffer). One can hold to a set of beliefs and still recognize that others have an equal right to hold to a different set of beliefs. The distance between scholarship and propaganda is too great to be classified as a tension; it is a contradiction. The distance between professionalism and partisanship is not necessarily more than a tension.

Robert Paul Wolff, a self-styled radical not associated with the Movement, was correct when he contended, "Those who would use the university as an instrument of political propaganda must answer for its death as a community of learning."[42] At the same time, Wolff is a man of partisan commitments, as is implied in the next sentence: "I can imagine conditions under which I would be prepared to sacrifice the university to a higher good, but nothing resembling such conditions exists now in the United States."[43] His main point is to deny the new radicals' assessment of the social condition in America and its universities and to demonstrate his ability to conceive of a higher good than the mere existence of the university. Only one with a value system could make such a judgment, and Wolff has that. He has a partisan perspective. His is a coherent and legitimate stance; Flacks's may be. Few of the new radicals have achieved anything like a coherent and legitimate synthesis of the conflicting loyalties and interests which comprise their roles in the academy.

Thought and Action

Radicals have taken great pains to try to reconcile thought and action, to keep their lives from becoming dichotomized by the two. But they complained that society frustrates their desires. Lynd observed, "Clearly current doctrine with respect both to academic freedom and civil liberties remains: Talk but do not act; instruct but do not obstruct; discuss but do not disrupt."[44] He found that this distinction "prevents a man not only from being a good citizen but also from being a good academic. At least in the social sciences, action may be essential to the search for truth itself."[45]

Theodore Roszak, who was only on the fringes of the Movement but who shared much of the new radicals' critique of academic life, proposed that "in assessing a scholar's intellectual quality, we be prepared to ask what the man's thought or the example of his actions has been worth in the defense of civilized virtues."[46] His emphasis was on action.

Suppose an instructor in American history takes an active part in organizing a thoroughly thoughtful, thoroughly well-conceived campaign against capital punishment in his state. He musters the students to the cause and succeeds in engaging public officials and people generally in a searching debate of crime and punishment. Now has he or has he not made a more real intellectual contribution than if he had authored a definitive study on the decline of cotton factorage in the American South for the period of 1865–1894? What should our "professional" assessment of him be?[47]

Roszak's example is an interesting one. Should the university give a person tenure or a promotion or a salary raise for leading a campaign against capital punishment? Should it offer these inducements to a person who leads a campaign to have the death penalty reinstated? Who will determine what is citizenly conduct? The individual involved? The university officials? Roszak? Does Roszak imply that assumption frequently made by radicals, that the virtues which they acknowledge are the ones to be rewarded? If so, a proposal which might merit consideration is vitiated by a politicization not intrinsic to it.

The radicals' drive to unify thought and action took precedence even over the matter of legality. Lynd stated flatly, "I reject the distinction between thought and action which would protect the teacher so long as he talks and would fire him if he acts illegally."[48]

No one would deny the beauty of congruity between thought and action in anyone's life, radical or not. Many academics confess that professional pressures tend to cloister them from everyday affairs, both public and private. The particular difficulty faced by the radicals was that the actions generally called for by their thinking were often at odds with the expectations of the academic life style, not merely superfluous to them. So the issue reverts to that basic one: is it possible to be both an academic and a radical? Some have answered in the negative and have left the academy. Lynd suggested leaving half-way and staying half-way.[49] But that suggesiton would seem to leave the radical professor a part-time thinker and a part-time activist, a part-time radical and a part-time professor—and all in the name of wholeness. The seemingly self-evident desideratum of linking thought and action turns out, in the radicals' case, to be baffling. Instead of resolving this perennial tension of academicians their radicalism has exacerbated it.

The Inevitability of Co-optation

Of all of the specific details of this conundrum of self-definition, the one which has caused the radicals the greatest anguish has been the matter of co-optation. To be true to themselves and their stated position without being co-opted by the system in which they work—this is the problem. Since the university trains personnel for a place in the establishment, how can a radical within its environs maintain personal integrity? His very presence validates to some extent the entire operation. Further, the profession places great demands on its members, and some of these are in conflict with the radical vision.

Herbert Marcuse, borrowing a term from the German student radical leader, Rudi Dutschke, endorsed "the strategy of the *long march through the institutions:* working against the established institutions while working in them, but not simply by 'boring from within,' rather by 'doing the job,' learning (how to program and read computers, how to teach all levels of education, how to use the mass media, how to organize production, how to recognize and eschew planned obsolescence, how to design, et cetera), and at the same time preserving one's own consciousness in working with the others."[50]

Marcuse's advice only sharpens the problem of co-optation; it does not help radicals toward its solution. To some radicals, Marcuse's chosen role is a prime example of co-optation. As long as he sits quietly in his office in San Diego and writes about revolution, the system can easily absorb him as a harmless eccentric. Kampf noted, in another context, "There is no apparent limit to the academy's capacity for institutionalizing, not merely innovations, but the most intemperate onslaughts against the Establishment."[51] Marcuse has become a kind of national institution. His attacks seem at times to soothe the liberal conscience by showing that academic freedom must indeed flourish if so dedicated an enemy of the establishment as Marcuse is allowed to function within it free from official harassment.

It is the tendency for the university subtly but effectively to shape the radical into its image, rather than the reverse.[52] Lynd complained: "We ought to take very seriously the fact that ... the university corrupts radicals more often than it destroys them. ... It is a very peculiar sort of radicalism which permits one only to be arrested in summertime, or obliges one to hurry home from Hanoi to be on time for a seminar. But that is the kind of radical one has to be so long as one's first commitment is to university life. ... The point is that whatever we may think, university life requires us to act as if our radicalism were episodic and of secondary importance."[53]

Not only does co-optation corrupt the individual radical professor, but it also vitiates the programs which the radicals propose—according to Chomsky, a fate "which not even the most radical program can escape."[54] The accuracy of Chomsky's lament will soon become apparent. Stripped of rhetorical display, virtually every specific proposal emanating from the radicals proved capable of being absorbed by liberal reformism.[55] So great was the fear of co-optation that radicals were frequently immobilized by the prospect that some of their ideas might be accepted and implemented by the establishment without the concomitant adoption of the total world view out of which their specific suggestions grew. This was an exact replay of the dilemma which Todd Gitlin felt concerning SDS's impact on the nation as a whole: that the whole of the SDS vision was more than the sum of its parts and that the adoption of one or more of the parts in isolation from the whole would be co-optive.

The net result of this fear was that radicals sought to insure that their proposals were of such a nature that they could not be co-opted—or adopted at all. They became grotesquely unrealistic. Rather than providing serious alternatives, they supplied only vehicles for the negative critiques which made up the actual substance of the new radicalism. That also cut the radicals off from the satisfaction of short-range achievements, a satisfaction they desperately needed to maintain morale and momentum. Deprived of the possibility of success, radicals either dropped out of activism in despair or turned their energies upon each other. The fear of co-optation forced them into a vicious circle from which there was no escape.

An interesting case study of the immobility enforced by fear of co-optation comes from a report by the NUC chapter at the State University of New York at Stony Brook: "A little over a year ago, Stony Brook NUC people were responding to university reform issues on campus. ... Basically we decided not to participate directly on the various 'study commissions' on governance, etc., because we wanted to be free to criticize all recommendations without being associated formally with the work of the commissions. . . . All interesting and important changes in power relations are barred by state law or a distant Board of Trustees. To fight them on such issues is, we think, not worth the effort."[56] When invited to contribute to reshaping the university, these radicals chose to abstain. Following the logic of all or nothing, they chose nothing rather than something, because they perceived that they could not attain everything. What turned out to have primacy was the need for maneuvering room which would leave the credentials of their negative attacks untainted by cooperation with the establishment. Once again, the anarchist strain of the new radicals surfaced clearly.

One radical took the notion of co-optation so far that he saw a kind of conspiracy in the distribution of radicals throughout the academic disciplines. His willful impugning of motives left entirely out of account those individual radicals whose natural proclivities led to selecting their own fields of study; rather, he implied that some master-mind(s) moved personnel about like chess pieces:

Neverthless, faculty radicals are disproportionately concentrated in departments which are not vital to the functioning of the American Empire. Most dissident faculty are found in the humanities and social sciences, with a sprinkling in the pure sciences. But departments of business, economics and the applied sciences, in which is trained a majority of the managers and technicians of the American Empire, are distinctly inhospitable to radicals.

It seems probable that the toleration of academic radicals is actually advantageous to the system, since such toleration hardly threatens the recruitment process of the system and allows the perpetuation of the myth of the university as a "marketplace of ideas."[57]

There is a modicum of truth to this assertion; just as workers are, according to Marcuse, given enough of the system's satisfactions to keep them inside institutions and out of revolt, so does the university provide enough satisfactions so that even the radical professors stay. For all their fulminations against it, not too many have left voluntarily. If they have been co-opted, they have allowed themselves to be so. It is a game which demands two players.

The resentment toward co-optation usually implied that it was an unfair tactic. But the real problem lay elsewhere. Others were not taking the radicals seriously. They thought of their struggle as a war, while others treated it as a minor nuisance. Second, their ideology forced them to reject the principle of a liberal university. Yet it was the only arena for the kind of work in which they wished to engage. The very nature of a pluralistic institution in a sense co-opts anyone who enters it with an identifiable world view of his own, a view which will perforce be one among many presented within the institution. But the radicals do not believe in pluralism, and the ground rules of the pluralistic university must seem discriminatory to anyone who rejects the very concept of pluralism.

Finally, a caveat can be lodged against radicals who complain about being co-opted, yet freely engage in a co-optation of their own, such as the manipulation which radicals practice in their drive to recruit followers. Even more important is the penchant of radicals to speak in the name of others. They blithely invoke the people, the workers, blacks, women, youth, students, Third World people, and those whom they seek to make their special constituency—inevitably without success. A particularly egregious example of this kind of co-optation is seen throughout a book by Lauter and Howe, even obliquely in its title, *The Conspiracy of the Young.* They spoke in the name of the counter-culture, in the name of the civil rights movement, and in the name of youth. Sometimes they had to admit that not all persons in those loose groupings responded to their radical leadership; but they quickly reverted to their pose as spokesmen for large blocs of people, many of whom were overtly hostile to their ideas.

Radicals as Elitists

In this light, it is ironic that many—if not most—radical professors found themselves within elite universities. It was not consistent with their egalitarian doctrine, though it was a natural outcome of the fact that the new radicalism preoccupied some upper-middle-class whites from affluent and cultured backgrounds. Numerous commentators have observed this phenomenon, and it has been acutely embarrassing to the radicals.[58]

NUC's egalitarian doctrine inveighed against the anti-vocational attitude endemic in elite universities. Barbara Andrews complained that "many people who teach complex courses in the University could not teach basic reading or composition skills in their communities. Academe has successfully put us into an ivory tower existence."[59] Academe, be it noted, was at fault—as if the radicals did not choose which course they would follow in their lives. While the thirst for prestige might deflect students at elite universities from pursuing such training, many teachers have prepared themselves to teach basic reading and composition. Academe makes such programs available, and they are well populated. The problem with the radicals was that, after reaching their political position, they realized that it conflicted with the practice in which they were already engaged.

Radicals spoke about the virtues of vocational education as if they were wide-eyed novices in the matter, as indeed they were: "We must also be careful to avoid the elitist and objectively reactionary position taken by many well-meaning liberal faculty members, who essentially call for the destruction of vocational programs, and their replacement with expanded 'liberated' humanities curricula. The implication that learning vocational skills is not a worthy activity serves no one but the ruling class. Rather, we should see as one of our tasks organizing within these programs."[60] This statement was not typical of NUC literature. It was a self-flagellation of the criticism/self-criticism type and grew out of the Marxist-Leninist doctrine adopted by NUC, which legislated establishing an identity with the working class. The statement also ignored totally the contradiction that vocational education is designed precisely to manufacture cogs for that American economic machine which is the chief enemy of the radicals.

The elitism of the new radicals, as evidenced by their presence primarily within elite institutions, again demonstrates the contradiction in their position. They work within those institutions of learning that are most indefensible from their point of view. The early New Left emphasis on the personal, existential dimension of their lives was not violated by being at elite institutions. It was only after the New Left became Marxist that their position was compromised. But their bodies did not follow their minds, which called for them to transfer to what they sometimes called working-class colleges.

It is intriguing to speculate why they did not do so. Intuitively or from experience and observation, they must have sensed that working-class students would make poor material for recruiting efforts. Although the doctrine declared that these students were the most likely future cadres of the revolution, SDS experience testified clearly to the contrary. Also, for all their inveighing against professionalism, the fact that they stayed at elite institutions may illustrate another tension within the radicals: the desire to do what ideology demands against the unutterable desire for the prestige and personal gratification coming from affiliation with an elite university. Finally, remaining in prestige positions was a hedge against the failure of the Movement. As a factor, this obviously violates the desire to be a totally committed and integrated person, but we have seen enough divisions within the radical to accept the possibility of one more.

— 6 —

Radical Analyses of and Proposals for
the University

The new academic radicals' lack of consensus on self-definition did not deter them from assuming other objectives. Negative critiques expressed by the radicals were not necessarily invalidated by the failure of the New University Conference as an organization, nor by the failure of efforts at individual self-definition. However, such lack of success cast a doubt over the viability of their proposed remedies for indicated defects.

Radical Analyses of the University

The University as a Reflection of Society

All radical criticism was based on the accusation that the design of the university inevitably supports the status quo. Rather than criticizing society, it reflects its values and priorities; as the society is corrupt, so is the university: "a society devoted to war and profit will always create schools equally dedicated to these goals."[1] A bureaucratic society needs a docile citizenry; therefore, "University attendance today is, for most young people, a four-year socialization process which is intended to teach obedience and moderation, and a trained incapacity for creativity."[2]

What was needed in a corrupt society, obviously, was some distance between university and society, as Richard Flacks suggested: "there is a fundamental conflict between those who stand for reason, freedom and humanism and the dominant American culture—a conflict which cannot be absorbed. . . . That the excision of these values is taking place is evidenced by, for example, the prevalence of narrow empiricism in the social sciences; by the publish or perish syndrome; by the rise of research factories under state and corporate sponsorship within the university; by the systematic down-grading of undergraduate education in the major universities; by the very character of mass, packaged education."[3]

Actually, many non-radicals might well resonate with this statement. Those who did, however, would have difficulty agreeing with radicals about the definition of reason, freedom, and humanism. According to one radical,

> the military—the baby burners and the people who study how to burn babies—are only the top of the educational iceberg. This whole knowledge industry is oriented toward precisely the same task that the military is oriented toward.... There is no real difference between the people who actually manufacture baby-burning machines and the people who design these machines.... For, in fact the entire university is oriented at the policy level toward the burning of babies—either the rapid burning of babies with napalm or the slow frizzling of babies' minds in the so-called educational system.[4]

Believing that the university is the mirror of society, the radicals were confused about whether the university or society should be the object of their reformist efforts. In either case, they assumed a perfect analogy between the two. To change the university was to change society, because the university was a central institution of the society. Yet one had to change society before one could change the university, since society shaped the university in its own image.

Either way, the radical analysis broke down if the university was seen as a unique institution, allowing or even encouraging certain attitudes and actions which society in general would not tolerate. The fact that the Movement flourished only in the university setting was *prima facie* evidence of the university's singularity. Though the radicals did not read the evidence that way, most of the non-university population did. Tolerance of student rebels was a sign that the university stood apart from society as a whole, and legislators and trustees were encouraged to bring it into greater conformity with social norms.

The University as Socializer

According to the radicals, the university—as a reflection of society—has the task of smoothly integrating its students into the established social order. This view of the university as socializer was elaborated by John McDermott, using the Marcusean thesis that the professed tolerance of the university is a sham. Rather than cultivating diversity, it homogenizes its students into what he called university culture. The main object of this repressive tolerance is the student of working-class origin, whose "indigenous culture" the university actively seeks to destroy. "Like medieval priests or missionaries to the heathen, we dispensed a culture to all our students, despite the fact that a scant few could participate in it. . . . To the extent that this majority of students acquired the external trappings of the university, they seemed both culturally pacified and made culturally passive. Pacified because they were acculturated away from their own historical values and traditions; passive because they could at best be spectators of a culture whose home remained an alien institution."[5]

He claimed that these partially acculturated students must remain onlookers in American society, because today's university no longer delivers the results obtained when its students were drawn exclusively from the privileged sectors of society.[6] Instead, institutions attended by working-class students can only promise their graduates "a passport to a life style of high consumption and of reasonable job security. But it will probably be an industrial life style, characterized by social and economic dependence on a large institution, by little or no political or social influence, and by participation in rationalized work processes wherein one must try merely 'to get by and not step on anybody's toes.' "[7]

Working-class students are not alone in being socialized into deadening roles; so are teachers, including those who have become radicals. They generally share what is "by far the most common campus prejudice: that a student benefits by exchanging his own culture for that of the university."[8] They, too, have been "socialized like all their fellows into a rigid professional role by their university, graduate school and early professional experiences."[9] It is this against which they personally must struggle, as radicals.

McDermott's belittling of a college education was unrelieved. He called professors missionaries, as if that presumably pejorative term was sufficient to dismiss professorial concern with enriching students' lives through their university experience. But perhaps it is not bad for professors to consider themselves missionaries. If one thought that he was not in a position to uplift and improve students, he would be a poor choice for the professoriat. Radicals like to say that teaching should not be limited to relating factual information, but should also convey moral and social wisdom; so it is strange that they should call others missionaries and mean something unfavorable by it. It was precisely as missionaries that they said they were staying within the corrupt universities.

Doubtless, McDermott was correct that professors prefer university culture (to keep his phrase) to the cultural philistinism which even he admitted the students had inherited from their backgrounds. If a university education is not to effect a change in this situation, what is its purpose? Shall society not tamper with the "natives"? The implication seems to be that university culture will only shear them of their indigenous culture and replace it with an ill-fitting pseudo-sophistication. Following the Marcusean logic of "the worse, the better" implicit in the notion of repressive tolerance, McDermott could and did offer no answers—par for the radical course.

Tracking: Education as Conspiracy

The major device for placing students in their predetermined social strata, according to the radicals, is tracking.[10] Since schools are designed to "institutionalize and maintain privilege in America,"[11] particularly "the special class privileges of white middle-class students,"[12] they must impose a tracking system. It is a valve which controls the flow of manpower into the economy and "helps ensure that the American work force is not 'over-educated.' "[13] The educational system is designed to insure the failure of lower-class students. "Higher education in the United States has had to manage an elaborate and delicate technique for diverting many of these students from goals toward which they have been taught to aspire, but which a stratified society cannot have them all reach. . . . Working-class students are tracked into second-class or 'junior' colleges, 'cooled out' and counseled into substitute curricula (a medical technician's program rather than a premedical course), or, if they get to a university, programmed for failure in large 'required' courses."[14]

What seems like a failure of the system—the lack of upward mobility among poorer students—is actually a success, according to plan: "What if the apparent 'failures' of the American educational system have served necessary functions in American society? Perhaps the schools, like almost all other American institutions have been terribly, indeed horrifyingly, successful."[15] The authors add, "Such a proposition may seem shocking, if not downright perverse."[16] And indeed it does seem perverse to anyone aware of the university's veritable lusting after minority students. Whether universities are motivated by genuine social concern or chic priorities, no fair-minded person can doubt their eagerness to recruit students from backgrounds which were previously underrepresented on campus and to see them through to a successful conclusion of their studies.

The open admissions program of the City University of New York might have been received by radicals as a genuine attempt to foil the general conspiracy. Such was not the case. CUNY's program was judged deficient because it did not totally end tracking, because it would tailor programs to the needs, interests, and abilities of the new ghetto students. Furthermore, the blacks admitted into CUNY were "those, on the whole, perhaps, with middle-class aspirations."[17] Surely, in the minds of most ghetto blacks, attendance at a university is perceived precisely as a means to escape the misery of their poverty; by definition those ghetto blacks who attend the university have "middle-class aspirations." To the radicals, CUNY's open admissions program is another part of the conspiracy of the mighty engines of academe against defenseless youths from impoverished backgrounds.

One sees here the logic of revolutionism at work. Ghetto blacks, claimed by the radicals as part of the natural constituency they are seeking to help, feel their benefactors' wrath when they try to improve themselves. Why? Could the radicals sense that these upwardly mobile blacks will be difficult to recruit for the cause? One questions the radicals' interest in improved conditions for the poor and oppressed. Radicals have frequently advocated open admission. Why, then, their hostility toward CUNY's attempt at it? Could success at CUNY demonstrate that measures short of a socialist revolution are adequate to cure the social ill under discussion? Only if the situation can be demonstrated as beyond the help of reformist programs can there be any rationale for revolution.

The conspiracy theory of education is a necessary part of the radical view of education, as shown by the specific issue of requiring standard English of pupils who have spoken non-standard English before attending school. The usual approach taken by schools today is what is called bidialectalism. Students with non-standard dialects—the black dialect for instance—are allowed to see the integrity of their own dialect but are also shown that they must master the standard dialect if they are to compete successfully for jobs. Radicals felt that such an approach imposes unduly on students with non-standard dialects, since they must learn two dialects while middle-class students need to learn only one. If black English is considered wrong by our social conventions, the radicals asked, "What is wrong with being wrong?"[18] The realistic answer, of course, is obvious. Such students are unable to improve their vocational and social lot. Radicals still considered bidialectalism an "ill-advised attempt to change people" which "should be rejected, eradicated."[19] Wayne O'Neil condemned it as "a modern, fancy, but false promise to help black people get into the good life while putting them on and keeping them down."[20]

How are minorities depreciated by learning the *lingua franca* of the society in which they must operate? It's quite simple. The idea is to give them the feeling that they have a real chance to get ahead, when they are actually programmed for failure.

[T]he enterprise of making lower-class speakers over into middle-class speakers was never meant to be successful except insofar as it has been necessary from time to time to recruit some few of them into the middle class. The main purpose was indeed part of the main purpose of popular education, i.e., to render schoolchildren skilled enough to be exploited but finally uneducated, used to failure, and alienated enough to oppose their exploitation; thus, for them to continue to agree that they had had their chances to succeed in a free and open society but that they had failed. No one's fault but their own.[21]

Bidialectalism is part of the scheme of the ruling class to insure that "the managers' sons will be managers, the laborers' sons laborers, etc. It puts people in their place."[22] This analysis, which its author guaranteed as "quite correct,"[23] leaves only one option open: "To change the rules of the game or its name."[24]

This gratuitous impugning of motives will doubtless come as quite a surprise to those teachers who hereby stand accused of being conspirators against their students. Perhaps they will be relieved to know that those cases which they had considered classroom failures were in actuality successes and that they had served their country better than they knew.

Radicals as Socializers

The charge that the university is an agent of socialization is, in general terms, true but truistic: true to the point of being embarrassingly obvious, even self-evident. Which society has schools that do not do this? Surely not the radicals' beloved Cuba or China. The only real question, then, concerns the values society should hold, since they are those which the schools will transmit. The radicals are not urging value-neutral education. They are expressing only their disappointment that the overwhelming majority of teachers are not radicals.

This analysis is validated by an examination of what radicals offered in the stead of the present socialization process. They sought "the creation of an alternative culture and ideology."[25] They did not seek change in the actual process of socialization, merely the revolutionizing of the socializing agent. Rich Rothstein stated with painful clarity the radicals' willingness to use the same process of socialization:

all teachers are civilizers, socializers, more exactly. That's all education is, the socialization of students to a particular culture and social system. . . . From a ruling class point of view, functional education is

that which socializes students to survive in a culture without challenging power relationships; dysfunctional education equips students
with attitudes and skills which are revolutionary. . . . A revolutionary
teacher socializes students to revolutionary culture; equips students
with revolutionary skills; creates conditions for the development of
revolutionary habits.[26]

At best, the radical critique of the socializing function is incoherent; at
worst, it is disingenuous.

The Control of the University

Searching to explain why the university socializes young people into
accepting the status quo, radicals found their answer in the institution's
control structure. The question of who controls the American university
was crucial to them. And their summary answer was that control is
handled by big business through providing the trustees and regents for
educational institutions. Government also plays a major role in university
operation; but there is a close connection between business and government, and in a capitalist society business ultimately controls government
and molds it to the purposes of corporate profit.

Radicals contended that "mass higher education is in the service of . . .
economic growth"[27] and that "the university has, in fact, become that
typical product of late capitalism, the corporation."[28] Further, the university is in the process of becoming involved with other social agencies to the point of domination: "If knowledge in a general sense is the
motor of economic growth, then the university, the producer of original
and theoretical knowledge, is on its way to becoming the dominant institution in the society."[29] Kampf warned that the man of learning—who is
assumed to be the radical—would have to forego an intimate university
relationship.[30]

It is a necessary part of their analysis of the university and its integration with capitalism that trustees be powerful. The widespread belief that
their power is not great obviously bothered the radicals and was one that
they worked to counteract, as in the following example: "Because they do
not act that often, there are attempts to minimize the role of the trustees.
Yet they only act irregularly because others are doing the controlling for
them, in most cases the administrators of the college. When those administrators fear taking an action to preserve the class and political bias of the
university because it will make them illegitimate in the eyes of the faculty
and students, the trustees are called on to make their move, and they do
it not at all reluctantly."[31]

The notion that liberal administrators are tools manipulated by the corporate elite was the basis of Hal Draper's attack on Clark Kerr. Draper saw Kerr, who liked the term *bureaucrat* for university administrators, as "the archetype of the *liberal* bureaucrat."[32] According to his analysis,

> The role of the liberal is to do the job of buffering the status quo which the Right-Winger *cannot* do.... The liberal always tells us, sincerely: 'Support me, even if I don't go as far as you would like, because otherwise the Right Wing will get you.' And the majority of you do support him (sincerely), with the best of intentions. It is only because you support him that he is able to do the job which the Right Wing cannot do, or rather cannot do as cheaply.... When the liberal exhausts his credit or shows himself unable to do this job effectively, he can be thrown away like a squeezed lemon.[33]

Again the radical analysis of the university relies heavily on the conspiracy theory. While the liberal bureaucrat may be innocent on this score, the right-wing lemon-squeezers are not. The right-wingers, who have traditionally accused the university of leftism, will find it a revelation to learn that they themselves are the ones in control of the institutions. If they can believe the radicals' analysis, it will turn imagined defeats into victories.

The radical analysis has helped to publicize some severe problems in the governance of the American university. Many non-radical academics agree that the intimacy between the university and other social institutions is dangerous to university independence. As usual, they will find little help from the radicals in providing viable alternatives. Vague references to participatory democracy and student power are inadequate, and they seldom showed the feasibility of some other form of governance.

Bruce Franklin scoffed at the slogans of "Student Power" and "Faculty Power," preferring "Power to the People": "In the final analysis there can be only one radical position: the overwhelming majority of people, that is, the working class, must run the universities."[34] His model was Mao's China, where "the universities are now run by the workers and peasants and are totally at the service of the needs of the people."[35]

To show that the successes of China were applicable in the United States, Franklin provided the following scenario:

> The interpenetration of the university and the state will increase, rather than decrease. The present supposedly radical, but objectively reactionary, demand for university autonomy will be dropped by students and retained, if at all, only by liberal arts professors. The present supposedly conservative, but objectively progressive, demand for more

control over the university by the political apparatus of the state now
being made by the ruling-class politicians and press will soon become
a middle-class demand, and it will then be implemented. The revolutionaries will gradually realize that this university–state synthesis
contains the potential to meet all human material needs, and they
will fight for a new form of this giant, to be under the control of the
working people and poor people.[36]

Franklin's viewpoint was far removed from the anarchist and libertarian strain of early New Leftism; there was no rhetoric about expressing
the radical discontent of one's life within the university. But the most
important element in this statement was its undercutting of the usual
radical analysis of the intimacy between the university and the state. He
recognized, as did almost no other radicals, that it was a conservative
position to advocate a clear line of separation between university and
state. Most radicals operated merely as reactionaries, rejecting whatever
was presently in practice without having an articulate ideological pattern
by which to measure specific social entities which they attacked. Franklin
did. He had moved through New Leftism to Maoism and Stalinism. After
reading Franklin, one wonders why other revolutionaries did not also
advocate stricter governmental control over the academy. The apparent
reason is that they did not really believe that the revolution would come
and the state be transformed. It is no surprise that a person such as Bruce
Franklin regarded New Leftists as only half-hearted revolutionaries who
did not believe their own rhetoric enough to act upon it. In the process of
enunciating his own position, he demonstrated a contradiction in the
stance taken by the new radicals.

The idea that the university is controlled by the corporate elite can
be viewed as internally incoherent and not based on fact. It is doubtful
that the university mirrors society and its controlling elite except in the
most general terms. The voting patterns of business executives and university people indicate a significant cleavage between the two. Only a small
percentage of university professors praise the corporate elite; rather, there
is a distinct distaste for big business on almost every university campus. In
addition, the universities house the most outspoken critics of the establishment, including the very radicals who claim that the university is in service
to business interests. One hard-headed radical, Robert Paul Wolff, dismissed the New Left view of the university as a "rather silly notion" and
a "grotesque misrepresentation of the character of a university."[37] Wolff
contrasted the New Left view with reality:

The moral relationships among capitalist, worker, and consumer are simply nothing like those among administrators, faculty, and students. ... Much of the frustration which students suffer in their confrontations derives from their knowledge that it is the forbearance of faculty and dean, not their own power, which keeps them from being thrown out on the spot. They are forced to rely on the fact that the university is precisely *not* a capitalist firm merely out to make a profit, but rather is an educational institution dedicated—for better or worse—to *their* intellectual development.[38]

The Attack on Research

The intimacy between the university and government has caused radicals to attack the current emphasis on research, since much of it is conducted under government auspices. Military research sponsored by the Department of Defense has been the primary target of radical censure. The Massachusetts Institute of Technology is as prominent as any institution in military research and at the same time houses one of the most active institutional collections of radicals in the humanities. One MIT radical, Noam Chomsky, expressed some of the ambivalence which the local situation elicited and offered his solution:

When radical students at MIT succeeded in raising a serious challenge to military research, the first reaction of the labor union in the university laboratories was to enter a suit in the federal courts to prevent MIT from dropping military work. The response was not irrational; the New England economy provides no alternative sources of employment. Similar factors will make it quite difficult for engineers, and many scientists, to dissociate themselves from the commitment to war and waste. ... The task for radicals, in this case, is to develop concrete alternatives and to show how they could be realized under different conditions of social organization.[39]

One notes in passing that a sense of realism tempers the black-and-white rhetoric when the radical spokesman is intimately involved with local difficulties. Quoting Chomsky, one also recalls that some radicals are tarred with the same brush with which they tar other professors whose incomes come from government money. As Wolff noted, "One of the most prominent radical critics of American foreign policy, for example, draws much of his substantial pay from a federal grant to an electronics laboratory, where he does brilliant work on—of all things—the philosophy of language."[40]

The radical attack on government-sponsored research on campuses finds a resonance among some conservatives. Robert Nisbet, for instance, criticized the same abuses.[41] Seymour Martin Lipset, who generally approves the pecking order among universities as determined by the prestige of research, argued that leftists and conservatives are likely to share a revulsion against research: "Both want the university to be a school."[42] What separates the two on this issue is the leftist's politicization of the matter. As Lipset noted, "The issue of teaching versus research . . . did not take on a political character until recently."[43] The leftist explanation of what underlies the prestige of research is, predictably, a political one. The conservative critique of research is based on differing, non-political grounds.

Their hostility to government-funded research led many radicals to broaden the indictment to cover all research, or at least the lofty status which research activities enjoy on campus. They saw the prestige of research as leading to the oppression of all teachers but the relative few at the top of the academic pyramid. Some radicals advocated a new kind of research in which the radical "is concerned with making his scholarship relevant to his live [sic] as a whole, to his radical ideology."[44] One even urged that a "research (and propaganda)" collective be established with an annual budget of $50,000, since radicals needed theoretical sophistication in order to counter the "bourgeois hangovers which all of us in NUC share."[45] But "NUC's aversion to academic research"[46] was so strong that instead of pursuing these suggested alternatives, the radicals concentrated on a negative critique of research itself.

> We must recognize that in our attack on the elite (or large) school's functions that there is a great deal of research done there which is either objectively useful, benefitting all of humanity, or at least appears to be so to those engaged in it. While this is most true in the natural sciences and medicine, it is also relevant to a number of other disciplines. The proper attitude to take toward such research is still problematic . . . . It is necessary to debate whether we should "open up the labs—that is, agitate for and support scientists attempting to democratize their professions, and where possible, serve the movement (by developing de-bugging devices, doing radical ecology studies, etc.)—or trash the whole business because it is hierarchical and elitist and cannot as a totality serve productive or humane ends, or pursue some other alternative.[47]

As presently constituted, research was discredited in their minds, and they were not even able to affirm the value of such obviously non-ideological research as that to combat cancer.

The Charge of Persecution

An immediate and personal cause for radical accusation of institutional bias was emphasized by *The Insurgent Sociologist*—a journal published by radical sociologists—devoting space in every number to accounts of alleged persecution of radicals. Chomsky wrote in 1969, "My personal feeling is that . . . repression on political grounds is not extensive, at the moment";[48] in 1971 he reported "a rash of firings, mostly at smaller colleges and universities, on what appear to be strictly political grounds" in the past year.[49] According to his interpretation, "The purge of radical junior faculty—I believe the term is fair—at 'nonelite' institutions is one element in the general campaign to reinstitute ideological unity and conformism of the postwar years."[50]

In its earliest days NUC saw itself largely as a defense group designed to sustain radicals who felt isolated, and to bring widespread pressures to bear on any institution which might be tempted to ostracize a radical faculty member. An early document of NUC outlined the dilemma of radical professors: "They have been told that they have not published enough by departments which have promoted those who publish less. They have been told that their scholarship was merely derivative by men who are praised for writing 'brilliant syntheses.' They have been told that they have not worked for an academic audience by those whose work is classified. . . . They have been told that their convictions interfere with their scholarship in departments where full professors boasted that their scholarship is their way of fighting communism."[51]

The implied line of defense in this statement is intriguing. There was no denial of the charges, only an observation that they were not even-handed. Supposedly if non-radicals were purged for not meeting conventional standards, the radicals would have no gripe. Furthermore, if even-handedness were the desideratum, radicals would second the calls by such conservatives as Ronald Reagan and William F. Buckley, Jr., for proportionate representation of conservatives on faculties.[52]

The radicals' appeal to fair play was based on the traditional notion of academic freedom. Would they apply it to others as well? Or were they using for their own ends a concept in which they did not really believe?

Another factor in the radicals' case was the assertion that their first loyalties were not to the institutions within which they served, but to some outside force which was fundamentally at odds with the university. They declared that they would betray their professional colleagues if such action was dictated by the needs of the Movement. Does academic freedom mean that persons who seek to destroy the university through subversion from within are to be accorded the same rights as those not seeking its destruction? Many trustees, administrators, and even other faculty members would like to see radicals removed from the campus. But before the charge of persecution has real substance, radicals must show that their use of the concept of academic freedom in their own defense is something more than strategic cleverness masking disingenuousness.

The real irony of the charge is that the pluralistic, tolerant, liberal university which the radicals have attacked provides them with more security from persecution than their politicized university would afford a nonradical. While Wolff agreed with the new radicals that the university is not neutral, he contended that they gained more than anyone else from that idea, since such a fiction provides them with a shield against persecution.[53]

Radical Proposals for the University

University radicals, sensitive to the perennial charge that the New Left offers no constructive suggestions, attempted to set forth some sort of viable alternative to the alleged corruptions of the university. The New University Conference published two positive proposals for revolutionizing the university; they were entitled OUTS (Open Up the Schools) and SHBI (Smash the Hegemony of Bourgeois Ideology).

The "Open Up the Schools" Program

NUC described the OUTS program as "an attempt to integrate a general analysis of the political economy of higher education with a specific plan of action for NUC." NUCers faced the problem of participating in an educational system which they claimed oppressed its students; therefore, even they were oppressors. Calling themselves "both oppressor and oppressed,"[54] they were caught in a phase of that tension affecting SDSers: desiring revolution for their own sake and for the sake of others at the same time. The tension appeared in their discussion: "OUTS is a perspective for building a radical movement in the higher education system which aims at destroying the important capitalist functions of that system and replacing them with activities which will serve the people and the movement. Based on an analysis of the colleges which sees them not only as oppressive places in which to be, but as increasingly central to the institutional structure of U. S. capitalism, OUTS seeks to provide a strategic basis for a sustained revolutionary movement in our schools."[55] Building the Movement meant the radicalizing of others; this is part of the personalistic emphasis, as is the notion that universities are oppressive places in which to be. But the analysis that they are central to the structure of U. S. capitalism is political.

Indecision about the establishment of close or distant goals showed the same kind of tension. NUC settled for both at once. "The OUTS perspective enables us to start building this movement by including both short and long range goals, both demands which are clearly winnable, and ultimately revolutionary demands, all as a part of a cohesive attack on the capitalist social role of higher education."[56] The demands presented by NUC to accomplish this revolution-building are:

1. Universal access to free higher education
2. Financing of all public higher education to come from ruling class
3. Elimination of all forms of tracking
   A. Elimination of all dismissal for failure (flunk-outs) and all course-load requirements
   B. No use of standardized tests
   C. No multiple levels of courses and curricula
   D. Grading should be abolished
   E. Curriculum should be based on the needs of the people, not the corporations
   F. Provision for client-controlled child care centers at every institution sufficient to meet the needs of students, faculty, and staff.[57]

What becomes abundantly clear (eventually even to NUCers) is that every point is reformist; if each were implemented, the university would still be far from socialist. There is nothing here which is not reformist. The basic structure of the university would not be altered significantly by the adoption of the OUTS perspective. One analysis of these presumably revolutionary points would be that they were proposed merely as an irritant to the body academic and were actually no more than a reverse statement of negative criticism about certain details in university life. In the name of positive alternatives, the OUTS perspective merely sharpened certain criticisms and remained essentially negative.

Some proposals are worth closer examination. Universal access to free higher education has not yet arrived, but many states have made serious moves toward that goal without any radical motivation; it is not an inherently radical proposal. The financing of all public higher education by the "ruling class" also is not inherently radical (beyond the terminology); any system of graduated taxes places a proportionately heavy share of the financing of education on the wealthy. While many details of school funding are subjects for debate among legislators and educators, the principle has long been accepted that the student should not be required to pay his entire cost since society receives some of the benefit from his education. The OUTS proposal sought merely to extend a principle already in force. Even the more far-reaching NUC call for stipends for all students can be seen as differing only in degree, not in kind.[58]

The elimination of tracking, with its six subpoints, is the main proposal of OUTS and is extremely problematical. Basing the curriculum on the needs of people rather than on those of corporations is largely a rhetorical flourish which begs the question. One must first accept the entire radical critique that universities are in alliance with big business before the proposal makes any sense. Even vocational education—the likeliest candidate for the description of education to serve the needs of corporations—is not perceived as such by working-class students training for well-paying jobs in the business world; they see such training as advancing themselves. The provision for client-controlled child care centers was undoubtedly designed to placate the feminists within NUC by declaring opposition in concrete form to sexism. It would accomplish nothing revolutionary.

The most intriguing part of the OUTS perspective is in the first four subpoints under the proposal to eliminate tracking. All result from an extreme egalitarianism which rejects competitiveness and the corresponding standards which enforce competition. Two NUCers, Lauter and Howe, have written elsewhere: "Extending the idea of pluralism from curriculum to admissions and standards is the crucially radical idea of the free university movement."[59] From the context it is clear that the radicals wished for such free-university destandardization to be imported into established universities as well. So what they saw as "crucially radical" was a lack of standards. The appeal to pluralism rings false coming from radicals.

The proposal to abolish multiple levels of courses and curricula is curious—and seems poorly thought out. Certainly it does not help the advanced student, who must now be held back to the pace of his slower classmates. Are not the advanced included among the people in whose name education is to be carried on? If the people are only the "oppressed," it is far from clear that an end to multiple courses and curricula will help them; placed in classes with students from better backgrounds, they will internalize a sense of failure—a point made by many radicals. Formal failure has been eliminated in OUTS, but students cannot help but know if they are progressing as well as others through the material assigned. If somehow such awareness is successfully kept from them, they will imagine a progress that they have not achieved. Their degree will be devaluated and debased, as will be the degree attained by the faster student. Also, how does opposition to multiple curricula equate with radical support of separatist curricula, such as black studies and women's studies? For most radicals these are so separatist that they automatically exclude large portions of the population from either studying or teaching the material. The excuse cannot be used that they are compensatory—to make up for past wrongs—since that is the reason given as underlying all forms of tracking. Are the radicals really against tracking in general? Or are they selective about which forms of tracking they will reject?

Obviously, this critique holds assumptions about man and his nature which differ from those of the radicals, and perhaps this argument—even about such details as multiple sectioning and grading—must ultimately debate such a fundamental issue as the nature of man. But the radicals must assume, to be logical, that all men are equal in the sense that they have the same capacities and innate abilities and that different backgrounds are not to be taken into consideration in planning curricula. The burden of proof is on them.

Concerning the proposal to abolish grading, "The OUTS Program" asserts: "Aside from the curriculum content, one of the central modes of their [students'] oppression is through the grading system. . . . Grades constitute an illegitimate form of control over students, compelling them to perform tasks that are meaningless, alienating and oppressive."[60] The present grading system is undergoing re-evaluation and may profit from revision.[61] Certainly, grades sometimes compel students to perform meaningless tasks, and radicals are correct to note that grading imposes expectations on students. But it is sheer assumption (about the nature of man) that all students will learn well without such impositions, an assumption unsupported by the experience of most teachers. Nor is it fair to imply that teachers who dispense grades are petty tyrants; they would almost universally be delighted to be relieved of this onerous chore. A world in which no one failed and no external incentives were necessary for high performance is certainly not the world of the university. Nor is it the world of the radical organizations, the histories of which are rife with personal competition, strife, and organizational failures.

One radical, trying to make his grading practices conform to communist theory, wrote that with a little help from their-friend-the-professor, his students "spontaneously (and excitedly)" came up with "a property model for understanding grading, with me as middle management, themselves as workers laboring in a piecework fashion for a share of the limited wealth (in the form of grades) that I was distributing, and the grades themselves as a very real form of wealth that determined their ability to survive now in the institution and later in the society."[62] In keeping with such perspicacity on the part of his students, Professor Zimmerman then suggested "that we grade on the basis of communist practice, to each according to his or her needs": "this would mean roughly that students with low grade averages, scholarship students, and students who were majoring in social science [his field] would all get A's, while those with high averages, plenty of money, or majors in other fields could take lower grades."[63] The only grading pattern on which this is an improvement is that in which the professor gives all of his students A's, and complains when the university disapproves of his practice. Zimmerman's way at least allows a radical professor to stay in the institution—unless he has a student who feels that he has been treated unjustly (has been oppressed) and complains to the authorities about it.

The OUTS perspective of NUC is so riddled with weaknesses that even its proponents eventually realized that the short-range successes which it virtually guaranteed did not materialize. The blame for its failure was placed, predictably, on society.

> The initial exuberance surrounding the Open Up the Schools program has given way to the sober realization that building a movement within education is a very long and difficult road. The OUTS program program [sic] was initially developed from a series of demands made upon Peking University during the Cultural Revolution in China. This little morsel of history is a clue to our own difficulties with the program. OUTS is a series of demands possible in a revolutionary society; but in a pre-revolutionary one, there are several intervening steps.[64]

The "Smash the Hegemony of Bourgeois Ideology" Perspective

The NUC response to the failure of OUTS was to come up with another program, "Smash the Hegemony of Bourgeois Ideology" (SHBI). In the Leninist spirit of criticism/self-criticism, NUC pointed out—as well as any non-radical could—what was wrong with OUTS:

> The OUTS perspective as it presently stands has many serious deficiencies. Although phrased in socialist rhetoric, standing by itself it is essentially a liberal program. Open admission of working class and Third World students into institutions of higher education which are run by and for the ruling class can readily lead to the cooptation and brainwashing of these students. Equal opportunity to learn sociology, economics and history, and then to be graduated into relatively privileged, although fundamentally oppressive, jobs ... does not lead to the development of a revolutionary consciousness or struggle.[65]

This statement confirmed the failure of a program which had recently excited them, the dread fear of unavoidable co-optation, and the increasing militancy and hardening of NUC's socialist line. It added, "For OUTS to become a revolutionary program it must incorporate an SHBI perspective as its central component."[66]

This component was not another set of specific proposals. Either NUC had no other proposals to offer, or it was so dismayed by OUTS' failure that it feared to try new plans. Nothing ventured, nothing lost. SHBI retreated to the safety of ideological generalizations, based upon an admission that NUC did not understand the role of the university in American society and thus had no strategy for using it to promote the revolution,[67] a rather large admission even for practitioners of criticism/self-criticism.

After the usual rhetoric about confrontation and struggle within and against educational institutions in order to transform them to serve the people, the SHBI perspective defended the role of the academician in building a revolutionary movement. This defense was needed to counteract Weatherman and other militant belittling of radical academicians. Resisting the criticism that they held privileged positions, NUC found "the contributions of head workers in higher education . . . central to a successful revolutionary strategy."[68] In an implicit reaction against the OUTS program, the SHBI perspective averred: "It is a mistake to concentrate our efforts on what are essentially secondary aspects of the university's role in monopoly capitalist society, e.g., its relationships with its employees as workers or its lack of day-care centers. We must move on to the heart of the beast."[69]

It also argued against extracurricular activities as the main revolutionary enterprises of radical professors, since "SHBI deals with the very core of our work and life."[70] That personalistic note was expanded: "SHBI is about our own oppression. Most educational workers do not suffer from material deprivation or from particularly uncomfortable conditions of labor. Nevertheless, we are fundamentally oppressed. We are channeled into performing the functions required by corporate capitalism."[71]

What did NUC propose to implement this SHBI perspective? The list is disappointing. Some of its more salient points are in this excerpt: "We should engage in struggles both on the departmental and university-wide levels for job control, i.e., determination of the kinds of material taught by students and faculty. . . . More importantly, demands that working class and radical material be integrated into regular classes and that a wide range of good radical classes be offered (if not required) should be put forth. . . . We should struggle to have the faculty and students on both the departmental and university-wide levels take radical stands on educational issues."[72]

The rest of the SHBI program was no more precise or helpful. From the radicals' point of view, it would be fine for departments and universities to take radical stands, to "require" courses with a radical perspective, and the like. But how are such goals to be accomplished? For this fundamental question there was no answer. SHBI's withdrawal from specific OUTS proposals and substitution of unrealistic rhetoric were clear evidence of a paucity of ideas. The only practical purpose served by SHBI eloquence was to help raise the sagging morale of those susceptible to such militancy. Rather like whistling in the dark.

The New American Movement's Proposal

That the new radicals never developed any genuinely workable proposals about revolutionizing higher education is evident in the two-page "Proposal on Colleges and Universities" set forth about 1971 by the New American Movement, that self-proclaimed reviver of the organizationally defunct New Left. It offered absolutely nothing new: the university should be under popular control and internally democratic; it must be open to all; it must serve the needs of the community; and it should now be funded by progressive taxes on wealth, looking toward the day of collective control of wealth. Its programs for action included stopping tuition increases, instituting democratic control of colleges and universities, and installing curricular programs in women's studies, black studies, labor studies, anti-imperialistic studies, and penal system studies. It urged community influence in curriculum formation. It called for radical course and text critiques, radical study guides and reading lists, and information on career and employment opportunities for radicals. Last but not least, it sought the building of campus chapters of NAM.[73]

These were the same ideas and programs which had failed before. The only thing new was the organization itself, and even that was composed of many of the same persons, now somewhat chastened by their previous failures but with a burning desire for a new start and eventual success.

— 7 —

Politicization and the University

The sum of all the radical analyses of the university and proposals formulated for it was the vision of the politicized academy. Whatever difficulties the radicals encountered in verbalizing specific, concrete details of this possibility, the ideal itself remained a compelling and guiding one. But it is reasonable to assume that the contradictions which emerged in attempting to formulate the discrete elements of the vision were only manifestations of contradictions in the general vision itself.

A common theme among the radicals was that intellectual life had been depoliticized. The chief villain in this process was the notion of the end of ideology which followed World War II. A sense of exhaustion regarding ideology then encouraged a flight from politics which—to the radicals—meant a flight from reality. Speaking of this "denial of politics," Richard Ohmann declared: "I think that in retrospect we can see the origins of our present malaise in the core of our earlier beliefs. We wanted to move out of social action; we wished politics out of existence. But as Georg Lukacs says, 'everything is politics'; every human thought and act is 'bound up with the life and struggles of the community.' "[1]

The goal of the new radicals, then, was to reinsert into academic life the understanding that everything is politics and that all reality must be measured against the political yardstick. If "everything is politics," then the university is political, too. If, along with the rest of society, it had been depoliticized, then it was high time that politics be reinstated.

The Contradictions of Politicization

In calling for the politicization of the university, the radicals generally meant two different things. First, the individual professor had to bring a political perspective into every aspect of his work—his classroom teaching,

111

his research and publishing, and his extracurricular activities. Second, the university itself had to take political positions. For example, by not taking a public stand against the Vietnam War, it was guilty of passive complicity, since its task included expressing enlightened values of society and silence did not fulfill this function.

Politicization Means Radicalization

Much ink has been spilled in rebuttal of the second point. A simple question will show its incoherence. Would the radicals settle for the university's taking a political stand with which they personally disagreed? If not, why should anyone else be expected to do so? It would be absurd to expect the university to take only a leftist position; yet that is exactly what the radicals advocated. As Lauter and Howe noted, radicals "argued that politics—left politics—had to inform any educational experiment."[2] So politicization means "left-ization"; it does not allow for any politics other than those which are satisfactory to the radicals.

As to the other element—that each teacher bring a political perspective to bear on his work—the same principle applies: politicization can mean only radicalization. One example was described by Robert Meredith: "*The primary project of the radical as teacher is to subvert a corrupt culture as it is internalized in his students.* 'Subverting' here means undermining and disorienting at a fundamental and immediately personal level, by definition possible only from a radical point of view."[3] Meredith's method of subversion was to show his students the values underlying their papers and to indicate what was wrong with those values. "By the end of the term, most students have been radicalized in permanent and deeply personal ways. They have become radicalized . . . because there has forcefully been established a series of connections between *their* private troubles and public issues."[4] To differ from Meredith's analysis, the task of the politicizing teacher is nothing other than proselytizing. Subverting culture means subverting individuals. Radical success is gauged, as always, by the gaining of new recruits.

The thinking which underlies the radicals' confidence in their own righteousness was clarified by Bruce Franklin's comments to John Howard, president of Rockford College, in a 1969 debate. The areas of their agreement and disagreement, as pinpointed by Franklin, are revealing: "Our question is not whether the university should teach values and build character. We agree on this, but disagree profoundly on *whose* values, what kind of character. I am arguing that the university should be building Socialist and Communist character."[5] And if one wished to challenge Franklin about which values and what kind of character should be inculcated? It would be fruitless to argue with him, Franklin assured us, for he and his antagonists have no common ground upon which to base an argument: "So I think we ought to recognize that we have two ideological systems confronting each other. It may very well be that you cannot have rational dialogue between them. There is the statement of one position and a statement of the other position and then one chooses sides."[6]

This is the true-believer mentality at its most pristine. It is why the radicals had such a strong distaste for the concept of the open marketplace of ideas and why they opposed the image of a pluralistic university. While radicals, on occasion, appealed to pluralism in defending their presence in the university, it was clearly an idea which was incompatible with their call for choosing sides. And such choice was integral to their concept of politicization.

Politicization: Future or Past?

There is a further ambiguity in the plea for politicization. The criticism that the university is allied with defenders of the political status quo is an implicit admission that the institution is already politicized. Jesse Lemisch complained: "Long before the New Left began to speak of 'relevance,' the historical profession had constructed an ideology which justified the discipline in terms of social utility; historians and their professional associations put that ideology into practice in World Wars I and II and in the Cold War."[7] If the universities were already politicized before the radicals came on the scene, their call for politicization rings untrue—unless they frankly acknowledge to outsiders, as they do to one another, that they seek radicalization rather than politicization. It is the use of the term *politicization* which is hypocritical. Their real objection was to the liberal consensus in the academy. In the wake of its destruction, they did not want a pluralism which would allow their viewpoint and others to flourish, but a new consensus—their own.

In some substantial ways the radicals have attained success in politicizing academic life. Scholarly associations did not take overtly political stands before the radicals prodded them into doing so. Radical pressures forced ROTC and some corporation recruiters off some campuses. But these are minor successes compared to what they had in mind.

The Attack on Scholarly Objectivity

The vision of a politicized university has placed the radicals in diametrical opposition to the widespread academic assumption that objectivity is the desideratum in scholarship. The editors of *Studies on the Left* took aim at the notion of objectivity at the beginning of the journal in 1959,[8] and the criticism has been echoed and expanded by virtually all radicals who have written about the modern university.

Perhaps the best-known attack on the "myth" of objectivity came from Theodore Roszak. His critique attacked the scientific method and the concept of the expert which it had spawned:

> An expert, we say, is one to whom we turn because he is in control of reliable knowledge about that which concerns us. In the case of the technocracy, the experts are those who govern us because they know (reliably) about all things relevant to our survival and happiness. . . . Very well, but what is "reliable knowledge"? How do we know it when we see it? The answer is: reliable knowledge is knowledge that is scientifically sound, since science is that to which modern man refers for the definitive explication of reality. And what in turn is it that characterizes scientific knowledge? The answer is: objectivity. Scientific knowledge . . . is a verifiable description of reality that exists independent of any purely personal considerations. . . . And that at last is how we define an expert: he is one who *really* knows what is what, because he cultivates an objective consciousness. . . . What flows from this state of consciousness qualifies as knowledge, and nothing else does.[9]

The Political Base

What separates Roszak's critique from that of most new radicals is that they gave the political element primacy. Louis Kampf contended, "Today the idea of independent scholarship is a mask for the commercial activities of the academic bureaucracy; it permits us to bow, in good conscience, to the impersonal demands of the office."[10] There is, said the radicals, no such thing as learning that is neutral, value-free, independent, impersonal. Claims of this sort merely camouflage political motivations of dubious propriety: "The term [objectivity] has been used less as a positive standard to measure all scholarship and more as a delimiting or negative device to deny the possibility of Marxist scholarship. It became, in a sense, a weapon in the Cold War. . . . The typical scholar of the political center came to regard himself as the sole custodian of the objective method. And because of his rather casual assumption of virtue he grew less and less able, or willing, to apply the standard to himself and his works."[11]

Claims of scholarly objectivity are claims of political neutrality and nonpartisanship. It is all a matter of semantics, according to the radicals; no one can escape being partisan: "The writer who advocates and displays disengagement, has already committed himself. The mildest reformer, in refusing to be anything but that, already supports the status quo. So that what passes for objectivity is often intensely partisan in fact, and what is openly partisan may be wholly objective. It argues a sadly fragmented view of human nature to deny that analysis can lead to and justify the most violent partisanship, or to deny that objectivity and passion may point to the same goal."[12]

The Rejection of Relativism

The radical opposition to the doctrine of objectivity included rejection of that relativism which assumes that the most important questions that man can ask can never be answered satisfactorily and leads to a devaluation of education by neglect of such ultimate concerns. Michael Novak, a theologian who sympathized with aspects of the Movement, has written an eloquent critique of that relativism:

> In the first place, the standing assumption is that ultimate questions are in principle unanswerable, and hence not worth asking seriously. ... The university, on principle, concentrates on statistics, historical facts, historical intellectual positions, logic modeled on the discourse of the physical sciences, and ample documentation. ... More fundamentally, it is possible—it is even common—for a student to go to class after class of sociology, economics, psychology, literature, philosophy, and the rest, and hardly become aware that he is dealing with issues of life and death, of love and solitude, of inner growth and pain. He may never fully grasp the fact that education is not so much information and technique as self-confrontation and change in his own conscious life.[13]

This indictment does not apply to every scholar–teacher, not even to all who are non-radical, but it does describe an ethos felt by many students.

Historically, the dominance of the scientific method coincided with the end-of-ideology mood, and there may be a causal relationship between the two. The end-of-ideology mood was accompanied by the notion that technology carried within it its own imperatives. The latter were of greater significance than past ideologies for giving normative shape to a view of the world, since this view was not dependent on the flimsy foundations of predetermined theories but conformed with reality as determined by scientific investigation. The prestige of the scientific method affected the methodologies of all academic disciplines, even the humanities. Objectivity became the watchword; personal reflection became suspect.

The new radicals believed in absolute truth. In the words of Jesse Lemisch, they "start with the assumption that there *is* something called truth, or at least that some statements more nearly describe reality than others."[14] It was a position which "goes against the grain in a profession whose dogmas include a heavy dose of relativism."[15]

Asymmetrical Application of Freedom of Expression

The new radicals were not alone in observing the dangers in this new ethos. By the force of their presence and tactics, however, they brought the issue to the forefront of academic discussion as no other critics of objectivity have done. While others might welcome this turn of events, one must be a radical to approve the foundation underlying their particular formulation of the critique of objectivity. For radicals seek not the reinsertion of personal viewpoints into the academic discussion, but the insertion of just one viewpoint—their own. They are far from defending the right of those with whom they disagree to express their opinions.

It may seem unfair for a group to advocate that it alone has the right to express itself; yet examples of this attitude abound. For example, Lauter and Howe complained that schoolbooks in America treat Communism as if it were sin; it is not treated favorably or neutrally.[16] Since radicals do not want value-free education, the only options left are favorable or unfavorable treatment of Communism in the textbooks. Unless there is only one value-oriented perspective allowed, either judgment of Communism must be acceptable. Yet it is precisely such a single value judgment which caused their complaint. The only option which Lauter and Howe approved was that American texts had to treat Communism favorably—for a reason which they apparently found obvious, but which is obscure to the majority of Americans, that Communism is deserving of favorable treatment because it is "objectively" good for humanity.

From Louis Kampf comes another example of the radicals' asymmetrical application of the legitimacy of expressing personal viewpoints. He argued against "the very notion of a 'policy science,' " because it "makes the whole activity a mockery of scientific procedure." As he observed, " 'Policy' implies a commitment; it involves the making of choices on the basis of what is considered to be the good. 'Science,' on the other hand, implies the neutral search for knowledge, the commitment to an epistemology and a method of research."[17] But this contradiction applies equally to the radicals, who called for research which would be of direct benefit to the cause of revolution and who spoke repeatedly of the need to put knowledge into the service of some preconceived ideological end. Most of those calling for a radical scholarship meant precisely that it should be policy science. While they might claim that theirs is negative, not in service to the established order, that chimerical distinction would fade away as soon as America found its own Mao or Castro and experienced a socialist revolution.

Marcuse's Doctrine of Repressive Tolerance

The new radical critique of objectivity agrees with Herbert Marcuse's doctrine of repressive tolerance. Marcuse contended that all-inclusive tolerance serves to reinforce the status quo, because the very rules of the game ignore distinctions between good and evil, true and false.[18] He recognized that "impartiality to the utmost, equal treatment of competing and conflicting issues is indeed a basic requirement for decision-making in the democratic process."[19] He could deny its validity for contemporary America only by imposing certain definitions of terms before making his case. Thus, America is "a democracy with totalitarian organization,"[20] the Left encompasses movements of peace and humanity, and the Right encompasses movements of aggression and hate.[21]

This loading of terms grew out of Marcuse's conviction that there is such a thing as objective truth. The all-inclusive liberal tolerance is based on a relativism which denies that anyone can decipher the truth. If that relativism is as untenable as Marcuse believes it is, so perforce must be the tolerance which is based on it.[22] One can believe that there is an objective truth, but confess a healthy skepticism about how much of it he personally perceives. Such modesty was not Marcuse's style.

Marcuse accurately diagnosed the plight of the radical minority in contemporary American society when he remarked its helplessness to change the whole of society if a majority of that society believed (falsely) that it had no reason to revolt.[23] What was needed was a way by which that minority could become a majority. While he conceded that "no government can be expected to foster its own subversion," he added that "in a democracy such a right is vested in the people (i.e., in the majority of the people)."[24] Marcuse could only envision his radical minority becoming a majority by their being granted preferential treatment. They had the truth, but in open battle with falsehood truth was losing; so the rules of the game would have to be altered in their favor. "This means that the ways should not be blocked on which a subversive majority could develop, and if they are blocked by organized repression and indoctrination, their reopening may require apparently undemocratic means. They would include the withdrawal of toleration of speech and assembly from groups and movements which promote aggressive policies, armament, chauvinism, discrimination on the grounds of race and religion, or which oppose the extension of public services, social security, medical care, etc."[25]

Since tolerance, in the Marcuse-designed America of tomorrow, must be withdrawn from some persons and beliefs and a favored status bestowed on others, the question arises as to which position among the many competing for the allegiances of men will be elevated at the expense of the rest. Marcuse claimed that "the distinction between liberating and repressive, human and inhuman teachings and practices . . . is not a matter of value-preference but of rational criteria."[26] He elaborated without identifying those rational criteria:

it is possible to define the direction in which prevailing institutions, policies, opinions would have to be changed in order to improve the chance of a peace which is not identical with cold war and a little hot war, and a satisfaction of needs which does not feed on poverty, oppression, and exploitation. Consequently, it is also possible to identify policies, opinions, movements which would promote this chance, and those which would do the opposite. Suppression of the regressive ones is a prerequisite for the strengthening of the progressive ones.[27]

While Marcuse was inexcusably derelict in not stating the criteria to be applied in the test of progressiveness and regressiveness, he was clear on one point: "The question, who is qualified to make all these distinctions, definitions, identifications for the society as a whole, has now one logical answer, namely, everyone 'in the maturity of his faculties' as a human being, everyone who has learned to think rationally and autonomously."[28] Obviously, this answer only pushes the question back one step further along the line of eternal regress: Who is qualified to determine whether one is "in the maturity of his faculties" as a human being? Marcuse's answer, though only implicit, was clear: himself and others who share his light on the subject. It should be no surprise (since the eternal regress must stop somewhere short of God) if Marcuse and company would decide that the most fully human beings in the world were Marcuse and company. Certainly, only those who see the truth are in the maturity of their faculties, and for true-believer Marcuse the truth is in his possession. The reasoning is totally circular.

Marcuse had the effrontery to call his brand of tolerance liberating. In one of the few passages of clear prose in his books, he asserted: "Liberating tolerance, then, would mean intolerance against movements from the Right, and toleration of movements from the Left. As to the scope of this tolerance and intolerance: . . . it would extend to the stage of action as well as of discussion and propaganda, of deed as well as of word."[29] There it stands, in all its grotesque nakedness.

Marcuse himself pointedly applied his doctrine of selective intolerance to the university setting: "This means that previously neutral, value-free, formal aspects of learning and teaching now become, on their own grounds and in their own right, political: learning to know the facts, the whole truth, and to comprehend it is radical criticism throughout, intellectual subversion. . . . The pre-empting of the mind vitiates impartiality and objectivity: unless the student learns to think in the opposite direction, he will be inclined to place the facts into the predominant framework of values."[30]

One response to Marcuse is simply to dispute his facts, to assert that the whole of society is not in the extreme danger which he affirmed, and to add that the burden of proof is on him to show the accuracy of his analysis, since all of his prescriptions were based on the assumption of its accuracy. As Eliseo Vivas said in his polemic, *Contra Marcuse*, "Marcuse is not satisfied with saying, 'My goal is the wrecking of the society in which I live.' What he says is, 'My goal must be yours, and until it is, you are not free, you are a contemptible flunkey of a repressive society.' "[31]

Vivas's book poses an interesting case study. The new radicals called for the abandonment of objective scholarship and the substitution of committed scholarship. This book is anything but objective. While Vivas seriously explicated Marcuse's ideas, he did so as an engaged scholar with an unremitting disapproval of them. In the abstract, it would seem that this is the kind of approach advocated by the radicals, but it is beyond belief that they would approve it. It was engaged on the wrong side of the struggle, and Vivas was not one of those "in the maturity of his faculties." Yet their refusal to tolerate it as even a legitimate endeavor would prove that they did not want committed scholarship *per se*, but only scholarship committed to their cause.

Response to the Attack on Objectivity

The insistence by Marcuse and the new radicals on manipulating theory in their favor is intellectually indefensible. It grew out of petulance rather than lucidity. Although they may have been attacking a real evil when they challenged value-free neutrality, they did so for invalid reasons. The conclusion is that the radicals raised a worthwhile issue when they defied the hegemony of objectivity in the academy, but that they did so from grounds which provide no basis for a viable alternative. In their rush to politicize the university in their favor, they raised the most important of all of their issues almost accidentally, not realizing either the dimensions of the problem or the egregious internal contradictions of what they offered in its stead. Their overriding concern to further the revolution blinded them to all other considerations. Their interest was not really in the issue at hand: how intellectual activities should be pursued. Any alternative views were seen only as obstacles to be overcome on the road to the new society.

The Merits and Limitations of Objectivity

The whole issue of the scholarly pose of objectivity needs a thorough airing today. It is the primary item on the agenda of the academy. It demands much more space than can be given it in this work, the focus of which must lie elsewhere; nevertheless, some observations are in order.

Objectivity functions only in those areas where the material under investigation is amenable to quantification or replication; there it functions well and is necessary. In many fields—the social sciences are the prime example, but the humanities show a marked tendency in the same direction—scholarship has become more and more statistical. Personal perspectives can be dismissed as matters of mere taste, as if there were no distinction between informed opinions and uninformed ones. It is more difficult to dismiss statistics; they carry with them the aura of the scientific method. That objectivity has become the primary guideline for the acceptability of scholarly production can be readily attested by a perusal of the scholarly journals in virtually every field. The problem is that there is much in human experience which is not amenable to quantification or replication. Huge areas of human concern are neglected. As Novak has said, these are the most important issues which face mankind. Thus, the insistence on objectivity as a method is severely restrictive. If it is a modest approach, such modesty is unbecoming the great issues which should be addressed by the academy.

It has become fashionable in some quarters to declare that there is no such thing as objectivity and that all scholar–teachers bring to their subject matter their whole beings, including their personal points of view. So far, this is mostly cant. The journals, publishing houses, and tenure committees still show a clear preference for scholarship which makes a pretense at being value-free.

Various academicians have spoken to the issue, albeit not definitively.

It should be noted that most of them have done so out of the motivation to argue down the radicals, who have been the catalysts for reopening the discussion on this crucial matter. One who has written usefully on the subject is Seymour Martin Lipset:

> This stress on the problems of scholarship in the social sciences and humanities does not mean that any such thing as objective or value-free scholarship occurs in any pure or absolute sense. Practically every major writer on these methodological problems has recognized that personal values, variations in life experiences, differences in education and in theoretical orientation, strongly affect the kind of work which men do, and their results. . . . Max Weber, who is frequently credited with being the major exponent of value-free, politically neutral scholarship in the social sciences, clearly enunciated the impossibility of such work. He argued, in fact, that the concept of ethical neutrality was spurious, and that those who maintained this "spuriously 'ethical neutral' " approach were precisely the ones who manifested "obstinate and deliberate partisanship." . . . A teacher, knowing something about his own political biases, should consciously try to negate them in class by presenting more materials contradicting his opinions than supporting them. He should make his values manifest to those who read his works or listen to his lectures.[32]

This citation deserves several comments. However many commentators admit the impossibility of value-free scholarship, it is still the goal of a majority of scholars. If the concept proves intellectually suspect, that does not mean that it has not seeped down through the professoriat into the minds of the graduate students who will soon, in their turn, take their places behind the lectern. Similarly, whatever Max Weber may have himself embodied, that does not mean that those who learned from him have learned the right lesson or the whole lesson. The history of learning is full of examples where a teacher's influence has been other than what he intended. It is intriguing that the context for this discussion displayed Lipset's motivation to counteract the radical probe. The tone of the passage indicated that he believed that there is not a major problem where the radicals say there is. But the problem is deeper than Lipset allowed: his exoneration of the scholarly world was more inclusive than it deserved. Finally, it should be underlined that few radicals are willing to follow Weber's prescription in the final two sentences. Richard Flacks warned his readers what his biases were in the opening pages of his book, *Youth and Social Change;* few other radicals followed his example.

To try to limit the validity of objectivity as a method of academic investigation is not to deny its legitimacy, though this qualification is only sporadically found in the radicals' writings. There is today a strong anti-rational tide running in the academy, which would make science the villain and dismiss the whole scientific method. This extreme rejection of objectivity is reactionary in the strictest sense. Once the limits of objectivity are properly circumscribed, it should be accorded the great value which it deserves.

The extent to which the scientific method is applicable even to study in the humanities was stated well by Stuart Hampshire:

> it is plain that the same unconditional requirement of accuracy and truthfulness is imposed on humanistic scholarship (historical, linguistic, critical, philosophical) as upon any investigation in the natural and social sciences. . . . The scholar and the natural scientist are equally committed to patience, skepticism, slowness, to minute attention to detail, and to the usual disappointment of large designs. . . . The really difficult issue of commitment, and of the morality of scholarship, is this: how are we to decide what questions are worth asking, what problems are worth raising, or, more strongly, what problems must be raised?[33]

Hampshire was right in calling for factual accuracy in the humanities, and he raised a crucial issue when he declared that values will determine in large measure which problems one investigates. There is the additional matter of the attitude subsequently expressed about the matter under investigation. Thus, there are two moments in the work of the scholar when viewpoint takes precedence over objective analysis—the first (which Hampshire noted) and the last.

Stated briefly, then, scholarly work grows out of personally held values in that they determine what is to be studied. Once the investigation is underway, all scholars must subscribe to canons of honesty and accuracy which insist that the intrinsic statement within the subject matter be given full expression, whether or not this is what the scholar anticipated. Finally, he is allowed the freedom to express his own opinion about the material under investigation—to evaluate what he has just analyzed. Using these terms, the analysis is objective and the evaluation is subjective. Analysis and evaluation need not be chronologically separated, but it is essential that they be logically separate.

To clarify this schema, anyone who analyzes a text is under obligation to represent its intrinsic statement as accurately as possible, even though its content may not be quantifiable or replicable. As an example, Joseph Conrad's thesis in *Heart of Darkness* must first be discovered before passing value judgments on it. In this task, personal bias is a detriment. Logically, it is only after the most accurate analysis has been completed that the personal element should be reinserted as a basis for evaluation, and the latter must be clearly identified as personal opinion.

Many areas of scholarly investigation are such that it is unlikely that analyses by different scholars will yield uniform results, though that is the desideratum. Even when they mutually recognize their obligation to abide by the canons of honest and accurate investigation, some scholars may represent the original text more honestly and accurately than others. In the final analysis, this complication adds an additional limitation on objectivity as a method, since it indicates that even in the ostensibly impersonal stage of analysis objectivity is often beyond our grasp.

All of this, while it shares with radicalism a mistrust of objectivity as presently practiced in the academy, is far from either the theory or the practice of radicals themselves. While it shares their penchant for perspectival scholarship and teaching, it does not share their rejection of pluralism. It is their yoking of these two elements that leads to the monolithic end of the new academic establishment, the politicized (*i.e.*, radicalized) university.

All radical arguments, in the final analysis, are reduced to the simple assertion that they are right, that they are the truth-bearers. All else is rationalization. They seek no middle ground between neutrality and propagandism. They do not try to transcend (or even to demonstrate the need to transcend) the dichotomy between intolerance based on absolutism and tolerance based on relativism. Here, as so frequently elsewhere, the radicals end up being strictly reactionary. It is no wonder that negative criticism is their forte and that close scrutiny finds their meager alternatives pitifully inadequate. They may well be correct that the purist proponents of objectivity constitute a greater menace to the university today than do engaged scholars like themselves. If this is true, it is so only because of the preponderant number of their opponents, not because of intrinsic coherence in their own position.

The Logic of a Radical University

If the attack on objectivity and defense of perspectival partisanship had been intended to resolve the radicals' plight of feeling unfulfilled and co-opted in the pluralistic university, they might have proposed establishing an institution that is clearly radical and makes no pretense at being pluralistic. Such a proposal might be declared impracticable for financial or other reasons—though it is not altogether clear that the financial barrier would be insurmountable. The idea has a theoretical intelligibility. There are plenty of precedents for such an institution, primarily those Catholic and Protestant colleges which claim to have an institutional perspective. The idea conforms well with the early New Left call for decentralization, though it agrees less with the later, highly ideologized New Left.

If the new radicals reject this idea, even in theory, they stand exposed as totalitarian. It would entail their competing for students in the pluralistic society which is the United States. (Might not this be a greater barrier to practicability than money?) But if they, with their all-or-nothing mentality, will settle for nothing less than total capitulation of American higher education to their viewpoint and its expression, they are both unrealistic and unfair.

The concept of establishing a radical university was proposed by John Howard in his debate with Bruce Franklin. Franklin dismissed it, but his rejection was weak since he did not deal with the theoretical issues raised by the proposal: "I think that this pluralistic tolerance is a tolerance only of one small group really, as far as control over the educational institutions is concerned. In other words, you need enormous resources of wealth and power in order to set up a university or in order to keep a university going. So to say 'Go set up your own pluralistic university' is preposterous."[34] Howard was not suggesting that radicals set up a pluralistic university, of course, but a perspectival, a radical one; but let that pass. Before the idea is to be dismissed as intrinsically worthless, radicals are called upon to present better reasons for doing so than Franklin offers—since his only concern was money.

As a radical, Robert Paul Wolff was more responsive than most commentators to the dilemma facing a person with an absolutist commitment who finds himself working within a university system the pluralism of which is grounded in relativism. In his view, "By permitting all voices to be heard, the university systematically undermines all those doctrines which claim exclusive possession of the truth and seek therefore to silence opposed voices. By permitting a Catholic to preach his faith only so long as he allows others to preach theirs, one quite effectively repudiates precisely the central thesis of the Catholic Church."[35] Although Wolff used Catholicism as his example, his statement pertains even better to the new radicals.

Wolff's solution was that which the Catholic Church has followed—and that suggested here to the radicals. "*It would make much more sense educationally to turn the curriculum over to one faction and permit those students and professors who find it uncongenial to seek a totally different undergraduate milieu elsewhere.*"[36] The College of Old Westbury, a branch of the State University of New York, seems to have been a partial fulfillment of this prescription; in this case—if the college catalogue is any guide—it was the radicals who controlled the educational process.

The question is whether this diversification of higher education would satisfy the radicals. Their ideological commitment to total revolution argues against it, but it may be the best they can reasonably expect. The further question, to which the answer is surely negative, is whether the radicals would approve the process of diversification if it meant, say, turning a branch of SUNY over to the constituency which elected James Buckley as the U. S. Senator representing New York.

Part III

The Radical Caucus in English
and the Modern Languages
and Radical Literary Criticism

— 8 —

Professional Literary Organizations
and the Radical Probe

In 1950 Lionel Trilling wrote, "In the United States at this time liberalism is not only the dominant but even the sole intellectual tradition."[1] As a good liberal, he found it "not conducive to the real strength of liberalism that it occupy the intellectual field alone."[2] But in resignation he mused, "We cannot very well set about to contrive opponents who will do us the service of forcing us to become more intelligent, who will require us to keep our ideas from becoming stale, habitual, and inert. This we will have to do for ourselves."[3] The liberal hegemony over culture is no longer secure; today Trilling's words smack of smugness.

The most direct assault on the liberal intellectual hegemony came from the new radicals. Early in its history, the Movement was interested in questions of culture, art, and literature. The role of art was discussed at length in the initial document of the Radical Education Project. Art as an instrument of propaganda would subordinate talent to immediate poster and pamphlet needs, an attitude which would pervert the Movement's "utopian ideal of a society where personal creativity is valued and each man is encouraged to develop and express the best that is within him."[4] It rejected—"obviously"—"the idea that the obligation of a radical artist is to produce art which serves and glorifies this movement," and equally strongly "the idea that the only art of interest to a radical is art with explicit political content."[5] It declared, "The ultimate goal of the REP program in the arts should be to bring to public consciousness the role of sensibility in sustaining or altering values and institutions."[6] While seeking to encourage radical art through the establishment of magazines of radical sensibility, the document designated research and criticism as the major area of concern.[7] Finally, it advocated reform of the academic disciplines, noting that "in the study of literature and the arts, formalistic analysis saps man's creative products of their social meaning and thereby, often, of their spiritual impact."[8]

With cultural and literary criticism, as with the criticism of the university initiated by SDS, the young faculty radicals of the later 1960s were the primary elaborators. By the time they appeared, the Movement had undergone such drastic change that the tone of most literary criticism was considerably different from what had been intimated by REP. It still reflected the whole gamut of concerns voiced by SDS throughout its variegated history; the literary radicals replayed the major contradictions experienced by SDS. As the early SDS was primarily personalistic, so the earliest essays were autobiographical and negative and did not move beyond protest—typical of SDS. As SDS subsequently sought an ideology of its own which would not be a mere rehash of old Marxist clichés, so the literary radicals set themselves to the development of a new radical theory of literature. As SDS eventually succumbed to the lure of doctrinaire Marxism, so a Marxist line was adopted in literary criticism. As the New Left split into separate camps emphasizing political or personal concerns, so did the literary radicals; feminism was the main example of the resurfacing of the personal element.

The same parallelism exists between the radical critique of literature and the literary profession and that of the university in general. Literary radicals saw literature teachers as prime agents in the university's socialization process. They wavered between devoting their energy to reform of the literary profession and to the revolution of society as a whole. They rejected pluralism in literary criticism and sought capitulation of literary studies to their own purposes, opposing objectivity and advocating politicization. Within literature they manifested the same all-or-nothing attitude of university radicals in general: the only positive alternative articulated was the development of "a revolutionary (that is, a communist) literary tradition."[9]

The Radical Coup: the Modern Language Association

While radicals made significant inroads into several academic disciplines within which they formed their own caucuses, the literary profession was affected much more than most fields. English professors were a substantial factor in the New University Conference. In purely organizational terms, the radicals in the Modern Language Association (MLA) had greater success than radicals in any other scholarly society.

MLA 1968: the Events

The crowning achievement of the literary radicals came at the 1968 convention of the Modern Language Association: one of their number, Louis Kampf of the Massachusetts Institute of Technology, was elected to the office of second vice president, which meant that he would become president of MLA in 1971. Another radical, former SDS member Florence Howe, served as MLA president in 1973. But the MLA convention of 1968 accomplished much more for the radical cause than Kampf's election. It indicated the direction which literary radicals would take in pursuing their insurgent goals within the literary profession.

Kampf and Lauter acknowledged that the radical presence at the 1968 MLA Convention had its antecedents in the student Movement.

The Little Bourgeois Cultural Revolution of MLA 1968 really began with the student sit-ins of 1960 and the organization of SNCC; Mississippi Freedom Summer, 1964; Berkeley 1965; and so down to the Columbia strike that spring, just prior to our meeting. . . . Just where in all the ferment, we wondered, were most literature teachers? To what extent could we further activate our friends and colleagues into the antiwar movement or into radical politics? Could the annual MLA convention—that job market and old boys' reunion—be used to focus the discontent people already felt with the profession, to gather and organize them, to move them into action?[10]

The radicals criticized the use of MLA meetings by English departments to recruit new faculty members and the smug complacency of the "big names" of the profession who control the affairs of the association; they criticized the association's slavish devotion to scholarship, excluding other concerns of persons who teach English. Their most accurate assessments of their own feelings were usually conveyed through vague and decidedly personal rhetoric. Kampf commented: "The singular quality of Modern Language Association (MLA) conventions, their capacity for spiritual corrosion, is difficult to convey. There is the terror of the unsystematic and unpredictable movements of crowds, the impersonal name tags, and the hundreds of papers to which no one listens. Yet one's fright stems from a misconception, from the perverse assumption that the MLA is concerned with intellect, that it is anything but a society devoted to trade."[11] All of it seemed to him petty and unimportant in comparison with the great affairs of the world outside the profession. "Instead of my fellow academics, I kept seeing the specters of Vietnamese villagers being burned by napalm. Did anyone at the various section meetings care? . . . I became obsessed with the following fantasy: if all 15,000 (10,000? 20,000? who knows?) professors and graduate students attending the meeting, outraged by the slaughter in Vietnam, decided to storm the White House."[12]

Richard Ohmann's justification of radical activities at the 1968 MLA meeting was less subjective than Kampf's. He remarked that "scholarship is far and away the most evident interest of the organization,"[13] and he explained this bias according to

> the general Marxist principle that each class creates an ideology to serve its interests, and to equate these interests with those of society as a whole. The ideology that justifies scholarship as the finest manifestation of culture and of the disinterested quest for truth is not contemptible in itself. It can be defended, as well as attacked. What I wish to note here is simply how very comfortable this ideology is for the professors who have risen to the height of their careers, and who therefore occupy ideal positions for inculcating ideology in younger aspirants to success; and how comfortable it is to maintain the reputations of their universities, and so confirm their own wealth and power.[14]

Ohmann's relative moderation allowed him to speak for many nonradical English teachers as well as for his fellow-radicals.

> The profession exists so that there may be a means of accreditation and advancement for people in the profession, not out of any inner necessity, and certainly not out of cultural need, or the need of individual teachers. Most of the latter, I think, are what William Arrowsmith called "conscript scholars"—people by and large of admirable sensibility who went into the field because they liked literature and wanted to teach young people, and who found that the way to convert these commendable tastes into an adequate living and the respect of others was to write what the profession seemed to want—but what it rarely read.[15]

This kind of insight helps to explain why the radicals found surprisingly strong support for their efforts at MLA in 1968.

Reading four major accounts by radicals of MLA 1968[16] makes it clear that the radicals did not have any cohesive plan worked out in advance. One said, "Our initial thoughts about just what to do at the convention extended little further than 'stirring things up.' "[17] Activism at the meeting was not spontaneous. A letter was printed in the *New York Review of Books* urging that interested persons meet at MLA to discuss possible

strategies for making the radical presence felt, and letters were sent to
five hundred persons whose names were culled from an NUC mailing
list.[18] It was the Modern Language Caucus of NUC which managed the
radical presence at the 1968 meeting.

Florence Howe gave the best chronological account of events involving
NUC at MLA 1968. It is summarized here since the *NUC Newsletter* in
which it appeared is generally inaccessible.[19] On the evening of December 26, an organizational meeting was held with an unexpectedly large
attendance of four hundred and fifty. Committees were formed which met
throughout the convention.

The next morning, two panels—one on "Student Dissent" and the other
on "The American Scholar and the Crisis of Our Culture"—were inter-
rupted by an announcement that Louis Kampf and two graduate students
had just been arrested for placing NUC posters on the hotel's marble
pillars and resisting their removal by hotel employees. Florence Howe was
given the floor during one of the panels to collect bail and to recruit a
dozen professors to discuss the arrests with MLA leadership. Thirty to
forty radicals formed a line in front of the platform in one of the meeting
halls in silent protest of the arrests. Participating in this silent vigil was
Paul Lauter, a former SDSer, who was scheduled to present the radical
option with his paper, "The Imperial Scholar," but refused to do so because
of the arrest of his colleagues.[20] MLA provided NUC with a room for an
open meeting of eight hundred or more that evening, on the topic "Student
Rebellions and the Profession of Literature." A film about the Columbia
University strike followed; then a caucus attended by about one hundred
was held to plot strategy for the rest of the convention.

On December 28, Noam Chomsky led a teach-in on the Vietnam war.
Caucuses met to discuss the problems of teaching assistants, women in the
profession, the teaching of literature to non-white students, curriculum
and grading, and high school experiments in teaching literature. When the
hotel refused to drop charges against the arrested trio, Bruce Franklin led
about thirty persons in a sit-in in the hotel lobby, attracting a crowd of
some two hundred. MLA leadership broke the impasse by asking the hotel
to drop the charges, which it did in exchange for the promise that it would
not be sued by the three radicals. A celebration party was held that night
at Columbia University.

The fateful business meeting was held on December 29 between
11:30 A.M. and 5:00 P.M. Louis Kampf was nominated by Richard Ohmann
and elected by a hundred and fifty votes, and four NUC-sponsored resolutions were passed. The first of these urged immediate repeal of "anti-riot"
provisions in recently passed federal legislation; it was provoked by the
government's policy of punishing student protesters by revoking federal

financial aid. The second declared opposition to the Vietnam war and demanded immediate withdrawal of all U. S. and other foreign military forces in Vietnam. The third opposed the draft and demanded its end. The fourth supported writers suppressed by authoritarian governments; those mentioned were Cleaver, Jones, Siniavsky, Daniel, Paz, and Fuentes. The only NUC resolution which did not pass was that urging termination of the Center for Editions of American Authors (CEAA), on the grounds that this use of MLA funds was wasteful and that the money would be better spent on more relevant problems of teaching. Also passed in the meeting, with support from the NUC people but not initiated by them, were resolutions to move the 1969 convention out of Chicago, where it was scheduled to meet, and to establish a commission to investigate the status of women in the profession. NUC held its final meeting of the convention after MLA adjournment.

MLA 1968 as Seen from the Inside

Those were the events; what they meant is more difficult to determine. Kampf's arrest undoubtedly provided the spark which ignited the whole convention. As Ohmann remarked, "Louis' arrest became the emblematic event, the charged event, of the three-day convention, and it is not fanciful, I believe, to say that almost everyone's response was tinged with irrationality, as was my own."[21] It raised much anti-establishment resentment that the radicals were able to channel in directions of their own choosing for the duration of the meeting.

The election of Kampf to the second vice presidency showed the radicals how much weight they had in the business meeting. NUC put Kampf's name in nomination only as a test of strength, with no expectation of winning.[22] Kampf told a reporter after his election, "We are flabbergasted. We didn't plan this or pack this meeting. Apparently, we all underestimated the resentment boining [sic] here against the system."[23]

Realizing their strength, NUC cadres then submitted their five resolutions, received by the Resolutions Committee of MLA prior to the convention, but not introduced.[24] Overtly political resolutions were new to MLA business meetings, and the argument raged as to whether MLA had any right to get into politics—an argument still not resolved.

It was the resolution to shift the site of the 1969 convention from Mayor Daley's Chicago, as a protest against police action at the 1968 Democratic Convention, which brought to the business meeting those non-radical members of MLA who gave NUC unexpected support for its own resolutions, as even the radicals admit.[25] MLA custom was to hold the convention in New York and Chicago on alternate years. A ballot about the site of the 1969 convention had been sent to the entire MLA membership before the convention met. The results of the mail ballot were two to one in favor of retaining the traditional schedule and assembling in Chicago in 1969, but the radicals and some others saw the mail ballot as loaded in favor of Chicago and therefore unfair.[26] Richard Poirier, not an NUC member, bought several thousand black and yellow "No Chicago" buttons and distributed them at the meeting.[27] During the business session Poirier asked that the results of the mail ballot be declared invalid "on the grounds that its language was biased, and that such language made it difficult if not impossible for members to make an honest choice."[28] Such a resolution was passed, as was one instructing the Executive Council not to hold the 1969 meeting in Chicago.

The radicals were ecstatic over the outcome of MLA 1968. In a report to her fellow NUC members, Florence Howe exulted, "From any point of view, NUC at the MLA was an incredible success."[29] Kampf and Lauter observed, "what strikes us most about MLA 1968 was the amount of political and intellectual energy our organizing helped to release."[30]

In addition to her account in the *NUC Newsletter*, Florence Howe joined Ellen Cantarow in a report published in *College English*. It is interesting to compare the two articles. The second spoke of the interest in the profession itself held by NUC people. "From first to last the activities of the New University Conference (a radical caucus) at MLA were a sign of concern and, hopefully, of revitalization of the profession."[31] It also suggested a large number of radical MLA members. "It is important, to begin with, to realize that the term 'radical caucus' indicates not some small group of 'dissidents' but a significantly large number of members of the profession, from graduate students to full professors, who gathered spontaneously to participate in the programs directed to the need for change."[32] Finally, it implied that the purpose of the radical presence was to improve and reform the MLA. "What was accomplished was no more than a beginning: a very small dent was made in a huge structure. But if the radical caucus succeeded in making this dent, then perhaps there is a hope—or at least an opportunity—of reforming the profession."[33]

However, in her report to NUC, Florence Howe spoke of cadre-building and recruiting for NUC rather than of reforming MLA. She also referred to small rather than large numbers.

> What were our concerns? To begin with, and to be most conservative, they were to recruit for NUC. How could we, six weeks ago, have thought in terms of changing so enormous a bureaucratic structure as the Modern Language Association? Any of its thousand tentacles was

longer and stronger, we thought, than all of us together. Moreover, we are movement people who think in terms of moving small groups of people to consciousness through discussion, decision-making, and action. Hence, we had not thought in terms of power to alter MLA. And hence, if I were asked to point to a single most important outcome of the convention, it is that now there are not a handful of people who know how to work together, but perhaps 50, perhaps slightly more than that.[34]

Far from being excited by the prospect of reforming the MLA, Howe was uneasy about the new-found power of the radicals. They would have to think in much larger terms now, since "Louis did, in fact," win the election, and we are, willy-nilly, engaged in changing the MLA."[35] Her report to NUC ended with troubling questions:

Here, then, is the final question of success. Is it desirable that we spend our time "reforming" the MLA, even if that were possible? Is it not diversionary for us to be engaged to a dinosaur, not only for this year, but for a number of years to come? Radicals shy away from assuming power inside institutions, and for a very good reason, I think. Many of us have argued against any attempt to gain control of institutions, since to do so one always has to attain the support of liberals, and once having gained power, one has to work to keep that support. We are and will be for a long time to come too few to hold power without the support of liberals. . . . Can we learn, as we learned at the convention itself, how to build from the small group . . . ? And hence, perhaps, to manage the job—instead of having it manage us?[36]

MLA 1968 as Seen from the Outside

The repercussions of the 1968 MLA convention were swift in coming. *College English*, edited by Richard Ohmann, devoted a twenty-four page section to "MLA 1968: Documents and Responses." One item in this was a memorandum from John Hurt Fisher, executive secretary of MLA. He complimented "the reformers" on their organizational skill and restraint in displaying their strength.[37] He conceded that there was no indication that the reformers deliberately set out to pack the business meeting, although "the net effect of the traditional lethargy of the MLA majority concerning business matters and the active distribution of pamphlets by the reformers was just that."[38] And he found it "appalling that a group of no more than 299 (the largest vote of the reformers) in a convention of more than 11,000 registered participants was able to control the Business Meeting."[39]

On the other hand, Fisher faulted the radicals for "attempting to place posters, pass out leaflets, and harangue in the halls in violation of hotel rules without warning the hotel or the MLA Staff that this is what they planned to do."[40] When he and the hotel sales manager met with spokesmen for the insurgents and agreed on what areas could be used for demonstration, the spokesmen "pointed out that they could not be responsible for the actions of their constituency."[41] He also attacked the radicals for their "threat of violence": "The arrest of three people on Friday, the threatened arrest of twenty-five or so on Saturday, and the statement in the newspaper about the plans for Sunday suggested that if the reforming group had not found itself in a majority, the tone of the Business Meeting might have been different."[42]

Twenty-four professors from Duke University and the University of North Carolina asked all MLA members to protest the politicization of MLA by signing a petition to be sent to the MLA Executive Council. Complaining that a small faction had packed the business meeting to block the regularly-nominated candidate for second vice president and "to enact a series of partisan political resolutions having little or nothing to do with the purpose and objectives of the Association," the petition called for a reaffirmation of "the professional character of the Association" and a mail ballot on the issues passed at the controversial business meeting to determine the wishes of the majority of MLA members.[43]

Richard Ohmann responded to the Duke–North Carolina petition:

The whole culture says with one voice that professionalism is good, and the literary academic man is no dissenter. The Duke–North Carolina petitioners recognized the clout that inheres in the word, so that when they came to their point (overturning the legitimate action of the Business Meeting, the attentive reader will recall), they said it this way: "We urge the Executive Council to affirm the professional character of the Association." That is to say, a professional group will not meddle in those matters that properly belong to other professionals— in this case, the military draft, the war, repression of writers, and threats to dissent on university campuses.[44]

While the Executive Council did not try in any way to rescind the actions taken at the convention, it did take the unprecedented step of asking the membership for an "expression of opinion" on the resolutions passed. The results delighted Ohmann:

Let it here be recorded that, to my own surprised pleasure, the general membership, lashing out, perhaps, in blind fury against the invisible, omnipotent, and procedure-crazed organization it had created, affirmed all four political resolutions, so that the Modern Language Association of America is now *twice* on record as asserting that "the United States is waging an immoral, illegal, and imperial war in Vietnam," as urging the immediate withdrawal of American troops, and as calling on colleges and universities to "refuse cooperation with the Selective Service System." This last makes the Association a conspiracy, but I suspect that the resolution will not be given wide publicity.[45]

Ohmann himself came in for severe criticism from a professional colleague, Bruce Harkness, whose letter Ohmann published in *College English*.

Specifically, you confused moral issues and facts, as in your attitude toward Chicago and the draft; refused to accept a majority vote unless a meeting could be packed, as in your attitude toward the mail ballot; acted with a happy willingness to exercise thought control, as in the motion to censure the Executive Council; displayed a lack of personal integrity, as in the conflict between your professed views and the academic positions you hold; led younger members of the profession into an attitude guaranteed to insure scholarly procrastination; and violated a number of good traditions of scholarship and teaching in the MLA by turning a high office into a political position.[46]

On the mail ballot about returning to Chicago in 1969, Harkness charged that of the 11,000 members who voted two to one for Chicago, "Very few people were misled by that ballot: they wanted to return to Chicago"; and he scored Ohmann for his "refusal to face the consequences of a vote."[47]

Not all the responses reprinted in *College English* opposed the radicals. G. H. Fleming denied that a small faction packed the business meeting, observed that the time and place of the meeting were widely publicized, and reminded MLA members that the radical caucus had not been secretive at all about their activities and intentions—that, in fact, these were the main topics of conversation around the convention. He added, "Those who did not take the trouble to go to the meeting should not cavil at those who were in attendance."[48]

Perhaps the most revealing document in the March 1969 issue of *College English* was written by Clare Goldfarb, a non-radical who voted with the radicals. It showed both the motivation behind outside support for NUC resolutions and the shallowness of that support. Since hard-core radicals probably were no more than one-sixth of the voting majority which they controlled at the convention, it is likely that Goldfarb's attitude was representative of a significant number of MLA members.

While supporting most but not all NUC proposals, he was reluctant about the politicization of MLA, conceding that "nowadays every group must be political. There are no alternatives."—but remembering uneasily that some of his best teachers were not at all politically oriented.[49] His conception of the primary task of the literature teacher showed clearly his deviation from the NUC line: "But with all the right targets and the right words, is being a radical our supreme contribution as teachers? Is that what we do best? It's not what I do best. What I do best is involved with literature, and I cannot surrender literature to the bonfires of revolution. I will not burn my books behind me. . . . I see no contradiction between being politically concerned and being proudly elite."[50]

Despite his support for NUC, he declared, "Whether they realize it or not, groups like NUC are absolutists; the choice is simple: 'Either you're with us or against us.' Humanists get uncomfortable in such an atmosphere."[51] He concluded by damning with faint praise: "Although more of my sympathies lie with the radicals than with the 'other side,' I am a reluctant radical. I become more and more uneasy as more and more greys disappear, as more and more lines harden, and as more and more radical thought becomes mere slogans."[52] With this kind of half-hearted support, it is easy to see why the NUC cadres could not follow up their 1968 triumphs with further gains.

While most establishment figures in MLA were clearly hostile to NUC's activities, a few attempted to "reach out" and work together with "the reformers." Maynard Mack tried to take seriously some of the radical criticisms of MLA and to explore ways to correct some of its failures.[53] The radicals considered this only an empty gesture, a classic case of attempted co-opting, since it explored only strictly reformist measures. A genuine, well-intentioned effort by a "big name" to bridge the gap could not be met halfway by the radicals because of the revolutionary component in their ideology.

Henry Nash Smith, MLA president, also offered an olive branch: "The militants have succeeded in waking us up; they have shown us that a good many received ideas need to be reexamined in the light of recent events both within the Association and in American universities generally."[54] However, he noted the radicals' major shortcoming. "In short, although the New Left has performed a valuable service in challenging conventional assumptions about literary scholarship and teaching, it seems conspicuously barren of suggestions for alternative ways of proceeding."[55]

These and similar statements suggest that the radicals, having successfully shaken things up, could have had a major impact within the profession had they been willing to work with non-radicals for institutional reform. MLA might have undergone substantial change. But the ideology of revolution prohibited the radicals from such compromise; the two camps, "us" and "them," hardened into combative postures.

MLA after 1968

MLA conventions since 1968 have devoted some sessions to topics of interest to the radicals. At the 1969 meeting in Denver, NUC sponsored thirteen workshops and placed a number of its members on the regular MLA program, such as forums on "The MLA, Politics, and the Study of Language and Literature," "Why Do English and Foreign Language Departments Do What They Do?", "The Economics of Departments," and "The Job Market." NUC-sponsored workshops were held on the MLA and politics, class bias and the teaching of literature, foreign language and the Third World, radical critical theory, English departments, foreign language departments, black literature and black studies, the media, women's liberation, teaching working class and other "non-elite" students, the relation of whites to black literature, radical American thought, developing radical research, and a report on a trip to Cuba by NUC delegates. Louis Kampf, as first vice president of MLA, arranged the program of the 1970 convention, devoting the first day and a half to forums and workshops on "NUC" topics. The forum on "The English and Foreign Language Teacher in the Political Economy" was followed by workshops on the English teacher as civilizer, cultural imperialism and the teaching of foreign languages, education and the textbook industry, cultural consumerism, the job market in English, the job market in foreign languages, and the intelligentsia and the political economy. That on "Women in the Profession" led to workshops on the economics of women in the profession, literary sexual stereotypes, the comparative (international) status of women in the profession, women writers, women teachers, women scholars, curriculum for and about women, and children's literature and texts. Workshops following "The Many Cultures: Communication and Social Class" discussed blacks and ghetto language, Chicano culture, American Indians as an internal colony, Africa, and Mexico. NUC cadres also led workshops in Victorian literature and American literature.[56] In addition to being on the program of MLA, NUC personnel manned literature tables at each convention.

If 1971 was a somewhat slow year for literary radicals, since NUC was collapsing, 1972 marked a renewed surge of interest in radical activity.

Two differences between 1969–1970 and 1972 are noteworthy. First, the radical presence was led by a newly-organized Radical Caucus in English and the Modern Languages, since the Modern Language Caucus of NUC had folded. The new Radical Caucus was an outgrowth of activity in the Northeast by former NUC cadres, and at the 1972 meeting there was a concerted effort to organize on a national scale; the newsletter of the caucus was distributed nationwide. Second, the influence of Marxism was overt. The main forum sponsored by the Radical Caucus was entitled "Marxist Perspectives on Literature." While the main organizers were still the same NUC people, participants included Marxists who would never have considered themselves New Left and had not belonged to NUC.

Since the topics at the 1969 and 1970 conventions were mainly designed to air negative criticism by the radicals, something of the same pattern observable in the history of SDS emerges. The first phase stressed negative criticism based on a sense of personal anguish; then came a period of confusion; out of this limbo emerged a new clarity of vision, but one which was pronouncedly Marxist.

Regional meetings of MLA also felt the presence of the NUC cadres. The opening address at the 1969 meeting of the Midwest Modern Language Association in St. Louis was delivered by Louis Kampf. NUC sponsored sessions on teaching the non-elite, a participatory project in radical teaching, black studies, and the profession and the media. Workshops were held on male supremacy and its manifestations in the profession, the politics of elementary language instruction, radical approaches to D. H. Lawrence's *Women in Love,* the appeal of unions to teaching assistants, foreign literature and foreign politics, and something called "How to Survive." At NUC instigation, the Midwest MLA also passed a resolution demanding immediate withdrawal from Vietnam and urged its members to participate in a monthly moratorium for the time required to compel a total U. S. pullout.[57]

The Radical Impact on the
National Council of Teachers of English

The other major professional organization of English teachers, the National Council of Teachers of English (NCTE), was not spared the radical probe. At its 1969 meeting, resolutions were passed on "ending the Vietnam war" and on "the need for courses reflecting the cultural and ethnic plurality of American society."[58] NUC campaigned at this meeting for the principle "that literature anthologies which discriminate against oppressed groups be excluded from commercial displays and that they not be advertised in the NCTE journals."[59]

Just as they did in MLA, however, radical successes had a backlash in NCTE. William A. Jenkins, NCTE president in 1969, later wrote,

Last November, expediency in the form of a need to preserve NCTE as an organization may have justified the excursion into political lands. There were members present at the convention who were intent on destroying the Council if it insisted on remaining neutral and non-political regarding Vietnam and several other issues of the day. . . . The resolution which passed represents an indiscretion that cannot be overlooked or forgotten, for NCTE has neither the knowledge nor the clout to impress. Last November in Washington we, at best, were quixotic; at worst, Machiavellian.[60]

Establishment figures in NCTE, including Jenkins, agreed that the council should be involved in politics—"it *is* involved in politics by its very existence, and has no other choice; the only real question for discussion was in *what ways* and *to what extent* NCTE should consciously and purposely involve itself in politics."[61] James E. Miller, Jr., a former NCTE president, cautioned against taking a "deeper plunge" and endorsing political programs and candidates: "The profession and the organization should remain broadly based, attracting liberals and conservatives, as well as neutrals, Democrats and Republicans, and radicals of both the right and left—all those with the common aim of improving the teaching of English."[62]

The Coup in Retrospect

Enough time has elapsed since the dramatic 1968 MLA convention to evaluate the long-term results. In retrospect, the spectacular 1968 successes of the radicals have proven to be ephemeral. MLA is little different from what it was before 1968. At the 1972 convention—while the radicals were encouraged by the addition of new names to the Radical Caucus mailing list and an unexpectedly good attendance at the Radical Caucus forum— the program included only the forum on Marxist literary perspectives (followed by some workshops), some women's liberation meetings, and a couple of stray papers by radicals. With the termination of Florence Howe's presidency for 1973, the radical influence was almost entirely washed out of the MLA system. The overwhelmingly non-radical majority had been sufficiently galvanized to more than offset any efforts by radicals to influence the organization. Some candidates for the recently-formed Delegate Assembly—a reformist measure to democratize the governance of MLA and avoid the possibility of the packing of business meetings—have run on the platform of ending the politicizing of MLA. The radicals once went beyond symbolic gestures of defiance and achieved a partial seizure of power, but that is past. Florence Howe had good reason to wonder whether it was worth time and effort to try to change MLA.

Radicals have often spoken of co-optation as the worst plague that could befall them. Was not the election of radicals to high offices the ultimate in co-optation? Since its inception, the new radicalism has been most effective when it acted in the role of critic, of outsider looking in on the operations of the powerful. Giving radicals power forces them out of this cozy position and demands that they produce something positive; they are open to attack by outsiders. The purity of their critic role is gone forever. Their failure is probably best explained by two factors: the smallness of their constituency and their own anarchist tendencies.

Although it is only speculation, perhaps in the final analysis it was the radicals who were the pawns propelled into prominence in 1968 by the arrrests and the "no-Chicago" sentiment, not the reverse. They never intended to gain power within MLA. When it came, they could not use it either to radically change the association or to further their own cause as a revolutionary movement of intellectuals. Moreover, it seems fair to say that neither Louis Kampf nor Florence Howe would have ever become presidents of MLA had they not been radicals. Certainly no "establishment" woman with Howe's credentials (no Ph.D., affiliation with non-elite undergraduate schools) would have had a chance. The same seems to be true elsewhere in the profession. Radicals are invited to speak at conventions and have their articles accepted for publication partly because these meetings and journals want breadth and excitement to mix with the dry-as-dust scholarship which is their ordinary fare. Radicals often complain about being harassed and fired, but it should be remembered that being radical has been tremendously helpful to some in their careers. They may call these advancements and opportunities examples of co-optation, but they do not turn them down.

This should not detract from the magnitude of the radical coup of 1968. That fifty radical literature teachers (Howe's estimate in 1969—and it is doubtful that the figure ever went much beyond that) could introduce such trauma into an organization of some thirty thousand members is no small feat. Since so much was accomplished easily and unexpectedly, the disillusionment and despondency which must have set in when the resistance later stiffened can be imagined. After accomplishing so much in 1968, the minor successes which followed—and which demanded more energy than the original coup—must have seemed anticlimactic. How could 1968 be topped?

It is perfectly legitimate to have a radical caucus within MLA trying to introduce an emphasis which it feels is slighted in the profession as a whole. There are other such adjunct organizations which meet at the MLA conventions, publish newsletters, and seek to promote perspectives not widely reflected in the association. Two in the religious field are the Catholic Renascence Society and the Conference on Christianity and Literature. But these groups do not take the attitude that what they emphasize should be the sole activity within the literary profession. Here they differ strongly from the Radical Caucus, which set itself as counter to the entire MLA and saw its efforts, not as supplementary, but as holistic and therefore as a substitute for business as usual. It was, of course, the ideology of the Radical Caucus which forced it to take the stance that it did. Cooperation would have meant co-optation.

Probably the most successful single venture of the radicals within MLA was the establishment of the Commission on the Status of Women. Kampf and Lauter call it "one of the most significant instruments in pressuring for change in the profession and in the literary curriculum."[63] But the proposals offered by the Commission at the conclusion of its major study would be palatable to the majority of non-radicals in MLA,[64] and one could easily assent to every point without having an ounce of sympathy for radical politics. The proposals are in no way revolutionary, but call for reformist measures. Another case, it seems, of co-optation. And another case supporting Kampf's glum analysis of MLA: "The monster has been shaken. But its response to every challenge is to create machinery that will absorb the shock."[65]

— 9 —

The Radical Critique of Literature
and Culture

If the radical surge at the 1968 MLA convention ultimately failed in the organization, it unleashed a spate of essays trying to analyze and to justify what had happened. It is striking how little of the present body of new radical literary criticism antedates 1968. In large measure, it was an effort to explain after the fact what caused the radicals to do what they did in 1968. Louis Kampf and Paul Lauter called *The Politics of Literature* "one product of MLA 1968."[1] It is a collection of essays which they edited and is the best single source for studying the thought of the new literary radicals. As always, action preceded theory on the New Left.

The Existential Dilemma of the Literary Radicals

The initial written productions clearly centered on personal concerns, and the main concern was to integrate the radicals' politics with their work as literary professionals. Like other academic radicals, those in literature faced the riddle of self-definition.

The Personal Need for Integration

Following the 1968 convention, Kampf and Lauter observed: "Many of us who had participated in Tactics meetings, high on our political successes, turned back to our criticism and teaching, seeing the distance between them and our radicalism."[2] Ruth Misheloff reported on a 1970 meeting of the Modern Language Caucus of the New University Conference:

Last year's ML Caucus meeting had occurred during the first flush of discovery that our training and teaching was demonstrably class-biased, chauvinist, racist, and that we had a lot to learn from each other about how not to do the capitalists' ideological job for them. This year, my impression was that the group seemed more doubtful about the efficacy of "radical teaching" or "radical criticism" (if it makes sense to use those labels at all). . . . The question will certainly be revived as we all keep trying to integrate our day-to-day lives with our conscious political aims.[3]

The citation is instructive. Integration was imperative, but there was serious doubt about whether it was possible: radical teaching of literature and radical literary criticism might not be viable entities. Nevertheless, the question could not be left unresolved, for it divided the person. Literature teachers had been impelled into the Movement by personal, psychological imperatives. Only subsequently did they see the significance of such major political categories as class and race—and these categories were still judged in the context of how they affected their own personal roles as teachers.

Radical after radical spoke of the felt need "to bring personal life and professional life into some degree of coherence,"[4] but they recognized the difficulty of that desired integration: "A department of English has its functions, a committed intellectual has his: how is the latter to work as an activist while performing his academic task? Are the two not subversive of each other?"[5] Furthermore, "what we haven't done is a reflection of how difficult is the process of repoliticizing our intellectual lives."[6]

The need for integration gave rise to a number of primarily auto-biographical essays which told "how I was radicalized." Ellen Cantarow's essay is a textbook case. She traced her undergraduate education at Wellesley College, finding its central truth to be that "it nullified . . . experience, rendered it invisible, as invisible as the life and person of the hero of Ralph Ellison's novel," forcing students to live "in a state of schizophrenia that we took to be normal."[7] From teachers' comments on papers, she learned: "When writing about literature, don't write about your own experience or feeling."[8] Graduate school reinforced the lesson: "I loved literature; when I reached graduate school I was given to understand that loving literature had nothing to do with literary professionalism."[9]

During a trip to Yugoslavia, she "began to consider the possible connections between my own experience, my political experience in particular, and literature."[10] Her first step toward integration came then: "Suddenly it became clear that at the heart of any great piece of literature was some profound human truth; any great piece of literature told of complex, miraculous relationships among human beings in society: relationships that might move one to wonder, to laughter, to tears. It occurred to me, finally, that such feelings of sympathy were much the same as the feelings with which one engaged in political efforts."[11]

Her conjunction of politics and literature involved both a gain and a loss. "In a paradoxical way my political convictions and my desire to put them into practice have reinvigorated my interest in teaching, but at the same time they have sharpened the difficulties of teaching."[12] One day, after giving "a brief rap on the idea that all literature has social content," she reflected:

> Such days as these raise the same questions. Am I a teacher of litera-
> ture, or am I a woman revolutionary socialist using literature as a
> means of groping through the paradoxes, compromises, and occasional
> exhilarations that constitute radical political work in the university?
> Is there, ideally, no split between being the one thing– "a teacher of
> literature"–and the other–"a woman revolutionary socialist"? I should
> be able to say, "I teach literature because I am a socialist." But such
> an answer, though theoretically right, is too simple to describe the real
> circumstances.[13]

This open-ended honesty forced her to consider going underground or helping to form counter-institutions, but she rejected such possibilities as methods of change which were incomplete or did not work.[14] She was sure that she would stay within the university, although her only theoretical basis for doing so was her faith that the United States was in some sort of pre-revolutionary period of transition; "what is needed is the creation of an intelligentsia a large part of which engages in active political work."[15] She clung to the belief that the student Movement of the late 1960s offered "a recent historical example of the ways in which radical scholarship, teaching, and action mutually reinforce each other."[16] Given the history of that Movement, this was a slender thread upon which to hang one's whole life, but it was all that she could find.

Louis Kampf tried to sort out the existential dilemmas confronting him by going back to the question of why the profession attracted him in the first place: "The impulses which led me to the study of language and literature are far from clear. Yet I am certain that I drifted toward the profession of literature and to the academy with the hope of doing work which would not be alienating. It was wholeness I yearned for: unity of ideological purpose and economic necessity, of leisure and the way I earned my daily bread."[17] But his high hopes had turned sour; something had gone wrong. Hope and reality did not converge: "That promise has faded for most of us: the young go into the profession with dread; the old can hardly wait for retirement; and those of middle years yearn for sabbaticals. The sourness begins to turn to acid as many recognize—finally—that teaching and writing about language and literature are indeed alienated labor."[18]

Some radicals have struggled to resist following Kampf's capitulation to despair. Robert Meredith suggested viewing "the pedagogical and critical enterprise of dealing with literature as *our* essay in (attempt at) liberation."[19] He hoped that work informed by the understandings of Marcuse's *Essay on Liberation* would show "that humanistic studies, broadly constructed . . . are among the most relevant and vanguard studies we can engage in."[20] Gaylord LeRoy offered the possibility that "the teacher of literature might eventually begin to feel that he can make as effective a contribution to the goals he cherished in the fifty-minute classroom hours as by marching on Washington."[21]

The Admission of Split Consciousness

Such optimism was unconvincing to most radicals. More common was the grudging recognition that their dual role of academician and politico caused a cleavage which could only be remedied by a communist revolution and the pursuant establishment of a communist culture. Kampf conceded: "To be radical means to live with one's head split. We have an idea of what social relationships ought to be, but the available institutions and the existing states of consciousness force us to settle for intermediate and historically transient cultural forms. Living with this split becomes bearable if the intermediate culture allows us a taste of the future, and thereby gives us the desire to continue the struggle for a just and humane society."[22]

Sheila Delany elaborated:

But for the radical teacher who is not himself a communist, that sort of split consciousness will be necessary until a revolutionary (that is, a communist) literary tradition exists. It is a split which can, I believe, be healed in the commitment to communist ideology and action, but it will continue to be felt by those who retain the illusion that capitalist society can fulfill their radical aims. As long as our greatest aesthetic achievements convey nonprogressive moral and political values, it will be impossible to gratify aesthetic and political convictions at once.[23]

Politics over Aesthetics

If a choice had to be made between gratifying political or aesthetic convictions, the radicals would choose the political. Indeed, their activism led some of them to lose interest in literature. Carl Oglesby confessed: "I don't read novels or poems or plays now with any of the excitement that I remember feeling ten years ago. That was a time, in fact, in which I not only read but wrote the things.... It was a very serious matter for me in those days, this literature.... That I no longer feel this way about it... means, to be sure, most simply that I have changed. But the situation has changed, too. It has become very wild, very confusing, and seems everywhere to bespeak most clearly our individual impotence and unimportance."[24] Kampf and Lauter reported that the effects of MLA 1968 led some radicals not only out of professionalism but out of teaching altogether.[25]

Donald Lazere scored the new radicals' "ineradicable bourgeois upbringing" and "the congenital limitations of even the bravest middle-class humanist."[26] His resolution of split consciousness lay in subordinating culture to politics: "The imperatives for resolving the self-contradiction within the humanities are the same today that they always have been: if we were really committed to culture, we would have to subordinate our cultural activities to working toward creating a society in which culture can exist in good conscience.... But what if creating such a society necessitated revolution, or at least full-time radical political activity...? Could professors... be counted on? Not bloody likely."[27]

Examples of Fragmentation

Some radicals in literature temporarily alleviated their split consciousness by writing on explicitly political subjects rather than on literary ones. Lauter and Howe authored a book on youth revolt; Roberta Salper had a regular column in the *Guardian* on the Puerto Rican independence movement; Noam Chomsky wrote columns on the Vietnam war. But teaching literature and language with the right hand and writing such pieces with the left does not cause integration. It is an analogue to the fragmentation which the radicals perceived to be a curse of professionalism as it is generally practiced.

As they could not settle for writing on non-literary topics, so they were not content to write essays of literary criticism which did not overtly express a radical perspective. Many were too young to have published before 1968. Those who had done so, for the most part, published books and articles which did not indicate the radical direction taken by their writings after 1968. This was true of such books as Richard Ohmann's *Shaw: The Style and the Man*,[28] Bruce Franklin's *The Wake of the Gods: Melville's Mythology*,[29] and Sheila Delany's *Chaucer's House of Fame: The Poetics of Skeptical Fideism*,[30] among others. Louis Kampf's *On Modernism: The Prospects for Literature and Freedom*[31] intimated things to come, but its radicalism was still embryonic and its style less fervid than almost anything that he subsequently wrote.[32] Since 1968 nearly everything written by the literary radicals has been overtly revolutionary, whether the topic was literary or directly political.

The Politicization of Culture

Academic radicals in general called for the politicization of the university, and literary radicals for the politicization of culture—yet both showed confusion in using the term *politicization*. Was there a need to introduce politicization into the realm of culture, or had the establishment already introduced it? If the latter, a new direction should be given to that politicization. The following quotation implied the former: "Culture without politics is a hundred flowers blossoming and being plucked instantaneously by the same folk who deplete our physical environment continuously. . . . Politics without culture, on the other hand, does not move the people."[33]

The literary radicals more often spoke in terms of the latter formulation. Kampf declared, "Hegemony in the realm of culture is a necessity for those who rule: in their hands, culture is a political instrument. This instrument will have to be appropriated—or substituted for—by the masses of people if the fundamental changes requisite for a humane existence are to come about."[34]

In either case, the radicals viewed "the concept of culture as an entity grounded in social and political reality."[35] Since "politics is cultural and culture political,"[36] it followed that "all culture serves someone's interest."[37] Culture is not politically neutral.

The Humanities as Pacifier

The view that establishment figures manipulated culture for their own ends—the perpetuation of the capitalist economy—allowed the radicals to play their accustomed role of negative critics. They charged that "the major forces governing the quality of the present culture" were "the oppressions engendered by the exercise of male supremacy and of racism"[38] and "the values of capitalism in its monopoly phase": "not justice and passion, but order and sophistication."[39] Since "we teach language and literature, whatever our intentions, not in some abstract realm, not in and for themselves, but within institutions," and since these institutions "serve a major function within the political economy,"[40] language and literature were ineluctably indicted along with the whole educational enterprise: "departments of literature are as deeply involved as departments of industrial management" in serving the economy.[41]

The device used by the ruling class to allow the English teacher to fulfill his "historic mission" of "the shaping of values"[42] was the notion of a liberal education. Barbara Kessel found a simple political connection: "Once upon a time I realized that the word 'liberal' in the phrase 'liberal education' was related to the political designation 'liberal.' "[43] Paul Lauter found it suspicious that "the service academies have recently been moving to institute a curriculum richer in the humanities."[34] Kampf explained why not all teachers of the humanities would find this move consoling: "We are the inheritors of an educational ideal intended for the training of elites. . . . This ideological relic . . . allows us the comfortable pretense that the functionaries we train receive an education which makes them whole, humane, and enlightened."[45] What society needs from its universities is technologists and experts, but "to perform their assigned tasks they must be convinced that they are serving the interests of Western Civilization and Freedom. And so they must all study their Shakespeare."[46]

Kampf saw the pacifying effect of the humanities not as an unintended ill side-effect, but as a successful conspiracy of sorts: "Thus the master task of the humanities becomes one of accommodating students to the social dislocations of industrial society by hiding their painful apprenticeship—their rite of admission to an appropriate office—behind the mask of a traditional culture. Confronted by the radical transformation of roles played by the educated, the liberal arts must assure us that the status quo is, after all, being maintained."[47]

The content of liberal education gives prominence to high culture, which the radicals saw as "a ruling class preoccupation."[48] It is produced for consumption by "the leisure class."[49] In all ages, it has been the product of men who traditionally shared the "ruler morality." Lazere elaborated: "Poets, painters, and philosophers have on the whole been more effective as lapdogs to ruling classes than as their gadflies. Matthew Arnold's gentlemanly 'culture' and Cardinal Newman's 'liberal knowledge' inadvertently served to bolster an unhumanistic power elite as effectively as today's service-station multiversity does."[50] He concluded, therefore, "The most substantial political accomplishment of the humanities . . . is the inadvertent one of diverting intellectuals away from radical commitment through the lure of cultural genteelness and prestige."[51]

While the humanities have traditionally served to pacify the leisure class, in modern American education they have acquired the additional task of keeping down the lower classes. Those who gain admission to the university "are invited to reject their own culture, and exchange it for the more valuable goods of the elite."[52] But it is a bogus invitation; the exchange cannot occur:

> Homer and Shakespeare, Vermeer and Mozart, Plato and Sartre—magnificent as they may be intrinsically—are largely incomprehensible to the "culturally deprived," and furthermore in their eyes become accessories to an oppressive class structure, names to be dropped by the educated bourgeois to flaunt his social advantage.
>
> Knowing thyself—the sublime and the beautiful—the best that has been thought and said—existential responsibility—are all, alas, the luxuries of those with enough leisure time and intellectual refinement to afford the egocentric indulgence of contemplation.[53]

Even the radical literature professors have not escaped the pacifying effects of the humanities. Becoming teacher–critics inevitably means complicity with the machinery of American capitalism.[54] Their perception of this perplexing situation explains why "the process of redefining a socialist literary practice has been slow and tentative."[55] It also explains why the contributors to *The Politics of Literature* felt compelled to scrap their original intention of "simply writing more committed, more 'relevant,' more overtly radical or Marxist critical essays" and to settle for a preliminary task: "to clear away the underbrush: to begin opening some paths toward a different practice, different roles."[56] The establishing of a positive socialist literary practice remained the long-range goal, but it would have to be delayed.[57]

The Need to Destroy Culture

Having dismissed culture as pacifying and often oppressive,[58] the literary radicals faced the problem of "where we are to turn after attaining such knowledge."[59] Bruce Franklin's answer was that they had to become conscious "class traitors."[60] With his typical exaggeration, he pontificated: "Each side is already fighting for particular class interests, though only one side recognizes that fact. Barbara Kessel, Kathy Ellis, myself, and a few hundred million others realize that we are putting forward ideas that serve the class interests of the oppressed and exploited masses of the

Amerikan empire."[61] His rejection of high culture was total and vitriolically sarcastic: "Only a totalitarian state would expect people to read Mao, who tells them that they are the real heroes of history, and that 'it's right to rebel' because the earth belongs to the people. Only a highly civilized professor would compel people to read T. S. Eliot, who tells them that they are trash stuffed with straw, or Jonathan Swift, who tells them that they are shit-smeared monkeys."[62]

Another radical declared, "Chaos must rule—anarchy within a framework."[63] He recommended that destruction take precedence: "What better way to learn than by first destroying the past, or even destroying one's art—to humble, humiliate, eliminate oneself from the taint of success? Often it is most important to destroy rather than pose another solution which will be construed incorrectly and misunderstood."[64] Kampf conceded that radical activity might entail anti-historical and even anti-humanist activity: "Our devotion to criticism demands a willingness to destroy received dogmas, to rid ourselves of the deadening burden of history: such anti-humanist activity may be the going price for a study of literature which affects life."[65] What this destructive activity has to do with life is understandable; in what way it is the study of literature is the question.

Sometimes the literary radicals' negation of culture was so thorough that it is difficult to believe that literature interested them at all. Lazere, for instance, in the climactic sentence of an article on the radical critique of culture, declared: "So perhaps it will be for the best when one melancholy day the militants focus their attack directly on humanists and revive the Dadaist chant of 'Down with culture.'"[66] Kampf sounded a similar note when he asked, "Why, then, the concern over something so seemingly trivial as culture? There are times when I find it difficult not to gag on the word."[67] He elaborated on the cause of his personal anguish:

> Why do I—a cultured man, my students and friends might say—choke on the word "culture"? . . . For a long time I have been obsessed with the emotional possibilities of baroque architecture. I have traveled, gotten grants, studied, looked and looked—and I have been deeply moved. But at whose expense were my sensibilities deepened by the experience of Rome? . . . When I last stood in the Piazza Navona, watching my fellow tourists more than Bernini's fountains, I hardly dared think of the crimes, the human suffering, which made both the scene and my being there possible. I stood surrounded by priceless objects—and I valued them. Yet I hate the economic system which has invested finely chiseled stone with a price. Our esthetics are rooted in surplus value.[68]

Since Kampf equated radical criticism and radical action,[69] he advocated the following as an exercise in criticism: "The movement should have harrassed [sic] Lincoln Center from the beginning. Not a performance should go by without disruption. The fountains should be dried with calcium chloride, the statuary pissed on, the walls smeared with shit."[70] This anti-art attitude, which is a concrete instance of his generalization that "the critic's function in the university will be the rather unacademic one of courting conflict,"[71] had its cause in the actual political situation. "When one of my students had her head banged against a truck by the cops it was hardly an occasion for civilized discourse; the thirteen stitches taken on her head did not lead her to contemplate the masterpieces of Western Civilization she had been studying in the classroom."[72]

This vehement anti-culture bias should not be attributed to all of the literary radicals, but it does expose the crux of their dilemma. Many statements by radicals implied the same emphatic rejection of culture, but not all of them were ready to embrace wholeheartedly Kampf's anti-culture stance, indicating their internal dividedness over this issue. They could not violate either part of their dual loyalty to politics and to culture, nor could they harmonize their service to these two masters. Even Kampf did not follow his own advice. He remained in his position of working with the monuments of culture in his professional duties; he did not attack the Lincoln Center with urine and feces; perhaps he has stopped applying for travel grants.

As early as in his book, On Modernism, Kampf saw the proper role for the critic as that of destroyer and concluded that "only an anarchist has the capacity to properly perform the duties of the critic, to destroy properly."[73] Perhaps, then, his call for such acts of criticism as well-aimed urination and defecation was merely the logical outcome of his anarchism. In that case, the unwillingness of his radical colleagues to follow his advice was caused by the conflicting strains in their political amalgam and their desire to be Marxists rather than anarchists—which forced them to suppress those anarchist tendencies that surfaced.

When Kampf equated criticism with destruction and cautioned that the intellectual should never put himself in the service of the regime under which he lives, he again manifested his anarchism. What if his announced goal of a socialist revolution and the subsequent establishment of a socialist culture were achieved? Would he then become a propagandist for the new regime and its culture? Or would he remain an anarchist to the end? The two positions are inherently in conflict. To what extent did radicals call for revolution as a serious political goal? Did their call for revolutionary culture merely satisfy their intellectual need for a coherent pattern which could then be used to explain their present discontent? In that case, they could go on being professors of literature in the present system, while having in their intellectual arsenal an explanation of why they acted as they did. Perhaps their revolutionary posture was only a theatrical gesture, as Robert Brustein has argued.[74]

The Problem of the Great Tradition

The existential dilemma of the literary radicals is revealed in stark form in their discussion of the Great Tradition of Western literature which it was their professional duty to transmit, but toward which they were generally antagonistic. Jonah Raskin's hostility was typical: "Tradition, the dominant idea in the minds of modern critics, is a fraud. What have you got when you possess a Great Tradition? Nothing."[75] Kampf agreed:

> The Great Tradition is dead. . . . It is surely dead for those committed to radical social change. Each component of the Tradition may be alive for me as an individual: Pope's late poetry moves me profoundly. Yet *An Epistle to Dr. Arbuthnot* does not exist for me as part of a humanistic continuum. Indeed, there is an anomaly—even precious-ness—in my reactions to Pope; I have taken an unnatural leap in time, and embraced someone whose historical location makes him my enemy. Pope, the last major voice of Renaissance Humanism! How is that textbook category a part of my culture?[76]

Here is a man with a personal taste for some of the cultural monuments of the past who must suppress that taste because it is incompatible with the political stance which he assumed after that taste was developed.

The Conservatizing Effect

The radical who has written most illuminatingly on the issue of the Great Tradition is Sheila Delany. She acknowledged the inherently con-servatizing effect of studying literature from the past, observing that "the masterpieces of English and American literature have usually supported conservative values: the sanctity of private property, the inevitability of social classes, women's natural inferiority, and an other-worldly rationale for the way things are."[77] Such subject matter posed serious problems for the teacher who wished to express the radical discontent of his life through his professional work: "If you teach English literature, the problem of relating radical convictions to teaching is more acute than it is for your friends in the social sciences: your job is to disseminate the monuments of a culture whose values you personally reject. You don't generally give courses that let you express political opinions easily."[78]

While her exposition of the dividedness imposed by the Great Tradition on the radical professor of literature was quite straightforward, she did not reject her professional life. Rather, she settled quite consciously for the less-than-fulfilling task of "teaching material you now know to be politically uncongenial,"[79] admitting that nothing "can fully compensate for conservative material."[80]

Faced with the problem of trying to introduce something of her radical politics into teaching the Great Tradition, Delany compiled an anthology, *Counter-Tradition.* Since there exists "a tradition of opposition to the values of official culture,"[81] she anthologized those dissenters. The writers chosen to "represent the main currents of oppositional thought"[82] were a curiously varied lot: Amos, Thucydides, Plutarch, Lucius Annaeus Florus, Walter Map, Bernard of Fontcaude, John Ball, Jean Froissart, Thomas Muntzer, Milton, Winstanley, Swift, Patrick Henry, Paine, Blake, Mary Wollstonecraft, Shelley, Carlyle, Marx and Engels, Thoreau, Frederick Douglass, Kropotkin, Elizabeth Cade Stanton, William Morris, W. E. B. Du Bois, Jack London, John Muir, Eugene Debs, E. M. Forster, Mao, Christopher Caudwell, Trotsky, Ho Chi Minh, Marshall McLuhan, Roland Barthes, Robert Jungk, Che Guevara, Malcolm X, R. D. Laing, and Wilfred Pelletier.

The only common denominator in this list is that all the writers dissented against something; but they criticized dissimilar particulars and were widely divergent in their viewpoints. For instance, many writers in the first half of the book were overtly religious. Delany treated their religion as only a matter of context, the heart of their concerns—according to her rendering of them—being revolt *per se.* Surely this was an unfair manipulation to support her viewpoint.

Milton was included because he defended the revolution led by Cromwell, but that was nothing like the revolution desired by Delany. Milton never would have defended hers, because it grossly violated the basic principles of his whole world view. If he and she would agree that one could revolt against illegitimate authority, they would disagree violently about what constituted legitimate authority. Similarly, Swift was a very conservative writer. Barry Goldwater and William F. Buckley, Jr., have as much right to be included in a counter-tradition as has Swift. On the one hand, Delany included Swift in the counter-tradition; on the other, she declared that the tradition is conveyed through its conservative practitioners.[83] In fact, conservatives often criticized their culture—starting with Aristophanes.

Amos, who was included in her version of the counter-tradition, was one of the Old Testament prophets who called Israel *back* to an adherence to divine commands, not onward to some progressive revolution. Delany's attempt to update Amos and put his issues in contemporary political language was manifestly manipulative: "Amos addresses himself to two related 'transgressions.' First, the Jews had begun to indulge in such foreign cultic practices as astrology, idolatry, ritual fornication, and other fertility rites. Second, the recent development of Israel's international commerce, cities, and government bureaucracy had generated sharp class distinctions: enormous luxury for a few, grinding poverty for many, the profit motive, bribery, and miscarriage of justice in the courts."[84] In her effort to make Amos a political rebel, Delany omitted entirely his sense of mission as a divinely appointed prophet bringing a word from God to his chosen people. That the entrants in her book all tried to counter something is true; that they form any kind of tradition is untenable. Nevertheless, her anthology stands as the most serious effort by a new radical to find a way to remain politically radical as a teacher of the literature of the Great Tradition.

Sheila Delany is by training a medievalist. At first glance, there seems nothing contradictory about being a medievalist and a radical. One need not agree with one's specialty to be able to teach it. There are Soviet experts who are not pro-Soviet. Delany could teach, say, the medieval view of hierarchy in order to show its error and/or irrelevance. While it may be more satisfying to read material with which one sympathizes, this problem is only psychological. The logical conflict for the new radicals comes from being part of the very society and culture which they wish to destroy. Here they move beyond the psychological conflict which a Soviet expert with anti-Soviet views might feel.

Delany's recognition that the reading and teaching of traditional literature has a conservatizing effect might itself seem open to challenge, and some radicals did not agree. One indicator that historically-ordered humanities disciplines like literature, history, and philosophy do indeed have the effect described by Delany can be seen in comparing the ethos of these disciplines with that of such analytic and essentially non-historical disciplines as sociology and political science. The latter have a much more contemporary focus as whole disciplines, and this difference creates a change in the ambience between the respective fields as a whole. This is what Delany recognized, and it gave her and her fellow literary radicals a conflict in addition to those faced by their colleagues in the social sciences.

Certain elements of the Great Tradition have come under special attack. Delany listed as particularly repugnant the values of "social hierarchy, the sanctity of private property, strongly differentiated sex roles, absolute morality, undiscriminating respect for law, and the wisdom of resignation to society as it is."[85] Jonah Raskin's list included "tradition, art for art's sake, the values of stability, order, continuity, the politics of liberalism, the feelings of pessimism, boredom, defeatism, egotism, alienation."[86] Four elements criticized repeatedly are hierarchy, individuality, the fixity of human nature, and the tragic vision.

Hierarchy

As the radicals saw it, "Hierarchy is the most valuable myth any powerful person has."[87] In a monarchy or an aristocracy, "ideas about natural hierarchy, order, and divine sanction clearly shored up the dominant institutions."[88] Since literature reflects social reality, it, too, is rife with praise of hierarchy. Delany explained:

Hierarchy is fundamental to western literature, and much of what is amusing, tragic, or interesting in the literature is concerned with someone's attempt to break out of an ordered system. Dante's hell is hierarchal, so is Milton's heaven; and though their spiritual geography is irrelevant now, we have internalized the map. Freud . . . offers a structure of mind that combines psychic and moral hierarchies: not only is the personality fragmented into id, ego, superego, but upon the proper ranking of these fragments depends all of Western civilization.[89]

Delany found contemporary application of this principle even in the stance taken by classroom teachers. "Hierarchal thought is hard to avoid: no wonder that teachers often become petty tyrants behind the desk; that they consider 'unprofessional' the very idea of organizing for protest or bargaining; that they decline to defend colleagues who have been fired for political reasons. They have absorbed the myth of hierarchy and are daily engaged in perpetuating it."[90]

Individuality

Another element of Western civilization which the radicals attacked was the glorification of individuality. Herbert Marcuse saw, as a central feature of the class character of high culture in the bourgeois period, "the discovery and celebration of the individual *subject,* the 'autonomous person' which is to come into its own, to become a self in and against a world that destroys the self."[91] In Ellen Cantarow's words, "Bourgeois literature

... celebrates individual exploits, individual sensibilities. It puts forward the perfecting of individualism as the best of social goals."[92]

Modern literature also propounds this individualism, because such a view is a natural outgrowth of the economic system of the society in which such writing is produced. Kampf asserted, "a totally self-centered individualism is not necessarily a sign of heroism or nobility; it may, in fact, serve as a mask for the competitive depredations of capitalism. The narcissistic obsession of modern literature for the self, the critical cant concerning the tragic isolation of the individual—these are notions which tie our hands and keep us from the communion necessary for meaningful action."[93]

The same sort of unhealthy individualism is observable in our society's attitude toward the artist himself. In Kampf's words, "The cult of the great artist is the cultural myth most natural to a competitive society. ... The existence of great figures in the arts is a reflection of social disease."[94]

Universality of Human Nature

A third element of Western tradition which the radicals found unpalatable was the concept of the universality of human nature. The radicals believed that "there is no unchanging, abstract, human essence."[95] Bruce Franklin explained why this was important to them in literature: "Then there is the relation between human 'nature' and art. The primary assumption here is that human 'nature' has always been, and will always remain, essentially the same. ... The most essential quality of this human 'nature' is that it's incorrigibly corrupt. The greatest works of literature are therefore hopeless, grotesque, tragic, or absurd. Hopeful works are silly, naive, or, to use the most revealing term, sentimental. Good characters are often unbelievable, but no character is too evil to believe."[96]

The truth, according to the radicals, is that human nature is class-determined, as is everything else, including literature and literary criticism. Such concepts as "Eternal truths, human nature, timeless judgments" are simply "the self-serving mystifications ... which uphold the class interests of professional criticism."[97] Rather than operating in terms of universal human nature, literary criticism should focus on "the feelings of real men, living at a specific time, and belonging to a specific class."[98]

Tragedy

A fourth element of the Western tradition opposed by radicals was the concept of tragedy. They considered the tragic vision of life as restrictive to revolutionary activism, which explained their animus toward it. "The tragic vision implies a ready willingness to die; indeed, in its all too passive abandonment of Eden, it masks an almost pleasurable abandon to oblivion; as a consequence of the fall, it sees labor as a means to life, rather than a need of life: these attributes make the tragic vision profoundly counterrevolutionary. Since it resigns man to fate, it forbids the possibility of politics."[99]

Kampf noted that in the eighteenth century there was a gradual abandonment of classical tragedy and a substitution of bourgeois tragedy, which "involved a loss of belief in elemental and implacable forces; disaster is caused, instead, by error, bad judgment and the ways of some men and women to other men and women: all of these being matters which may be subject to change."[100] Then, he added, "Predictably, for most modern critics bourgeois tragedy has been shallow, classical tragedy profound"[101]—apparently, in Kampf's mind, a judgment based not on intrinsic literary criteria but on political convenience. Thus, he contended, the tragic vision plays a major role in the cultural pacification practiced by the university. "Brutes, we all know, should be humanized. And what better instruments of humanization, what better repositories of the great tradition than our colleges? We deposit the uncultured in one for four years so they may become imbued with the tragic sense before venturing into the arena to discover their inevitable fate."[102] One task of radicals was "to divest tragedy of its nobility."[103]

The Issue of World Views

One could argue with each of these four points in the radical critique of the Western tradition. It might be indicated, for instance, that the radical critique of hierarchy extends to themselves as well. This was what the feminists among them charged in regard to male supremacy within radical organizations. One could recall the manipulativeness which many radicals conceded was practiced in their endeavors. Or one could point out the contradiction between rejecting individualism and establishing a political Movement on the basis of the need for personal liberation. There is an incongruity between the anti-individualism propounded and the autobiographical nature of the essays in which it was propounded. Conflict could be demonstrated in denying the universality of human nature in favor of a view of human nature as class-determined and then presuming to speak for those of another class. There is an irony in absolutist ideologues opting for relativism on this crucial issue. One could argue that radicals dismissed only a reductionist version of the tragic vision and that their anti-tragedy viewpoint flattened out some of the diversity in life by dismissing mystery and wonder.

But such arguments would be beside the point. The radicals did not argue for the positions which they took; they merely asserted them. These points are manifestations of the presuppositions underlying their world view. It is important to see that these are matters of presupposition, for here lie the real differences between the literary radicals and most non-radicals. The differences are not literary or even strictly political—unless one has presupposed that politics is everything. The real differences are those in world views. Every time the radicals challenged their readers to choose sides, they were implicitly acknowledging the centrality of pre-suppositions and world views. Many of their criticisms can be seconded by persons holding other world views; the sharing of other criticisms depends on agreement with the presuppositions on which those criticisms depend. The four points traced above are of this second type.

One corollary of this matter is that those points of difference in literary criticism which can be discussed fruitfully between radicals and non-radicals are limited. Strictly literary debates will miss the real point of the difference. Another corollary is that radicals in literature have done very little actual literary criticism so far because they must first turn their attention to developing a fully orbed world view which can serve as the basis for its practical application.

In the light of this discussion, one can specify a chronology of four steps through which the literary radicals must pass before they will have established anything that might merit the designation of a new school of literary criticism. First, they must bring a negative critique to bear on current practice in the profession. They need not have any coherent theo-retical framework before doing this task, only visceral reactions. Second, they must develop a coherent world view, a view which encompasses all reality. Third, they must develop a literary theory which is a logical exten-sion of this world view. Then—and only then—can they apply that theory with any consistency to a discussion of individual texts. One sees here a parallel with the whole New Left enterprise as reflected in the three stages of its history. The literary radicals have restricted their efforts so far mostly to the first task. There have been inchoate, embryonic attempts at the second. The third and fourth steps are so far only prospects in the future.

An interesting parallel with the radical enterprise in literary study can be found in what is loosely called Christian literary criticism. Here is another attempt to criticize literature from the perspective of a compre-hensive world view. The great difference is that this world view has been two thousand years in the making. Thus, Christian literary critics can now apply those insights to the practical task of criticizing specific literary works. Their relative success is indicated by the large body of Christian literary criticism now available and even by the establishment of doctoral programs in theology and literature at some major universities. These critics need not endeavor to develop a world view simultaneously with their attempts to apply it in literary criticism. That the radicals must try to do both tasks simultaneously goes a long way toward explaining why they have been unsuccessful in the sphere of practical criticism of texts. Their experience suggests that such simultaneity is impossible.

Radical Alternatives to the Great Tradition

The discovery that the literature of the Great Tradition provides them with material for their professional work which is largely inhospitable to their political convictions led some radicals to look for substitute material which would alleviate this conflict. Kampf and Lauter called for "reconstructing the canon of what is studied and taught,"[104] and this goal was shared by others.[105] Martha Vicinus, a Victorian specialist, suggested that a body of nineteenth-century "working-class literature has been almost completely ignored" which is available to radical teachers.[106] She admitted, however, that this literature lacks high quality.[107] Her candor on this point was not always found in similar prescriptions by other radicals, but aesthetic quality was a problem to which their professional training had made them sensitive.

Radicals also advocated the teaching of ethnic literature—Chicano, native American, black. Such courses are burgeoning at the moment, but radicals have their own particular interest in them. They view them "as weapons in a struggle for liberation."[108] To seek out literature for use as a weapon in a political struggle is to minimize aesthetic considerations, though the radicals generally would phrase it differently. They would agree on "the urgent need drastically to revise traditional norms for evaluating literature according to the WASP pattern in order to include such variations as explorations of the 'black experience' by black writers, as well as the experience of other ethnic minorities by their own indigenous writers. To deny that a narrow prejudiced pattern of evaluation has existed in the past, and does still exist, is to compound error with self-righteousness and arrogance and to invite the complete rejection of school and college literature by the brightest and most sensitive youths of this generation."[109] Clearly, there was a need to get around the standards of aesthetic quality generally invoked by literary critics.

One black literary radical found the current rash of black studies programs "only the latest phase in America's domination over us."[110] As she explained it (with a good dose of conspiracy theory thrown in):

> a look at the so-called "black" programs which white, racist institutions are letting us have, reveals that colleges are conceding space not out of fear of our power, black power, but from a sense of their own strength. Administration and faculty members can feel secure precisely because they know that elementary and secondary education is efficient enough so that by age 18, the students who demand Black Studies will themselves devise programs which mirror the tendencies of inter-institutional and inter-personal competition, brain drain and diaspora which American institutions are organized to perpetuate in everyone—white, black, or red—whom they educate.[111]

Whether or not to have a program of black studies was not the issue with the radicals. It was—always and only—whether the curriculum would be made over in their image.

There were other suggestions for counter-courses. Barbara Kessel suggested teaching dialects in place of standard English in language courses and Cuban poetry under the rubric of Contemporary Literature.[112] Paul Lauter has taught a course entitled "Revolutionary Literature."[113] Kampf and Chomsky have co-taught a course entitled "Intellectuals and Social Change."[114] Of six courses offered in language and literature at the College of Old Westbury, with one of the most radicalized faculties in the nation, four were entitled "Politics of Language," "Introduction to the Study of Black American Literature," "Literatura y Revolución: Cuba," and "Tragedy, Justice and Law." Courses in "Literature and Psychology" and "Representative Contemporary Novelists" complete the offerings.[115]

The interdisciplinary program at Old Westbury followed the advice of Kampf and Lauter "to break out of our closed-in specialties" and teach such subjects as "Revolutionary Literature," "Imperialism," and "The Antislavery Struggle."[116] One radical went still further and recommended the establishment of revolutionary disciplines: "There are, unfortunately, no explicitly revolutionary disciplines within a counter-revolutionary culture. We find, for example, no departments of 'Exploitation Studies,' 'Counter-Imperialism,' or 'Socialist Planning,' or not yet anyway."[117]

Such off-beat suggestions did not appeal to all literary radicals. Some urged their colleagues to repossess traditional literature in one way or another. Gaylord LeRoy, a Marxist who has been active in new radical literary circles, dismissed "the ultra-left notion that radicalized literary study entails a wholesale break with the present curriculum" as "a socially oriented reductionism" and counseled: "The literature we have been teaching all along represents one of the great achievements of Western man; it is not less relevant for a revolutionary movement than for the establishment; on the contrary, it is more so. What serves the establishment is not the body of literature we teach, but the way we teach it—that is, the interpretation we put upon it, the world view with which we connect it."[118] LeRoy did not follow up this general encouragement with specific instructions on repossessing the Great Tradition.

Restructuring the Form of Courses

Some radicals, while not disavowing efforts to restructure the content of literature courses, suggested the urgency of restructuring the form of those courses. H. R. Wolf wrote up his experiment to break down hierarchy in the classroom structure, and he described his result as hovering between an ordinary class and an encounter group.[119] There were similar efforts to establish student-centered courses. James E. Miller, Jr., once president of the National Council of Teachers of English, advocated establishing an "anti-curriculum in English" which would be "anti-formal, anti-traditional, anti-rigid" and "pro-human, pro-imagination, pro-creation." This anti-curriculum would "focus not on subjects but on students, and not on students in lock-step, but students who develop different interests, in different ways, at different times. This is why the anti-curriculum must hang loose."[120]

The Radical Caucus in English and the Modern Languages has given wide circulation to a pamphlet which sought to go further. It observed that many radicals have embraced student-centered teaching "as the natural pedagogical form of our radicalism,"[121] but while it accepted that goal, it found student-centered teaching an inadequate fulfillment of it. It urged radical teachers to offer "not more intimate relationships in the classroom, but a purpose for relating; not just freedom from outmoded academic discipline, but a useful and exhilarating new discipline; not freedom from necessity, but freedom as the consciousness of necessity—of the specific material basis of one's thought and of one's dialectical relationship with books and other forces in society."[122] This entailed following four concrete steps in the study of a literary work:

1) Description of the model of the world and of the model of behavior proposed in the fiction, both by the depiction of characters behaving in various ways with varying degrees of success or attractiveness, and by the style itself—that is, the behavior of the artist himself in the work.

2) Analysis of the relationship between the author's social experience

and the literature into which he puts his energies.

3) Analysis of the relationship between the reader and the fiction: the relationship, that is, between the individual's experience of the world, his *modus operandi*, and the fictional model.

4) Critique of the work based on the above. Not just the strengths and weaknesses of a given work in its own terms, but the ways in which it strengthens and weakens us. The relative acceptability of the fictional model.[123]

This suggestion tried to accomplish three things at once: treatment of social background, which Marxists have emphasized and formalists have slighted; treatment of style, which formalists have emphasized and Marxists have slighted; and attention to the personal needs of the students, but not at the expense of the weakening of intellectual rigor likely to emerge from student-centered teaching. Whatever its intrinsic merits and demerits, this proposal was at a higher level of sophistication than the reactionary anti-authoritarianism of the early essays by literary radicals. It is no coincidence that it appeared only after the Movement took a Marxist turn.

At least one radical disapproved of all efforts by radicals to experiment with the form of their teaching. Since he posited that our civilization is discredited, he concluded, "No acumen about the social arrangement of class-rooms, no exchange of prescriptive for self-appropriated learning, no restoration of the voluntary character of pedagogical relationships will make acceptable a civilization which is inherently suicidal to own. Quite the contrary, enlightened or radical pedagogy under such circumstances constitutes a heinous deception."[124]

The View of Art as Inherently Subversive

Many literary radicals contended that the literature of the Great Tradition has an inherently conservatizing effect and works toward passive support of the status quo. However, sometimes there appeared a counter-theme: that literature is inherently revolutionary and thus subversive of the status quo. Kampf suggested: "The panorama of literature lies in the scholar's full view. It is more than a collection of words framed by the limits of his visual perception: it is history. And history is full of beautiful subversive possibilities.... By its very nature, in spite of our academic merchants, literature is not a commodity, but the sign of a creative act which expresses personal, social, and historical needs. As such it constantly undermines the status quo."[125]

The person devoting the greatest effort to explicating this notion of art is Herbert Marcuse. Marcuse's prose is always opaque and never more so than on this subject.[126] A major portion of his book, *Counterrevolution and Revolt*, was devoted to it. The book had the dual aim of encouraging the Movement during the dark days following the collapse of SDS and at the same time trying to correct the errors into which, in his opinion, the Movement had fallen.

One of those errors was an anti-intellectual tendency to reject art altogether. He sought to save art for the revolutionary cause.[127] He believed he could do so because of the inherent subversiveness of art by virtue of its presenting a "second world," one which shows how things could and should be and which therefore is ineluctably a critique of the actual social order.[128] Thus, even in literature which "carries a regressive political message"—Marcuse's example was Dostoevsky—"the message is canceled by the *oeuvre* itself: the regressive political content is absorbed, *aufgehoben* in the artistic form: in the work as literature."[129] Art and revolution, he contended, are related but not in any superficial or mechanical way: "The relation between art and revolution is a unity of opposites, an antagonistic unity. Art obeys a necessity, and has a freedom which is its own—not those of the revolution. Art and revolution are united in 'changing the world'— liberation. But in its practice, art does not abandon its own exigencies and does not quit its own dimension: it remains non-operational. In art, the political goal appears only in the transfiguration which is the aesthetic form. The revolution may well be absent from the *oeuvre* even while the artist himself is 'engaged,' is a revolutionary."[130] As part of "The Great Refusal" in which all virtue resides for Marcuse, art is inherently political whether or not it is overtly so: "the arts persist, and they even seem to assume a new Form and function: namely, they want to be consciously and methodically destructive, disorderly, negative nonsense anti-art. And today, in a world in which sense and order, the 'positive', must be imposed with all available means of repression, these arts assume by themselves a political position: a position of protest, denial and refusal."[131]

Besides the limitations imposed by his obfuscating style, Marcuse's discussion of art was severely restricted by his lack of specific cases to illustrate his points; he theorized in a vacuum. That a work of art creates a second world in a commonplace concept. That there is some reason to find in this commonplace the subversive power of art which Marcuse found is far from obvious. At the very least, the thesis needs supportive evidence, but Marcuse offered only bald assertion. His thesis will not be persuasive, not even to the literary radicals. Their widespread intuition that the Western tradition is hostile to them is a much sounder reaction.

Resisting the Distracting Power of Culture

Whether or not the radicals found value in the literature and culture with which they worked, they were faced with the question of its being a distraction from the pressing tasks of the moment. In Carl Oglesby's words, "Most coldly, the question I want to get at is this: When the house is burning down around the poet's head, on grounds of what if any dispensation can the poet continue the poem?"[132] The question is in the spirit of Theodor Adorno's famous dictum, "No poetry after Auschwitz." Marcuse was aware of the dilemma, and he inclined toward the side of interrupting the writing of the poem to put out the fire, though he vacillated: "I remember the familiar statement made long ago about the futility and perhaps even about the crime of art: that the Parthenon wasn't worth the blood and tears of a single Greek slave. And equally futile is the contrary statement that only the Parthenon justified slave society. Now, which one of the two statements is correct? If I look at civilization and culture today . . . it seems to me that the first statement is probably more correct than the second. And still, the survival of art may turn out to be the only weak link that today connects the present with hope for the future."[133]

The tension between urgent demands of the moment and persistent pressures for taking the long view is very real and has been felt by many, not just by the radicals. Some answers have been given. C. S. Lewis asked why one should continue studying during the Second World War. His answer (stripped from its religious context) was that society is and always will be in crisis and that the ongoing tasks of civilization must be assumed during those crises or the whole process of civilization will grind to a halt.[134] David Daiches concluded that "the notion that we can and should shelve humanistic culture, the nurse of the imagination, while we man the barricades seems to me to be naive."[135]

These and similar answers from humanists will not be convincing to the radicals, just as they will not be convincing to those professional anti-communists who advocate throwing all energies into the fray until the Red Menace is vanquished. Radicals do not share Lewis's enthusiasm for historical continuity and Daiches's confidence in the intrinsic humanizing powers of culture. Their inclination will be to opt for immediate urgencies. By so doing they give some indication of the superficiality of their allegiance to literature *per se* and to the other elements of culture. That they do not abandon literature, however, shows their ambivalence; they have imbibed too much of the spirit of the humanities to follow their anti-cultural bias to its logical conclusion.

— 10 —

The Radical Critique of the
Literary Profession

In addition to their attacks on literature and culture, literary radicals have taken dead aim on the literary profession. Their critique extends both to the style and aura which accompany contemporary professionalism and to particular styles and schools of literary criticism, especially the New Criticism.

Life Style

Radicals have been particularly caustic toward that personal style of life among professors of literature which is designed to give an impression of their sense of superiority.[1] They scoffed at the "foppish, dilettantish" discussions which reduce literature to "the cultural trappings of class privilege and of professionalism."[2] In their view, "The English professor tends to portray as a model his own ironic, faintly self-mocking life-style."[3]

The worst effect of this posturing of literary professionals is the damage which it inflicts on students, especially those who are seeking entry into the profession. "Graduate students are supposed to be measuring themselves by 'professional standards.' This means that they must be constantly faking, constantly trying to give the impression that they do, in fact, carry the whole of the literature of Europe within them (and a lot of the criticism of that literature besides), or else they must adopt an apologetic attitude toward whatever they do know."[4] Standards are such that the "rare successes implied that only a chosen few, an elite, really could appreciate literature; the additional implication was that they would go on to be the future academic professionals, the future teachers of other, future exceptions."[5]

Scholarship

According to the radicals, the most scandalous aspect of literary professionalism is what passes today for scholarship, "nearly all" of which "is written to fulfill professional requirements."[6] This is far removed from the lofty goals attributed to their efforts by scholars in the humanities: "We think of ourselves as scholar–critics making our contribution to the body of useful knowledge, and refining the taste of the general reader; but we write articles and books to get promoted or to sustain our self-respect. A few other scholar–critics might read our productions; some might even review them; still, their destiny is to become items in a bibliography consulted by graduate students suffering through their theses. What does this have to do with criticism as an instrument of perfection?"[7]

Katherine Ellis outlined the approach in a typical scholarly article: "It begins with the hypothesis that, with a few exceptions, everyone who has ever written about the particular author in question has missed the point, and goes on to prove that only the present writer, working alone and in competition with his fellow academics, is capable of finding, with the help of a long misunderstood or overlooked passage, the interpretation that will render further interpretation superfluous."[8] If "the scholar's responsibility is not to the literary work, not to history, not to his culture or to (God forbid) life, but to other scholarship," it is to be expected that in "an unending stream of literary critiques, there is to be found very little real criticism."[9] Scholarship is turned into a closed circle which serves no purpose outside itself.

The imperatives of academic scholarship as it is practiced today require narrow specialization, and this fosters the sterility of literary studies: "specialization breeds privilege, privilege generates more specialization; both isolate teachers from the concerns of students and, often, of the society generally."[10] Whether or not the literature professor recognizes his "oppression," he generally opts for the self-interest of cynical careerism which characterizes the competitive society fostered by capitalism: "The end of the academic pursuit is advancement in one's office."[11] Thus, " 'gentlemen scholars' have been replaced by entrepreneurs, and the art of criticism by the arts of grantsmanship and social climbing."[12]

Response of the Non-Radicals

It is perhaps the radical critique of professionalism which has struck the greatest number of resonant chords with non-radicals in the profession. Those going to MLA meetings have seen displayed the role-playing-become-life-style which irked the radicals. From their own experience many know that most graduate school programs in English have a tendency to dehumanize students and to deaden the life-giving power resident within literature. Many would agree that scholarly articles are generally dull and trivial, not inspiring to the spirit or stimulating to the mind, and therefore unread. (Who reads *PMLA*?) Along with the radicals, they ask whether this publish-or-perish regimen encourages the best use of the energies of those in the literary profession. Does it not discourage interdisciplinary research efforts, partly because they demand a wide range of background and expertise which takes years to develop and therefore comes too late for initial tenure and promotion considerations and partly because they do not correspond to the atomized structure of university and department curricula? Does it not encourage a rushing into print by young scholars? Does it not discourage in many the most serious devotion to classroom teaching of which they might be capable, since classroom performance is not where the university pays off? The radicals have indeed fingered a real weakness in the literary profession.

Nevertheless, on two points they have gone too far. First, with their usual absolutist mind-set in operation, their charges are totalist, not selective. For all the dross, there is also some gold to be found within literary scholarship and criticism. Not to acknowledge this is to vitiate the effectiveness of one's critique. Second, there is no necessary relation between the attack on professionalism and the economic model of capitalism which served as the context for the radical attack. The radicals' political and economic position need not be adopted in order to levy the same general charges against the profession. Perhaps the minor caveat should be added that sometimes the tone of the radical critique has been that of the self-pitying and envious outsider; needless to say, this stance is not necessary to criticize the vices of professionalism.

The Attack on the New Criticism

The radicals have denounced literary scholarship for being arid and trivial, vices which, according to their claim, are displayed most clearly by the New Criticism. Although the New Criticism is no longer new, its influence continues to dominate the teaching and criticism of literature.

Sometimes the radical attack on the New Criticism was unconscionably coarse and unfair. Bruce Franklin, for instance, charged: "Modern New Criticism began as a conscious counter-attack on rising proletarian culture. It was crude and frankly reactionary formalism. We should continually remind ourselves of where and when the most influential New Critics arose. Brooks, Warren, Ransom, and Tate all developed within that citadel of reaction, Vanderbilt University, and then received further training in elitism at Oxford."[13] Franklin saw the New Criticism as an essentially political phenomenon: "New Criticism, which emerged in the 1930s to halt the advance of proletarian culture, gained complete ascendancy in the early 1950s as part of the triumph of anticommunist ideology."[14]

Not all radical attacks, even on the New Criticism, were as vicious as this sample, though the difference was generally one more of tone than of substance.

The Separation of Literature from Life

Richard Ohmann, whose critique of the New Criticism was the most sophisticated and searching of the radical attacks, credited the New Critics with seeking to maintain and even to reinstate a relationship between literature and life, with purging the literary profession of such vices as sloppiness and imprecision, and with contributing to a humane critique of some of society's inhumanities. Other radicals sometimes agreed that the New Critics' original intentions were wholesome, but they were less concerned with intentions than with effects.

If the New Criticism sought to revivify literature by moving away from that accumulation of factual background which passed for literary history and toward examining the text itself, the actual result was quite different. Instead of successfully restoring texts to the reader, the New Criticism accomplished "nothing short of the elimination of the reader."[15] Kampf charged that "the New Criticism, which began as an attempt to force a critical confrontation between reader and poem, has (inevitably, one feels) become a method for avoiding thought about the poem altogether."[16] In place of flesh-and-blood readers of literature, the " 'reader' who is admitted by the New Critics is Lockean man, empirical man, an abstract perceiver who comes before the poem a tabula raza [*sic*] purged of his interfering desires, experiences, and ideologies. He is forbidden to bring his life to bear on the poem and certainly never encouraged to bring the poem to bear on his life."[17]

Ohmann alleged that the chief fault of the New Critics was that they separated literature not only from life, but from politics. (Since "everything is politics,"[18] this distinction is not a real difference.) According to Ohmann, the New Critics "see art as freeing man *from* politics by putting him above his circumstances, giving him inner control, affording a means of salvation, placing him beyond culture."[19] This "flight from politics" met a particular need in the post-war era of McCarthyism and end-of-ideology thinking:

"What those of us who studied and taught literature particularly needed
... was a rationale for our divorcing work from politics, for lying low in
society."[20] On this watershed issue of relating literature and politics, the
New Criticism performed little differently from the competing schools of
literary scholarship. Whether it is the scholar's approach to the work from
the outside or the critic's approach from the inside, "Either method will
suffice to withdraw the work from *our* history and politics."[21]

It was the excessive emphasis on form which effected the New Criticism's divorce of literature from life. The vice of close reading was that
"it perpetuates an interest in form or explication for its own sake."[22] New
Criticism effected "a shift in emphasis from 'responses' to 'techniques,' by
a substitution of 'scientific methods' for what had been the sole constituent
of literary criticism up to the nineteen-thirties: the sensibility of cultured
gentlemen."[23] While elimination of that old elitism was desirable, it did
not result from the New Criticism: "It simply reclothed it in the irreproach-
able garments of science."[24]

Meredith Tax recounted her student experience: "The one thing we
never discussed about any cultural monuments was their *meaning*—just
their barefaced everyday philistine literal meaning.... At most, we had
heard that form and content were the same in great works, so that there
was clearly no importance to discussing anything but form."[25] Jackie Di
Salvo effectively elaborated the radical attack on formalism:

> Imagine that the human eye in disinterest or distaste abandoned its
> perusal of the world and rolled inward to observe only its own pro-
> cesses and you get some sense of the withdrawal from reality which
> passes for contemporary literary criticism.... Modern criticism has
> removed art from all human consequences, emasculating it of its
> potency to transform either personal or social experience. Milton
> thought he was writing to enable personal redemption and social
> revolution; we note merely that he revived certain epic devices. For-
> malism is the heresy of the age.[26]

Or, in Franklin's memorable turn of phrase: "Here we see the essence of
New Criticism: the ostrich sticks his head in the sand and admires the
structural relationships among the grains."[27]

The triumph of formalism achieved by the New Criticism far out-
weighed all its other achievements. And the compartmentalizing of literature into a self-contained entity is apparent throughout the literary
profession as a whole, not just among self-avowed New Critics. Literature
has been cut off both from its social and political matrix and from relevance to current social and political issues. It has been elevated to a status

above time. Speaking of her own schooling, Katherine Ellis said, "During these twelve years I have taken scores of literature courses, in each of which the point was made that great literature is timeless and that its heroes are Everyman."[28] Teachers of literature consider the literary works which constitute the great tradition "supreme human achievements" which "stand above time and constitute the furthest advances of culture and civilization."[29]

The Anti-Revolutionary Influence of Matthew Arnold and Northrop Frye

It was Matthew Arnold and Northrop Frye who drew the radicals' fire on this point—Arnold for enunciating a principle repugnant to the radicals and Frye for seconding it. Frye rejected revolutionary action because it leads to the dictatorship of one class over the others, and he urged, instead, "attaching ourselves to Arnold's other axiom that 'culture seeks to do away with classes.' The ethical purpose of a liberal education is to liberate, which can only mean to make one capable of conceiving society as free, classless, and urbane. No such society exists, which is one reason why a liberal education must be deeply concerned with works of imagination. The imaginative element in works of art, again, lifts them clear of the bondage of history."[30]

Two essays in *The Politics of Literature* drew their titles from this passage and took it as their point of departure. The radicals denied "the existence of such an ideal order of cultural monuments in whose presence all class distinctions disappear."[31] Also, they pointed out that culture could do away with classes only if class was defined, as it was in Arnold, "not in terms of economic conditions but in terms of taste."[32] Since this was in conflict with Marxism, it had to be rejected. Ellis concluded that "it would be better to rephrase Arnold's axiom to say that culture seeks to do away with the awareness of class."[33]

The irony, as the radicals saw it, was that Arnold's desire to transcend class had had the opposite effect. Even the academic intellectuals "do not, as Matthew Arnold had misleadingly taught them, transcend the class system."[34] Far from furthering classlessness, "The Arnoldian notion of culture—as civilized and mature discourse—became, perhaps unwittingly, an instrument for the maintenance of American class structure.... Culture—something we can all attain to—is above politics. Since culture represents that which is best in us, institutions can safely be ignored. To be cultured thus becomes equivalent to ignoring the material sources of power. Arnold's ideas can lead only to the practice of cultural elitism— an elitism which is directed toward making the present system more 'civilized.' "[35]

The view of literature as above time and class leads not only to using it for escape, but to substituting thought for action.[36] For most literature professors, "the *study* of great literary achievements is more significant than taking social or political action."[37] Franklin stated the matter with his typical verbal overkill: "Why are most professors shocked when a few professors use their bodies to effect social change? Why do they find this not only nonintellectual but 'mindless'? Because bourgeois values teach that there are two different kinds of activity—physical and mental. On one side, we have beings who work with their bodies. These are mindless, less than human. Then there are those who think, intellectuals, disembodied intelligences whose physical existence is essentially irrelevant to what they think."[38]

Merits and Limitations of the Radicals' Accusations

Doubtless, many New Critics would deny that the radicals have described their school of criticism accurately and fairly. They would deny that technique is all that they are interested in, that they are merely formalists. They would assert that they seek to approach the larger issues of literature and life, but only through a careful textual analysis which would preserve the integrity of literature and keep it from blatant appropriation by propagandists. There is some truth in this defense, especially as it refers to the better New Critics, mainly the originators of the school.

New Critics and their defenders might also wish to challenge the radicals' assumption that everything is politics. This assumption is the crux of the radical critique of the New Criticism, as of everything else. One wonders at times if the literary arguments of the radicals (as distinct from the political ones) were intrinsically important even to their proponents—so totally politicized were they and so often did they declare that they were, above all, classroom organizers seeking recruits for the Movement. Perhaps these arguments were rhetorical devices to expose the fallacies of the professoriat in order to facilitate recruiting. But it is safer and probably more accurate to see these arguments as important to the radicals because they have a genuine investment in the literary profession and really do care about such intramural debates, even if this interest clashes with their usual image and even if it suggests that they have not yet shed all of their "bourgeois" values.

Nevertheless, at least three things must be said in favor of their critique of the New Critics. First, the New Criticism is perceived by many as striving for a value-free approach to literature which cloaks literary study in the aura of science. The radicals' attack on the New Criticism is part of their general attack on scholarly objectivity, and to the extent that there is validity in the wider charge, there is validity in this specific instance of it. Radicals derogate the concept of the disinterested scientist because they say it serves to reinforce the status quo and to suppress revolutionary implications in literature. The real problem has nothing to do intrinsically with politics. It is simply that literature has values and cannot be treated adequately by a methodology which must, by its nature, declare values off limits. The radicals have made a valid criticism of the New Critics, but they have done so for the right reason only if the world-view which governs their criticism is true and accurate.

Second, many camp-followers of the New Criticism have been unable to resist the lure toward pure formalism and have in fact removed literature from any real concern with life. Whatever the intentions of the original New Critics, the effects have not always been wholesome and humanizing. It is fair for radicals (and others) to focus their criticisms on the effects, disregarding the intentions. (What is not fair is to impugn motives and to declare the intentions themselves to be base, for that charge lacks evidence.)

Third, the New Criticism has a validity only as long as it is seen as part and not all of the critical enterprise. It is essentially a technique of literary criticism, not a world view. When a critic allows it to become the whole of his critical endeavor, the New Criticism has a deleterious effect on literary study, and this has often happened. As a technique it can be applied by persons with widely differing world views. This is not a critique often made by the radicals; they are more inclined to inflate the New Criticism to the stature of a world view—or at least to assert that it is a natural concomitant of only certain world views, which they label counter-revolutionary.

A few radicals have seen that this need not be so. Ira Shor, for instance, pointed out the usefulness of close reading for even the Marxist critic.[39] Lillian Robinson spoke, albeit cryptically, of a "radical kind of textual criticism" and "radical criticism of texts"[40]—presumably some combination of a Marxist world view and the methodology of New Criticism.

There is no inherent incompatibility between the New Criticism and Marxist criticism. A work of literature can be seen as a reflection of the social history of its time and also as an artifact to be scrutinized according to the intrinsic criteria for judging its aesthetic worth. The same person can perform both operations on a single work, first giving it a close reading to discover what the text actually says and then evaluating it according to the external criteria for truth against which he wishes to measure it. Analysis and evaluation are two discrete mental processes. When the radicals express the desire to bring their own life into relationship with a literary work, they speak as evaluative critics; but this says nothing *pro* or *con* about the process of analysis.

Michael Novak offered an analogy which illuminates this point: "As the New Criticism is to art, so is critical theology to religious awareness. Theology, like the New Criticism, has a role to play, but it is neither necessary nor sufficient for religious life."[41] To rephrase this with the literary term primary, New Criticism has a role to play, but it is neither necessary nor sufficient for literary study. Still, it does have its role, and the radicals have overstated the case against it.

The Search for a Radical Literary Criticism

Since the radicals shared the New Critics' rejection of the old school of literary history and also rejected the New Criticism, they were in need of a way to study literature which was distinct from both major approaches of literary criticism currently in practice. By their own admission, while a new radical literary criticism is not yet clearly developed, the hazy outlines of a new approach are apparent.

Respectability of Propaganda

To clear the way for radical criticism, "A beginning would be to desanctify literature itself by showing that it is a means of persuasion, in the service of a vision controlled by political as well as aesthetic values."[42] Propaganda is at the opposite extreme from objectivity, and therefore the radicals have been at pains to make it respectable. Kampf and Lauter commented on one of the essays included in *The Politics of Literature:* "One virtue of Franklin's essay is its openly propagandistic manner, its clear intent to agitate for a set of ideas in the most direct manner possible. We have been taught to be offended by the notion of propaganda, and shrink from it as by reflex. But all language use, as Kenneth Burke tells us, is rhetorical and therefore propagandistic."[43]

The literary radicals saw their defense of propaganda in criticism as an honest recognition of the facts of the case—an honesty not reflected in the widespread claims of scholarly objectivity. Carl Oglesby wrote: "In our time and place, one simply *is* a partisan—of something, of some cause; even silence is no escape. The business of the critic is to grasp and elucidate the fullness of all these circulating partisanships and—like the writer he scrutinizes—to take a stand. It should go without saying that the stand will be complex always and often ambivalent."[44] This was a typical radical statement, except for the final sentence, which conceded much more than did most radicals. Kampf and Lauter, for instance, when praising Franklin's direct agitational manner, were consciously approving a partisanship totally lacking in the qualifiers of complexity and ambivalence urged by Oglesby.

This partisanship means that "a radical literary criticism would surely wish to deal with the quality of the vision it has described."[45] The radical critic must "ask a question that is as old as literature itself: in what sense do poets 'speak true'?"[46] In Jonah Raskin's words, "When we step into a novel we do not trash the values we live by. If we do not accept tyranny in society, there is no aesthetic reason why we should accept it inside the covers of a book. The things, people and events which exist in a novel are vulnerable to the same standards of truth we exercise when we eat, work, make love and dream."[47]

Literature as Political History

The rejection of the New Criticism and the adoption of Marxism dovetailed to cause the literary radicals to emphasize that literary works are social-historical documents. "Like philosophy, religion, and the other arts, literature grows from a particular historical environment: it incarnates people and moral problems in magnified proportions."[48] So the task is one of "rewriting 'literary' criticism as historical and cultural criticism,"[49] of trying "to integrate our study of literature and culture with an understanding of the dynamics of class, economics, and history."[50] Literary criticism must be posited on the assumption that "literature is the interior of history.... Literature is ideological in spite of itself. Ideology is the product of man's connections to the material world that surrounds him; all ideas serve material interests in the real world. The writer cannot avoid taking a stand; his work will reflect a struggle to accept, to defend or to criticize and alter his milieu."[51]

To decide that "literature is most essentially a form of history, something which makes propositions about the human experience of a time and a place," is to subordinate, inevitably and rather strictly, all aesthetic concerns. "Whether or not these propositions are also elegant, they ought to be in the first place significant and in the second place true."[52] Relegating literature to the status of being a branch of history and nothing more deprives it of all autonomy. The critic can then focus on the politics in a work and disregard its aesthetics: "It is the politics of an artwork which we have to elucidate, explore, and—finally—judge."[53]

Judging the politics of a work of art is vital not for the purpose of understanding the work itself but for the purpose of a contemporary personal appropriation of it. Kampf set the tone in his pre-1968 book, *On Modernism*, when he declared, "The critical attitudes which control this book derive from a personal sense of current needs: not the needs of criticism, but those of life."[54]

The inevitable consequence of this focus on current needs is that the critic's "commitment must be to what is ephemeral."[55] Exaltation of the ephemeral is a logical consequence of the radical position. The past is available to use for our own purposes. Since literature is "an instrument for agitation," the study of it "demands that we react to a specific text—yet somehow in our own way. Shaping its meaning to our own desires, we help make its fate; doing so, we not only explore the limits of free thought but learn how to make conscious use of the past."[56]

Some radicals have admitted the danger that they could fall into the trap of "some easy extraction of ideas which happen to be useful for contemporary purposes."[57] For instance, Paul Lauter saw the trap, asserted that it could be avoided, but offered only unsatisfyingly vague generalities about how to do so:

> Discovering lessons for today's social problems in Shelley is, obviously, a vulgarization of Shelley and of politics. Similarly, "applying" Freud or the New Testament to Whitman is mechanical and reductive. But to approach them from a life and a classroom informed by, alive to, the political and social currents of our time will be to rediscover Shelley and Whitman and to reinvigorate one's political life. . . . Our problem in reading or discussing them is the radical reconnection of man thinking, man teaching, man living. That entails a struggle, with ourselves and with this society, which resists integration of self and politics.[58]

The Culmination of Culture in Action

If the radicals used the literature of the past as a device for therapy in the present, that was only an intermediate step. Therapy is useful only as it clears away obstacles to a life of action. One plank in the radicals' credo was the primacy of action. "The meaning of life is in action—whether the acts be physical or mental. Fulfilled action frees us; it makes us independent. When we can relate our thoughts, our yearnings, to activity; when our vague projections issue in conscious work—then we may rightly feel that we have our lives under a measure of control."[59] This cult of activism led Kampf to reject "the myth of heroic scholarship" and to assert that "too many radical academics have used Marx's twenty years at the British Museum as an excuse for their own inactivity."[60]

It would be quite logical to call for unity of thought and action without going the further step that the radicals took to insist that all action must be political. That they took that step is significant; and it is even more significant that they took it without arguing for it, simply assuming its rightness. Kampf asserted: "The field of action is necessarily politics, for a true union of thought and action cannot take place in the society we presently live in. The study of literature escapes being an elitist exercise in self knowledge—it escapes being counter-revolutionary—only as it takes place within the context of a movement for radical social change."[61] Indeed, Kampf found the "exhilarating" activities of the Movement during the 1960s to be "amongst the few reasons for remaining in the profession."[62]

The Nagging Question of Aesthetics

Some radicals realized that the attitude toward literary criticism imposed by their politics de-emphasized the aesthetic aspects of literature to an unacceptable degree. Consequently, they urged their colleagues to pay attention to both aesthetic and political aspects of the literary work. Gaylord LeRoy saw the need for both foci, and he conceded the difficulty of maintaining both: "One of the difficult problems for the radical critic is to handle the tension between a book's literary merits and its relationship to revolutionary goals and strategy.... The radical critic cannot assume, as many do, that if the writer does well what he sets out to do, that is all we need to be concerned with. But it is not easy to keep the two different considerations in mind."[63]

The radicals faced this dilemma whether they were studying radical literature or non-radical literature. LeRoy knew that this dilemma had to be resolved, and he attempted to do so:

> One way to handle this problem is simply to live with it, trying always to take account both of the artistic and the radical dimension in the work we study. But there is another solution, and a better one. In so far as we are able to move toward a radical movement capable of really profound understanding of the nature of our time, the tension between literary and literary-political considerations would be dissipated.... This would be a radical movement in which people had achieved a measure of common agreement concerning the roots of our disorder, the goals that man has the capacity to achieve, and the strategy for achieving them. If knowledge of this kind were deep enough

and sufficiently available, you would no longer have an antagonism between literary and radical considerations; instead they would blend into a synthesis in the writer himself.[64]

This is a pathetically inadequate answer. The first suggestion, which LeRoy rejected because it would mean living perpetually in a fragmented state, he was correct to reject. It was merely a recognition of the dilemma, not a resolution of it. The second answer, which he advocated, would do away with the problem by eliminating its real cause: aesthetically good literature with politically bad content. If only the Movement became so large as to encompass everyone, including all literary artists, there would be no conflict between aesthetic and political considerations. All literature would be of the right kind, and the path of criticism would be easy—though there would not be much need for criticism. (Even then, there would be that large body of past literature to reckon with, but LeRoy conveniently ignored this problem.) At best, it was an answer which fit only radical criticism of radical (or right-thinking) literature. And even here LeRoy himself had to admit that his proposed answer was not for the present, but only for the devoutly desired future: "I am not implying that this strengthened radicalism is within reach. On the contrary, we have a long way to travel before we get there. Until then, the student of radical art will have to use all the tact he can command to be aware of the polarity between art and politics—and to do justice to each in such a way as not to do violence to the other."[65]

LeRoy ended exactly where he began. This concluding statement was really a reiteration in other words of that alternative which he earlier had dismissed as inadequate—that the radical must live with the dilemma of what to do with a literary work in which literary quality and political "correctness" do not jibe—either one being higher than the other. This is a crucial issue for the radical critic (indeed, for any critic who works from a perspective grounded in a world view). Until the literary radicals can resolve it, their position will remain ultimately incoherent. The most straightforward resolution is that offered by Bruce Franklin: "as Chairman Mao points out, 'All classes in all class societies invariably put the political criterion first and the artistic criterion second.' "[66] LeRoy and similarly sensitive radicals may not like this frankly anti-literary approach, but they have no cogent response to it.

The Sine Qua Non of a Revolutionary Culture

LeRoy's favored resolution, which he admitted could be realized only in the distant future, indicated a line of thought which was prominent among the literary radicals: their task as radical literati never could be wholly self-fulfilling and unalienating until there was a body of literature congenial to them, that is, a revolutionary literature. Sheila Delany expressed the need for "a literature in which the radical teacher will feel at home, a tradition that will not require him to be 'what he is not thinking of.' "[67]

Thus, in the words of Kampf and Lauter, "ancillary to expectations of a radical literary criticism must be demands for a radical literature, or beyond that, a radical culture."[68] But antecedent to establishing a radical culture is the need to establish a radical politics. The pressure on the literary radicals was "how to develop a socialist literary practice"; but that "cannot, when one comes down to it, be separated from developing a socialist political practice."[69] So the criterion by which a radical intellectual should measure his work was "how helpful our writing becomes in creating a humane and socialist society."[70] This explains why many literary radicals wrote on non-literary subjects, since the furtherance of the revolution took precedence over professional work. Even in their literary essays their interest in literature had to be subordinated to their interest in the revolution. After all, "the revolution is just not going to be made by literary journals."[71]

Kampf devoted an entire article to delineating the rough outlines of what a radical culture would be: "These notes are mainly for the eyes of my brothers and sisters in the movement. For to discuss radical culture is, at the present time, to discuss the culture of the movement."[72] He hoped that the Movement would be able to provide a context for the development of a genuine radical culture, but he admitted considerable uncertainty about it, since the very concept of culture was culture-bound—by the wrong culture. He wrote that

> given the movement's stress on community, intellectuals may be able to plant their roots in the movement itself. This implies that the movement must become a culture—that is, a way of life. The very forces which have brought about the alienation of intellectuals and the young have propelled us toward that historical moment appropriate for creating a radical culture.
>
> These notes are written toward that uncertain end.
>
> Uncertain and puzzling, because the very concept of culture is rooted in social elitism.[73]

Ignoring his own warning that a radical culture might be a contradiction in terms, Kampf asked, "What is the task of a radical culture? Answer:

to bring about a social revolution; to make institutions democratic; to make us free; to make life more beautiful and humane."[74] This answer also showed Kampf ignoring the logical demand that the social revolution precede the establishing of a radical culture. But since Kampf was already a radical and a cultured man and since the social revolution had not occurred, he had no choice but to invert the logical order. Also, he put culture totally in the service of the revolution. His conclusion was especially disappointing, for after stating what a radical culture should do, he confessed to not knowing how to identify and describe it.

> In conclusion, I must admit to not knowing what a radical culture will really look, sound, smell, or feel like—although I have a clear sense of the contours of the larger Culture in a socialist society. . . . We are beginning to shoot Niagara, and the social transformations we envision imply something more deep—and hopefully less elitist—than experimentation with new art-forms. What is at stake is a new conception of the relationship of art and knowledge to the larger Culture.[75]

His title had suggested a groping toward some positive formulations of the concept of radical culture. The essay was overwhelmingly negative; a better title would have been "Notes Against the Great Tradition (or Present Culture)." Kampf's call for a "new conception" in the last sentence was typical—whether the subject was culture, literature, art, politics, ideology, personal interrelationships, or whatever. Always a brand new conception was ordered; never were any brand new conceptions forthcoming.

Some Ingredients of the Revolutionary Culture of the Future

While radicals were unable to describe the overall outlines of a revolutionary culture, they did specify certain ingredients which would necessarily be parts of it. Cantarow's musings on the subject contained an embryonic definition:

> I had asked myself whether revolutionary art was possible in America. And by revolutionary art I meant art that responded primarily, not to the need for individual expression imposed on artists by bourgeois society, but to the need for collective expression called forth by collective struggle. I meant, moreover, art that responded neither latently nor manifestly to the imperatives of the publishers' market, but instead responded to the imperatives of the movement out of which it arose. Finally, I meant art whose style expressed the culture of the struggling

class, not art that slavishly imitated the style of the class in power.[76]

The concept of collectivism was crucial here, and it was emphasized by other radicals as well. Revolutionary art was to be anti-competitive, anti-individual, anti-expert:

> Again, a revolutionary art should develop those forms which are irrelevant to the market or to mutual funds. Toward this end, there are many possible intermediate steps. As with scholarship, we should work to make individualist heroism in the arts unnecessary, for it is a sign of competitiveness and elitism. What is at stake is the collaborative participation of large numbers of people. This can happen only at the expense of what we ordinarily call quality—that is, at the expense of high culture. . . . Meanwhile, a revolutionary art can be practiced by anyone, almost anywhere, using almost anything: painting one's car or besplattering a wall; writing a song or singing it; coining a slogan or chanting it; knitting a sweater; playing a drum; or writing or reciting or acting or taking pictures or building or playing a game.[77]

This was an unusually candid statement. It virtually consigned to oblivion the field of literature as presently constituted. And it did not flinch from the logical conclusion that revolutionary art would be deficient in quality.

It also recognized the need for new artistic forms in a revolutionary art; pouring new content into old molds would not do. (Radicals were professional enough to recognize the unity of form and content in literature, even if they disliked the use to which the New Critics had put this nostrum.) The only way to bring forth new forms was to be part of the new content, the new social reality which the new art would reflect.[78]

Since the new social reality would give all power to the people, the new art would necessarily be a people's art. It would avoid the pitfalls of both of those kinds of art which the radicals saw as reinforcing the status quo and serving the end of cultural pacification: high culture and mass culture.[79]

The Current Paucity of Ingredients of Revolutionary Culture

Radicals had little to indicate as examples of the emerging new art which they desired. Some praised rock music and other art emanating from the youth culture,[80] but most of this was unsatisfactorily apolitical. Some saw the beginning of a radical culture in anti-war poetry inspired by the Vietnam war, even though being a radical was not needed to oppose that war or war in general.[81] For the most part, the Movement had to try to manufacture whatever might be seriously considered as even embryonic radical art. A series of short-lived periodicals was devoted to cultivating radical art; SDS, for instance, sponsored *CAW*. Todd Gitlin edited a volume of poetry which chronicled the Movement's history through the 1960s, though the tone of the introduction was more elegiac than progressive.[82]

Perhaps the most serious attempts to initiate a radical art were those which departed from the usual format of an individual composing a production to be transmitted on pages of print or in picture. The Living Theater was probably the best-known of these departures. Judith Malina described the structure of its play, *Paradise Now*, which sought to take the audience through parallel steps of personal liberation and social revolutionary action; the first step is physical, the second intellectual. "The third part we call the Action. That is where we stop and say to the audience, 'See the capitalist structure of New York and change it!' 'Be the Vietcong!' And the audience responds, doing nothing or everything. We join in whatever they initiate."[83] But even Herbert Marcuse, who expressed "solidarity" with the Living Theater group, found its "systematic attempt to unite the theater and the Revolution, the play and the battle, bodily and spiritual liberation, individual internal and social external change" to be "an example of self-defeating purpose."[84]

Liberation ran an article praising the political murals painted on the walls of Chicago tenement buildings as a new form of "people's art." It allowed the artist "a socially-politically significant role," placed art in the service of the revolution, sought "to restore an image of full humanity to the people, to place art into its true context, into life."[85]

Such experiments in participatory art caused Leah Fritz to lyricize about its future: "What is emerging is a folk art which, like folk dancing, is more fun in the doing than in the watching. Participatory art is replacing spectator art as participatory democracy seeks to replace spectator democracy. The striking individual forms which expressed the ego of the competitive artist are disappearing with the dissolution of that ego and the dying of the marketplace—declared goals of the Movement."[86]

That was in 1968. Few radicals talked so optimistically later. Marcuse was correct: "A revolutionary literature in which the working class is the subject–object, and which is the historical heir, the definite negation, of 'bourgeois' literature, remains a thing of the future."[87]

The Current Paucity of Practical Literary Criticism by Radicals

If the radicals have had little to offer in the way of positive creative artistry, the same has been true regarding their practical literary criticism. The fact that even in their literary essays the radicals must subordinate aesthetic concerns to political ones explains why this has been so. Criticism of individual authors and works contributes little to the cause of revolution. So most radical criticism of specific writers and works has been conveyed through fugitive, off-handed comments buried within essays primarily devoted to other subjects.

For instance, Bruce Franklin dropped the off-the-cuff remark, "Herman Melville was a consciously proletarian writer."[88] Nowhere had he developed this thesis. Similarly, he asserted, "The novel is the main art form of the bourgeoisie, rising with that class and mainly concerned with individual class status (from Richardson, Defoe, Fielding, and Jane Austen through Henry James to Faulkner, Malamud, Bellow, and Styron)."[89] No one has developed this intriguing thesis for a radical treatment of the history of the novel. Sheila Delany commented on Yeats: "When one of Yeats's editors warns us that the political poems 'must not be read as a record of historical events or of Yeats's political opinions,' poetry is not absolved of its services to the ruling class. On the contrary, criticism is implicated in the attempt to mystify experience by distinguishing class relations as eternal truths."[90] According to the radical perspective, must Yeats simply be dismissed as counter-revolutionary? Is there some sustenance for the human spirit to be gained from a reading of his work? It is the kind of question which can be answered only through a detailed study of Yeats by a radical. General principles enunciated elsewhere by radicals suggest that he is not worth our time.

For instance, Ellen Cantarow's fleeting comments on Spenser are not promising. She said, "I suggest Edmund Spenser as an example of a writer one might prefer not to teach, in comparison, say, with Bill Haywood."[91] She then suggested that to look at him "with a political eye" would be an alternative to rejecting him: "You might, instead, teach Spenser's work both as a particular kind of literary construct, and as a piece of writing that had a social function in Elizabethan society—more specifically, for the Elizabethan court. For example, a social function of *The Faerie Queene* is to substantiate and raise to the level of allegorical norm the standards of the Elizabethan aristocracy."[92] This is consonant with the radicals' view of literature as historical documentation, but it leaves no room for aesthetic considerations or for broadly applicable insights.

While there has been a dearth of full-length journal articles by radicals devoted to analyzing an individual author or work, a few have appeared. Sometimes these were little more than efforts to place a writer on the political spectrum. J. P. O'Flinn's attempt to reclaim Orwell for the left was one such.[93] It was long on society and short on literature. An ostensibly radical article which was more pedagogical than critical was written by James E. Miller, Jr., and posed the question of how to teach Poe, Hawthorne, Melville, Emerson, Thoreau, Whitman, Twain, James, and Dickinson in the 1970s. Miller's solution was to avoid the best-known works of these authors and to select lesser-known pieces which could be used to discuss themes of interest to radicals. He admitted that his reading list might be "capricious" and explained that "all the works included in it may be justified solely on artistic or aesthetic grounds. What my students and I make of them is up to us."[94]

Of greater interest than these examples was a discussion of D. H. Lawrence at an MLA meeting in which radicals participated along with nonradicals. Martha Vicinus, a radical spokesman (spokesperson), expressed the dilemma which always confronts radicals as they study literature not totally congenial to their point of view. She acknowledged the greatness of the novel *Women in Love,* valued its diagnosis of society, but could not accept the solution it offered. "Given this problem, I find myself forced to break the integrity of the novel by accepting only part of it, and it is in this issue that the notion of a radical aesthetic is raised."[95] Vicinus candidly confessed her present inability to resolve this conflict: "I do not feel that I have yet solved such problems as how we can agree to 'like' or 'accept' half a man's work, what principles we can use in such a selection, and the implications implicit in our critical judgment."[96] Since she could not resolve the dilemma, she simply embraced it: "My own partial solution to this dilemma is to accept the notion that one can approve of part of a novel and not its whole."[97] But when she applied this "solution" to *Women in Love,* the result was bland and imprecise: "My own basis for judgment is whether a work of art furthers life or exploits it, a general enough concept, to be sure, but one that puts the life-destroying powers of Gerald and Gudrun in a clear perspective and has as its base Lawrence's own concept of life. Thus, we can, I think, reject those parts which seemingly further life, yet in the process of granting a 'freer' life to some, must deny it to others. The freedom of the four main characters is based on the nonfreedom of the ferret-like colliers."[98] Just what is radical in this is not clear. And what is aesthetic (her goal being to apply a radical aesthetic) is even less clear.

Another radical essay in practical literary criticism—one which lacked Vicinus's modest tentativeness—was by Bruce Franklin in 1972. Franklin attacked "the profound pessimism of capitalist writers" as reflected even in science fiction, which had generally "tended to be much more optimistic than 'literary' fiction."[99] He found this pessimism rooted in "a now common reactionary idea: Human nature is irrational and evil; therefore a rational and just society would be inhuman."[100] The apocalyptic mentality of capitalist writers, Franklin argued, is misplaced. The world is not coming to an end; only the capitalist order is ending. "Common people have long understood" that "all culture reflects objective reality, and in the real world the people are winning, from Vietnam to Lordstown, Ohio"; and now "Some writers are beginning to see this."[101] Franklin concluded with his characteristic black-and-white distinctions: "Writers inside the empire can choose. They can identify with a doomed system and ruling class and then imagine the possible forms of their own doom. Or they can take the side of a rising class and system, helping, through their use of art, to create a better future."[102] Franklin assumed that his vision of the reality of the future was correct; he did not argue for it. From there he could proceed to berate those writers who did not accept this supposedly self-evident reality. Once again, the concern was overwhelmingly political and not literary.

The only full-length book by a radical which engaged in practical literary criticism was by Jonah Raskin. Considering imperialism to be "the total reality of our time," he envisioned his book as "an attack on the empire, a weapon for the revolution," since "culture has a crucial part to play in dismantling the Amerikan Empire."[103]

Dedicated to Ho Chi Minh, this book was a revision of a doctoral dissertation and was done while Raskin was an officer in the Youth International Party (Yippies) and engaged in political activism. The dissertation was written between 1964 and 1967; the revision was made from December 1969 to November 1970. It is easy to tell which passages were in the original and which were part of the rewrite. Passages redolent of the style of Jerry Rubin's *Do It!* are grotesquely interspersed among stretches of pedestrian prose typical of dissertations. Diction is startlingly uneven. In the middle of a passage prosaically describing the sea in Conrad's works, Raskin inserted the sentence, "Without the sea Conrad is a nowhere man."[104] The staccato style, with its verbal violence, attested to the energy which Raskin brought to his subject; it also reflected the level of his subtlety of thought.

The book treated Kipling, Forster, Conrad, Cary, and Lawrence, offering qualified approval of the last three and reserving unqualified condemnation for the first two. He set in contrast Kipling against Conrad and Forster against Cary. Raskin's reading of Conrad is especially curious. "Kipling was an imperialist. Conrad was an anti-imperialist."[105] "Kipling celebrated the white man's burden. Conrad deflated it."[106]

Raskin devoted a chapter to Conrad's *Heart of Darkness*, a work which he described as "a voyage into hell, the hell of colonialism."[107] Conrad demonstrated "that European civilization rests on the exploitation of Black people by white people, that European society rests on the annihilation of the wretched of the earth, on the theft of the riches of the planet."[108] Although Kurtz had engaged in "crimes against humanity," he

188 RADICALS IN THE UNIVERSITY

repented; therefore, "Kurtz is Conrad's hero because he judges, because he speaks out. He chooses and acts. He rebels. He is no liberal. He does not tolerate. He is not like the hypocritical pilgrims on Marlow's ship. Kurtz is an extremist. He wants no compromises—only hostilities, battles. At the end death is the only possibility for him. . . . He must die so that we can begin to make an outcry."[109] Still, Conrad disappointed Raskin somewhat. "Conrad says two things about corruption and evil. He seems to say that imperialism is responsible. But then he turns away at the last minute and says it is the Black man. In that moment he fails us. He does not look with steadfast eyes. It is as if there is too much that is evil about colonialism, too much horror about the white man and his history for Conrad to place all the blame only on colonialism. He must find the Black man guilty too, guilty because that is his innate nature."[110]

If Raskin's praise of Conrad is surprising to non-radical readers, it was surprising also to some radicals. James G. Kennedy, for instance, found *Heart of Darkness* "an expression of the irrational racism by which nineteenth- and twentieth-century Europeans have misunderstood Africans and justified exploiting them."[111] Kennedy did not share Raskin's view of Kurtz. He declared, "Kurtz is only remarkable as an expression of Conrad's sense of the white European's superiority to Africans."[112] Far from expressing solidarity with the wretched of the earth, "In *Heart of Darkness* Conrad indulged his taste for the ineffable experience of the solitary egocentric individual, and used as a palliative Marlow's allegiance to law and order."[113]

The contrasting statements of Raskin and Kennedy raise an interesting issue. When radicals venture into practical literary criticism, they do not always see things the same way. There is nothing wrong with this. But it raises the question of how useful ideology can be for guiding practical criticism. Something is needed in addition to (or prior to) an evaluation according to ideology. Radicals must first decide what Conrad is actually saying before they know whether to praise or to damn him. At this point ideology is of no help. They stand in need of some aesthetic criteria—perhaps of close reading, perhaps of some of the qualities of the New Criticism. Revolutionary ideology is no substitute for this initial step of recognition. If it is useful at all, it is so only as a criterion for the evaluation which can be made after analysis is completed.

Although there was a dearth of both creative art and literary criticism on the New Left, there was more of the latter than of the former. The reason is obvious: the new radicalism was essentially a cult of academics and would-be academics. It had signally little success reaching beyond the campus, and its dearth of creative artistry was one more evidence of its "ghetto" status.

— 11 —

The Diverging Paths of the New Literary Radicals

Just as the Movement as a whole in the late 1960s divided into camps of Marxist ideologues and of those who returned to the personalist themes of the early SDS, so did the literary radicals. In the early 1970s, Marxism became the dominant note in radical literary study. *College English* devoted a 1970 issue to "A Phalanx from the Left," large parts of which were incorporated into *The Politics of Literature;* by late 1972 the special issue given to the literary radicals was entitled "Marxist Interpretations of Mailer, Woolf, Wright, and Others." Similarly, the session at the 1972 MLA convention sponsored by the Radical Caucus in English and the Modern Languages was labeled "Marxist Perspectives in Literary Scholarship and Teaching."

Among the literary radicals, as in the Movement at large, the leading exponents of the revived personalism were the feminists. *College English* devoted an issue in 1971 and another in 1972 to feminism in literature, and most of the contributors were radicals. While some of them continued to operate within the Radical Caucus, radical feminists also organized their own separate meetings, workshops, and literature tables. These developments breathed fresh life into the Radical Caucus, with sessions of both groups well attended.

The Turn toward Marxism

The 1972 forum on Marxism held by the Radical Caucus had an attendance of five hundred and overflowed the hall to which it was assigned. Protest activities were evident, though they were muted in comparison to the raucous days of MLA 1968. Perhaps the presence of the Old Marxists

189

tamed the new radicals to some extent and forced the flow of radical energy into more academic channels than was formerly the wont of the free-swinging new radicals.

The greatest heat seemed to be generated not from proposals for protest action but from arguments over the varying degrees of Marxist purity expressed by workshop participants. Literary discussions were punctuated by citing the authority. The ultimate putdown was, "But that is not what Marx says." Tempers flared. In one case the moderator, a new radical, felt so badgered by doctrinaire Marxists that he finally stomped out of the room in a huff—to the scoldings of other participants that his action was uncomradely and irresponsible, and not in the spirit of criticism/self-criticism. In fact, this workshop was a microcosm of the fragmentation endemic to leftist groups. Marxism's boost to the new literary radicals came at a considerable cost.

If Marxism revived the flagging spirit of the new literary radicals, it is equally true that their vigorous presence in the profession gave Marxist literary criticism a shot in the arm. The new radicals have vociferously called the profession's attention to some of the concerns which Marxist critics had long been reciting. There is, of course, a substantial and ongoing body of Marxist literary criticism, but it lies outside the scope of this study. Our concern is with the effect of this ideology on the New Leftists in the literary profession.

The Marxist turn of the new literary radicals is too recent to have effected much practical Marxist criticism, and it is too early to make definitive statements on how helpful this turn will be in reinvigorating the new radical study of literature. Along with the Radical Caucus forum on Marxist perspectives at MLA 1972, the November 1972 issue of *College English* was designed to be part of a concerted effort by the new radicals to renew their vitality. One workshop at the MLA convention was devoted to discussing this particular issue.

From the introductory essay, written by Richard Wasson, it is clear what the radicals hoped to accomplish. He explained: "The issue was conceived at the time when the repressive forces in America had begun to assume their present dominant position and the left began to suffer from a sense of confusion, defeat, and invisibility."[1] He was referring to the slump which followed the salad days of the new radicals immediately following MLA 1968. He observed, "The 'phalanx from the left,' which had emerged at the 1968 MLA convention and filled the pages of the March 1970 *College English*, was in disarray."[2] The optimism generated in 1968, which had caused such effusive remarks as "What is far more amazing is the fact that the Modern Language Association, through our efforts, is now in a . . . 'vanguard' position among professional organizations!"[3] had

been quickly followed by this disarray. Out of desperation the new radicals turned to Marxism—not as the natural and inevitable outgrowth of
their visceral reaction against the established forms of literary studies, but
as an imperfect but still acceptable substitute for their initial efforts, which
had failed. Wasson explained: "The situation demanded an act of intellectual resistance. Marxism offered not only an intellectual position more
coherent than the ideas which had previously informed our action, but the
genuine possibility of an international movement aimed at changing the
world. . . . Our aims, then, were to sustain the left by a gesture of critical
resistance, to speak to the larger professional audience, and to free both
from the stultifying clichés of American intellectual life and the absurdity
and nullity of its emotional life."[4] The order here is important. The chief
aim of the turn to Marxism was not to bring a new dimension into the
professional world in general, but to sustain the left which had suffered
great loss. Once again, the political were dominant over literary concerns.

The new radicals were quite aware that Marxist literary criticism had
come under severe fire "as excessively sociological, as incapable of dealing
with form, as prescriptive in nature, and, as fundamentally abstract, dull,
and boring."[5] They themselves, in their more self-confident days, had occasionally echoed such charges, just as the early SDS had spoken negatively
of Marxism in general. Wasson admitted that these charges were "not
without their grain of truth,"[6] but he pleaded that it was at least better
than the historicism and formalism which had dominated the critical
enterprise and that it offered a concrete way to reintegrate literature and
life. His New Left residue was seen in his typically anti-academic conclusion: "Yet finally that debate, since it is about the nature of reality and the
future of humankind, will not be settled in the pages of literary journals,
but rather by correct actions in history. . . . The most we can hope from
this issue is that it gives to oppressed men and women within the profession a few of the critical tools and insights so long denied to them by the
bourgeois intellectual establishment, tools with which they can begin to
fashion their own liberation and the liberation of all people."[7]

If Marxism was not what the new radicals had initially had in mind,
it at least provided the kind of world view which the radicals knew they
needed in order to practice their kind of literary criticism. Frederic
Jameson formulated overtly the generally unspoken presupposition which
allowed the new radicals to take refuge in Marxism: "Is it necessary to
ridicule the idea that it is because the critic is himself a Marxist that he
practices a Marxist interpretation of literature rather than some other
kind? Not we, but reality itself is Marxist in its structure; and the Marxist
is not a member of some peculiar sect, with its own determinate beliefs
and terminology, but rather one who tries as best he can to approximate

that reality and to come to active terms with it, in literature as elsewhere."[8]

The overall impression of the Marxist issue of *College English* was quite different from that of the "Phalanx of the Left" issue of 1970. There was less of the autobiographical element in these essays. Fewer contributors had been associated with the New University Conference. More essays were devoted to commentary on specific writers and works, and the tone was more "academic," even pedestrian. This issue lacked the blazing protest of the earlier one; it was less exciting to read. The difference in tone was one of the main objections that the new radicals had had toward the old Leftists. They saw the latter as settling for being an academic subgroup, one voice among many. Rather than becoming just another subgroup, they wanted to revolutionize the totality of the profession. Their adoption of Marxism might provide them with the basis for a more sustained professional presence, but it was a significant compromise with their original desires—just as adulthood generally entails a gearing down of the enthusiasm and idealism of adolescence in preparation for the long haul.

Ira Shor contributed two items in the issue. The first showed both the earnest desire of a new radical to utter the right Marxisms and the awkwardness of his attempt: "*Marxist* critics, teachers, doctors, carpenters, and mechanics inherit standard tools for each trade, but they don't inherit bourgeois consciousness, and hence can expropriate old tools to make a new society, while rejecting those tools which had served only the bourgeois interests."[9] But he did identify what motivated the shift in posture from New Leftism to Marxism; protest, he explained, gives no basis for a positive restructuring of one's professional role: "What has unified us in practice has been opposition to the Vietnam war, but that has been difficult to translate into daily teaching of literature. What can unify us, vis à vis our domestic situation, is the dimension of class. A class dimension must incorporate, not exclude, the real exploitation based on race, sex, and age. More importantly, a class dimension gives us a common antagonist—bourgeois ideology and institutions."[10] His second piece mainly comprised a long list of questions, most of which were admittedly "primarily theme-and-content-oriented."[11] Perhaps its most significant aspect was the concession that there is some virtue in the formalistic approaches to literature represented by the New Criticism: "A marxist formalism becomes possible when a materialist intelligence reads texture and structure as closely as do New Critics. The deepest level of literary experience occurs through diction, imagery, patterns of language and character, structures of incidents, motifs, figures, and gestures."[12]

The need for Marxism to deal with literary form was remarked several times in this issue of *College English*. Radicals and Marxists had become sensitive to the allegation that Marxist criticism is unable to do so, and they were at pains to disavow the charge. Gaylord LeRoy, for instance, contrasted an outdated "vulgar" Marxism and an up-to-date sophisticated Marxism, insisting that "The function of literature is not to illustrate truths that can be arrived at by other disciplines; on the contrary, literature is in itself a unique mode of cognition, not replaceable by anything else. Marxist theory is sufficiently comprehensive so that it can be applied to *all* art. The goal of Marxist criticism is to throw light on artistic value; it is a study of *art*."[13]

Annette Conn voiced a similar concern. While recognizing "the centrality of ideological questions in any Marxist approach," she concurred that "the dialectical relationship between form and content" was "an absolutely central concern of the critic," even the Marxist critic.[14] This is easier said than done; so in her comment on one of the articles, she decided, in not atypical Marxist fashion, "to try to deal with a few very central issues in his [the author's] analysis of content rather than to 'casually' comment on a great many points made, this in spite of the fact that I feel that formal concerns must be made an integral part of our criticism."[15] Nevertheless, the repeated expressions of concern about form manifested a significant departure from the unsophisticated literary radicalism which Marxism had been called upon to bolster. They indicated an increasing interest in literary issues *per se,* and that Marxism was helping the new radicalism to settle down into more conventional academic styles, whether or not that was the intention of the new radicals.

The remainder of the Marxist issue of *College English* was composed of articles, each followed by a comment by a fellow-Marxist; and a concluding bibliography on "Marxism and Literature"[16] was significant chiefly for its dearth of entries by American critics. The list of articles was also revealing: "The Great American Hunter, or, Ideological Content in the Novel" (on Dickey and Mailer), "Beyond Student-Centered Teaching: The Dialectical Materialist Form of a Literature Course" (reprinted from an earlier pamphlet, which has already been discussed), "A Wilderness of Opinions Confounded: Allegory and Ideology" (on Langland, Spenser, and Bunyan), "Joyce's Political Development and the Aesthetic of *Dubliners,*" "The Content and Form of *Native Son,*" "Socialization in *Mrs. Dalloway.*" These titles form quite a contrast with representative titles from *The Politics of Literature*: "Why Teach Literature? An Account of How I Came to Ask That Question," "The Teaching of Literature in the Highest Academies of the Empire," "Teaching and Studying Literature at the End of Ideology," "Free, Classless, and Urbane?", "Why Teach Poetry— An Experiment," "Up Against the Great Tradition."

The Marxist issue gave much more attention to practical criticism than

did the earlier radical manifesto; it moved beyond protest. If these Marxist essays were the tools for personal and social liberation, as Wasson
suggested, they were so only very indirectly. That is, they allowed the
radicals a way of staying in the university and competing in the game of
"publish-or-perish," while at the same time expressing their leftist convictions. They provided models for other radical scholars to emulate. But
they did little to overthrow the "Amerikan Empire," which could easily
absorb tons of such exercises. Compared to the earlier radical essays, these
would seem to have had a greatly diminished power to radicalize students.

There is an appropriateness in the new radicals' turn to Marxism. If
their essays are now more in conformity with the expectations of the
profession and consign them to being just one among many competing
schools of literary criticism, they were always just an intellectual cult—but
with an ideology which denied that this could be the case. While they still
would deny vigorously that this is their situation, their acts of writing such
academic essays reinforce the unpalatable fact of the matter.

The Feminists' Revival of Personalism

In addition to the turn to Marxism, the other main direction recently
taken by radicals was the return to the personalist objectives of the early
New Left. This was seen among literary radicals almost exclusively in the
women's movement. *College English* once again reflected the trend: as it
devoted the November 1972 issue to Marxism, it devoted the preceding
issue, October 1972, to "Women Writing and Teaching." A 1970 issue had
been on the new radical "Phalanx from the Left"; its subject in May 1971
was "Women in the Colleges." There is the parallel between these two
tandems that as the "Phalanx from the Left" was heavy on autobiography
and protest and the Marxist issue gave more attention to practical criticism, so the earlier feminist issue was more concerned with the professional status of female English teachers than the later issue, which gave
more attention to practical criticism of literature written by women. However, the distinction is not as sharp in the case of the two feminist issues
as it is in the case of the two general leftist issues. Elaine Hedges, the guest
editor of the second issue, found anger to be the keynote of most of the
essays included.[17]

The striking contrast between the feminist and the radical issues was
the general lack of political discussion in the former. While there were
occasional routine remarks about the social-political milieu determining
both how writers treat women characters and how women read literature,
the overriding concern was with the personal liberation of women from
sexist bondage. Radical politics was at a minimum, although a major share

of the contributors have been associated with the radical cause.

Florence Howe's "A Report on Women and the Profession" was representative of the personalistic concerns of the two feminist issues. Formally devoted to reporting and interpreting statistics amassed by the MLA Commission on the Status of Women in the Profession, it contained a long autobiographical excursion explaining why she, a Ph.D. dropout at age forty-one and after fourteen years of full-time teaching, is still an assistant professor who teaches heavy loads and has never had a sabbatical.[18] (This is the same person who was president of MLA.) Howe's article was totally devoid of radical politics.

Elaine Showalter brought radical politics into her article, but just barely. In her concluding paragraph she suggested: "For the more radical teacher, male or female, teaching women could be the new frontier of education. The willingness of women teachers to make relevant aspects of their personal lives accessible to their students, the willingness of men teachers to forego the privileges of male authority, could have enormous influences on the ways women students visualize themselves and their future roles."[19] This was not much of a connection between radical politics and feminism, even though it was more than what was conveyed through most articles in the two feminist issues of *College English*. Her one point of contact was gratuitous. What she suggested radical male and female teachers could do has no organic relation to their politics at all; non-radical males and females could logically perform the same services for women students.

Of the twenty-four articles in the two feminist issues, only one offered a clear, direct linkage between feminism and radical politics, that by Lillian Robinson. Her essay insisted that feminist criticism is "criticism with a Cause, engaged criticism."[20] It concluded, "New feminism is about fundamentally transforming institutions. In our struggle for liberation, Marx's note about philosophers may apply to critics as well: that up to now they have only interpreted the world and the real point is to change it."[21] Pleading that feminists "must construct a method that applies radical insights about culture and politics, but does so in the context of a coherent feminist analysis,"[22] she recognized that one could be a feminist without being a radical, and it was this danger which she sought to counteract. She insisted that feminist criticism is "necessarily alienated" from bibliographical, textual, contextual, and archetypal modes of literary criticism because they are bourgeois modes.[23] A feminist criticism which employed them would be "simply bourgeois criticism in drag."[24] The crucial question, as Robinson saw it, was: "can women be liberated in our present political economy, or is more fundamental change required? For those of us who choose a radical response to this question, there is a more pressing problem. I am referring to the tension between 'feminists,' narrowly defined as those who believe that the basic social conflict is between the sexes and that all men benefit from male supremacy, and so-called 'politicos,' who believe that the fundamental conflict is between classes and that sexism is part of that struggle."[25]

This statement was a clear reflection of the reality of the split in the radical Movement. She wanted to heal the rift, but she did so quite unsatisfactorily—by declaring that women are "the other" in a male-dominated system (some men also are excluded from the domain of high culture), that women are not generally bourgeois: "Aren't there many bourgeois women, after all? Well, no. The wives and daughters of the ruling class do not somehow mystically partake in *someone else's* relation to the means of production."[26] Thus, there is no conflict between class analysis and sex analysis, between the feminists and the politicos. This was all presented very vaguely and briefly. For the crucial issue separating the radicals into two camps, Robinson provided meager resolution.

After denying the "standard lit-crit assumptions,"[27] Robinson was faced with the problem of demonstrating how radical insights could further feminist criticism. Her solution: radical textual criticism.

It was Sartre, I think, who asked whether it would be possible to write a "good" anti-Semitic novel in the wake of Nazi genocide. Someone replied that Celine had done precisely that. I imagine we would all counter by asking, "What do you mean 'good'?" A radical kind of textual criticism might well be able to answer that question. It could usefully study the way the texture of sentences, choice of metaphors, patterns of exposition and narrative relate to ideology. I call such an approach radical and insist that feminism is part of it.... Radical criticism of texts would obviously be more meaningful than a standard that simply said, "This is acceptable, that is not" without showing how this and that worked.... Radical criticism should be able to do more than point out a "correct line" on sex or class. Applying our analysis to texts will determine, as dogma would not, what it *means* to keep saying, "That is a sexist book—but it's great literature."[28]

The fact of the matter is that Robinson did not explain or demonstrate just what this radical textual criticism would be or how it would work; she merely called for its development. Her article was a plea that the feminists and politicos not part company; it offered nothing substantive toward that end. At that, it was the only article in these feminist issues of

College English which sought to keep the sisters from going their own way.

*   *   *

We have seen, then, that the literary radicals have, at point after point, replayed the conflicts which developed during the history of the student Movement. That these conflicts have never been resolved even to the satisfaction of the participants is evidenced most forcefully by the eventual disintegration of one radical organization after the other. At every point along the way, it has been the unresolvable conflict between personal aspirations and political positions. The literary radicals' division into Marxists and feminists allows them to maintain a serious presence within the profession, but it is at the cost of denying their original impulse to attempt to resolve this polarity.

Concluding Essay: The New Radicalism
as a Quasi-Religious Phenomenon

This study has analyzed the new radicalism in terms which give greater weight to its personalistic and existentialist elements than is generally the case in other analyses. It is based on the conviction that viewing the New Left as a primarily political phenomenon is a deficient approach for understanding its incredible outpouring of energy—energy which was usually vaguely focused and inchoate. Perhaps this new wave of radicalism should be seen as a phenomenon which is at root spiritual rather than political. What follows essays to test how helpful this analytic model can be in illuminating the most fundamental reality of the Movement.

Analyzing the Movement in terms of a quasi-religious phenomenon is not integral to the preceding chapters of this book; they stand or fall on their own merits. This essay is, rather, an addendum seeking to extend some of the conclusions reached heretofore by offering a paradigm which casts fresh light on the subject.

An interpretation of the new radicalism in religious terms has nothing to do with organized churches. While some of the new radicals come from religious backgrounds, seldom did they make any direct connections between their religious rearing and their political activities; hence the use of the term *quasi-religious* as opposed to *religious*. Rather, the category of religion may be illuminating if it is defined as does Paul Tillich: that ground of ultimate concern out of which grow all of one's thoughts and actions. For most Americans politics is a matter of mediate concern; for the new radicals it is a matter of ultimate concern.

Religious Analyses by Outsiders

Many interpreters of the New Left have found it convenient to allude to religious categories. For instance, in his book, *Remembering the Answers*, Nathan Glazer entitled a chapter "Religion, Culture, and the New Student Activism." Praising the early New Leftists for "their sensitivity to human social, ethical, and moral problems,"[1] he declared, "In the moral, and yes, one may say it, in the spiritual sphere, their achievement is greater than in the political sphere."[2] Quoting the Port Huron Statement's affirmation, "We regard *men* as infinitely precious and possessed of unfulfilled capacities for reason, freedom, and love," Glazer commented: "That is a remarkable statement to appear at a key point in a political manifesto. How can we say that a movement of social action with such a conception of man is not religious? Certainly that is in some sense a more spiritual, a more religious sentiment than one often hears from the spokesmen of religion."[3]

In an essay which was included in an anthology edited by two radicals, Philip Altbach also treated the early New Left against the backdrop of religion. Altbach scored the vacuity of organized religion and its inability to inspire young people to engage in social action based on a religious commitment. Calling for a revitalization of the churches, he concluded, "Until that time, one of the most potent forces for justice and peace will remain without meaning for large numbers of concerned and active students."[4]

Paul Goodman's *New Reformation* contained another example of a religious analysis of the new radicalism. The theme of the book was that "there is a crisis of belief, the times are like 1510."[5] And it is "an upheaval of belief that is of religious depth."[6] While Goodman acknowledged the imprecision of his analogy between the Reformation and the current period, he meant it to be taken seriously, not merely as metaphorical frosting. He understood that what was at stake was not merely one's function in a single arena of human endeavor (politics in this case) but one's very self-definition.

Arthur Waskow, a sort of fellow-traveler of the student movement, wrote two essays discussing the Movement in religious terms. He observed that the New Left showed "a remarkable interest in religion, magic, astrology, and other 'opiates' of [i.e., 'opiates' as judged according to] traditional Left ideology"; and he considered this an important distinction between New Left and Old.[7] He advocated "treating our own religious impulses seriously,"[8] and he called for the establishment of "small, free-floating religious organizations in some sort of loose network: what might be called Free Churches (and Synagogues, and Mosques, and Temples) in which social-action programs are central rather than peripheral, the clergy are community organizers and mystics as well as philosophical teachers, large buildings are avoided, and fusions of traditional and new religious ceremonies are sought that can address the traditional adherents of each faith and embody its particular urgencies and history, while simultaneously binding together the radical adherents of them all."[9]

Kenneth Keniston noted "the importance of religious upbringing in some of these [young radical] families."[10] Regarding those who did not have religious rearings, he reported, "For some, the beginning of adolescence was followed by a great intensification of largely self-generated religious feelings, often despite a relatively non-religious childhood and background."[11] Keniston cited an interesting case of the secularization of an initially religious impulse in a young radical:

> But my vision had always been that all of a sudden a million people would march on Washington, singing "A Mighty Fortress Is Our God," and the government would come tumbling down. I would feel much more identified with that than if a million people marched on Washington singing "The Internationale." . . . My basic rhetoric is a very theological one. . . . Maybe if I were born three or four hundred years earlier, I'd be a preacher. I'd say that the people should reform, that they should stop being sinners, that they should realize that the world has to be built on different foundations. . . . My initial thing is to get up and preach to people and expect them to follow me. That's where my impulse is, to speak out to the world.[12]

Keniston commented: "Here the underlying appeal to moral principle is clearly stated: the call to sinners to reform and repent. He [the young radical quoted above] went on to note, however, 'My problem is that the basic rhetoric is one that's irrelevant. . . . [It] just doesn't work.' "[13]

Religious Analyses by Insiders

Some of the new radicals themselves have invoked religious categories to understand their own Movement. Edward Schwartz contended that "the radicals of the New Left pay great attention to the religious instinct itself."[14] He located the New Left not in the traditions of liberalism or of Marxism, but in a long and honorable tradition which demands justice as a basically religious proposition.[15] This same tradition explained, for Schwartz, all radical movements in American history: "*Religious justice was the central demand of virtually every major radical movement in the United States throughout the nineteenth century. It was central to the philosophy of the American democrat.*"[16]

Even Staughton Lynd, for all his Old Left background, found the religious metaphor useful for making the distinction between radicalism and liberalism, for highlighting what was new about the New Left:

> what I think I mean by being a radical is functionally equivalent in

many ways to what people have meant for two thousand years by being a Christian. . . . He feels himself systematically or diffusely at odds with the existing scheme of things, and in this he differs from the liberal. The liberal is a person who is always discovering with astonishment that something else is wrong, but nevertheless refusing to conclude that there is a relatedness to these discoveries.

It seems to me that the radical, like the Christian in the best sense of the word, is a person who insists on talking about certain qualitative or systematic characteristics of the whole shooting-match, like private property, like competition, like arbitrary authority of one man over another. . . . the radical is or should be someone who has a coherent vision of a better way that men can live, a paradise, as it were, which he continually endeavors to create on earth.[17]

Paul Potter is another Movement person who has analyzed the new radicalism with the aid of religious terminology. He opined that "the movement has failed to make contact with the people who are in it, has failed to comprehend itself,"[18] and he proposed religion as a category for accurately understanding the Movement: "Increasingly I am attracted to religious *images* like love and communion and soul and spiritual and church. . . . The corollary of this is that I am less impressed with hard political words like strategy and tactics and organize and struggle and action than I once was."[19]

Similarly, his vision of the organizational form which the Movement should take drew on a religious parallel: "If these images correspond to any former images I have in my mind, it is not that of a political party or a 'radical organization,' or a club or a friendship group. But it is very definitely that of a church. Not of any church I have directly known or experienced, but of the church I have heard some churchmen talk about, the early revolutionary church, whose followers lived in caves and shared their bread, their persecution and their destiny."[20]

The minds of many new radicals ran readily to religious metaphors to describe their most basic experiences and motivations. Todd Gitlin gave as a reason for his joining SDS that its members "integrated their political and personal salvation at once."[21] Even while calling for socialism, Carl Oglesby declared, "But it cannot be too much emphasized that the interest in developing other social forms, however acute it will become, follows, *does not precede*, the soul-basic explosion against injustice which is the one redemption of the damned."[22] Young radicals seeking to adjust to adult life came to see that the expected life style of a Movement worker entailed "the basically religious stipulation to leave all and cleave only unto us."[23] Numerous examples could be offered of the use of such terminology as conversion, brother and sister rather than comrade), and the making of the new man. Radicals spoke repeatedly of the need to transform themselves—a basically religious concept. They also acknowledged the need to be free from a feeling of guilt—"the politics of guilt" was a common refrain of derogation. The term "Babylon" even appeared occasionally—it was a favorite of Eldridge Cleaver, for instance.

Certain practices of the radicals also echo religious practices. At the initial Radicals in the Professions conference in 1967, "There was virtually unanimous agreement around the need to give at least ten per cent of one's income to the movement: in one workshop, someone suggested that a tithe was 'chintzy'—to which everyone applauded."[24] The New University Conference carried over this idea of tithing and even sacrificial offering. The Vocations for Social Change commune asked for support of its work just as missionaries appeal for money.[25] Barbara and Al Haber noted that "the experience of the movement is one of voluntary and involuntary poverty. ... Poverty is thus a de facto prerequisite to full status is [sic] the radical community."[26] The parallel with the vows of poverty taken by religious orders is obvious. One of Keniston's interviewees told of attending the Camp for Social Responsibility which had the same effect of motivating him to go home and become involved that summer church camps are designed to have.[27]

While these parallels with religion are generally applicable to the vision of the early New Left, religious analysis of the radicalism which emerged in the late 1960s is also possible, and some radicals have employed it thus. If, for example, the spiritual quality of the early SDSers had become submerged, the "true believer" mentality had surfaced clearly. In such terms did Herbert Gans foresee the factionalism into which the New Left was to fall and warn against it: "The danger is that it will become another quasi-religious movement, whose first priority is to define True Radicalism and to set admission and exclusion policies for members rather than to determine and implement radical political action programs."[28] Calvert and Neiman, after likening early SDS assemblies to a cross between an encounter group and a Quaker meeting, found the image of the revival meeting particularly apt for SDS in its Marxist-Leninist stage: "It was like a revival meeting with the old tune 'I am weak but Thou art strong, Jesus save me from all wrong.' But in this case, the Lord had become Marx or Lenin or Mao."[29] Similarly, David Doggett employed a religious analysis to explain what had gone wrong in SDS:

SDS. . . is rapidly becoming a new fundamentalist religion. Antiquated classical Marxist-Leninism is the gospel; the works of classical Marxists make up the Old Testament, the Trotskyites have the Apocrypha, and Mao has written the New Testament. The decision-making body of the church (the SDS National Council) interprets the gospel for the people and anyone who opposes the "correct position" utters blasphemy. The world is divided into the saved and the damned. Anyone who does not meekly accept the "correct line" is automatically an "agent" of Satan (the ruling class capitalist pig).[30]

Extending the Religious Analyses

The evidence herein cited is by no means a comprehensive cataloguing of religious references by and about radicals. And it does not (nor would a comprehensive catalogue) *prove* anything. These references, rather, are illustrative of the ease and naturalness with which radicals (and some commentators on them) turned to religion for analogies to apply to their experiences. They are stimulating and provocative. They suggest the possibility of picking up these hints and extending them, of pressing them more rigorously than do most of those who offer them. Perhaps those who made even fugitive references along this line had found something which, for one reason or another, they did not pursue to its conclusion.

The first and perhaps most important component in an analysis of the New Left according to a religious model is the influence of the Student Nonviolent Coordinating Committee (SNCC) on the early SDS. Many Southern blacks who engaged in the sit-ins of the early 1960s were acting from explicitly religious motives, following the example of Dr. Martin Luther King, Jr., and the Southern Christian Leadership Conference. In 1960 SNCC adopted a statement of purpose which opens as follows: "We affirm the philosophical or religious ideal of nonviolence as the foundation of our purpose, the pre-supposition of our faith, and the manner of our action. Nonviolence as it grows from Judaic-Christian traditions seeks a social order of justice permeated by love."[31] SNCC's moral force served as an inspiration for SDSers, who saw their work among the poor and deprived of the Northern big cities as a white counterpart to that of SNCC. They generally secularized the underlying motivation for these good deeds, thus separating morality from its original religious matrix; but their original model, SNCC, did not entirely do so.

We have seen earlier the great importance which the early New Left attached to personal liberation, to principles which existentialism enunciates, and to the moral basis of their protest. Without reiterating the evidence, it can be seen that this whole constellation of concerns is what lies at the heart of the religious quest. As religion (meaning Christianity, the dominant religion of the West) is concerned fundamentally with the inner well-being of the individual and the ministering to his felt needs, so was the early New Left. Religion and the new radicalism were both concerned with providing a unifying core of beliefs by which to measure all of one's thoughts and actions, thereby developing personal wholeness and integrity. Both were concerned with the outworking of personal salvation in social actions which demonstrate that morality which salvation is intended to foster. Finally, both nurtured a sense of community among their adherents.

Most of the young radicals came from families with high ethical and moral standards, but in most cases these standards had become detached from traditional religion as early as their parents' generation. As Keniston and Flacks have amply documented, the young radicals generally were acting on principles taught by their elders rather than rebelling against those principles, and in most cases their parents approved of their activities.[32] Most of these parents were liberal or radical. So when the moral passion of the young radicals sought a political outlet, they followed the path marked by their elders. The only rebellion against parents was that against the perceived hypocrisy of not always transforming morality into action. The secularization and even politicization of the moral passion had already been accomplished by their parents, albeit usually in milder forms than those adopted by the radicalized offspring. What these young people did was to take modern liberalism's unacknowledged assumption that politics is the ultimate category of human concern and follow it to its logical conclusion: they made a virtual religion of it. Politics is what they had instead of God. While this substitution entailed a conscious rejection of religion, it does not rule out the interpretation that turning this ultimately spiritual energy to political account qualifies as a kind of religion, or as quasi-religious.

The fact that the new radicals' forays into politics have never been able to bear the desired fruit suggests that politics has been a poor receptacle for their spiritual and moral energy. If a substitute for God must be found, politics has been inadequate. There is no inherent relationship between the morality which motivated the New Leftists and the political activities in which that morality was expended. As Glazer concludes, "Do we have a substitute for or fulfillment of religion? Perhaps we have a fulfillment of religion; but it is not the best one, or the true one."[33]

Nevertheless, that moral energy was definitely the paramount motive force of the New Left; and it is, in the final analysis, more fundamental than the vehicle which the radicals chose for carrying it. Furthermore, it is when viewed as a moral force that the New Left is seen at its best. It was when morality took on the cloak of radical politics that it disfigured itself, sometimes even to the point of making the morality appear ugly. Stripped of its political garb, this morality is impressive indeed.

Analysis of the New Left as quasi-religious helps to explain what went wrong as it evolved during the 1960s. In its increasing ideologization it moved further and further away from that spiritual and moral vision which originally brought it into being. Numerous radicals have lamented SDS's loss of confidence in its initial impulses. If it is granted that these were fundamentally spiritual and moral, it becomes clear just how far SDS departed from its original motive power.

As we have seen, even the later SDS can be analyzed according to a religious model, though now it is seen to parallel the worst aspects of religious fanaticism rather than the life-affirming character of true spirituality. Sectarianism, after all, is a term which originally referred to the ecclesiastical scene, not the political one. Marxism has frequently been viewed as a form of secularized Christianity, even as a Christian heresy. And the New Left's adoption of Marxism replayed in brief the unpleasant history of Old Leftism. It was replete with the squabbling, heresy-hunting, nit-picking proof-texting, appeal to infallible authority, and holier-than-thou self-righteousness which characterized Old Left factionalism—and all sectarian religion, for that matter. As the sectarians represented a degeneration of that primitive Christianity which Potter and Lynd urged the New Left to emulate, so the Marxified New Left represented a degeneration of the primitive New Left's spirituality and morality. The parallel is quite exact.

The religious analysis is consonant with what has happened to many individual New Leftists since the Movement's organizational collapse. Andrew Kopkind, who had been active in the Movement, has documented and analyzed the drift into mystical religions—especially Oriental ones— of a large number of former politicos. While mystical contemplation and political action seem to be polar opposites, Kopkind explained how both could appeal to the same person: "Although a community of yogis and a collective of radicals may see their lives and their work as vastly different in context and purpose, . . . they appear driven by many of the same incessant impulses, haunted by the familiar fears, baffled by the old perplexities. . . . The energies which create and destroy social movements act on the cosmic ones as well."[34] This compatibility between apparent opposites was explainable because "the *Zeitgeist* of the political generation of SNCC, SDS and Weatherman—the 'student' radical movements—always had its existential and spiritual side beneath the hard edge of political action."[35]

Central to this whole study has been the recognition that the main goal of the New Left was to hold in tension the personal and the political and the judgment of the ultimate impossibility of their doing so. Kopkind, while believing that for a time there was a successful balance of the two, confessed that such was no longer the case.[36] While he stopped short of contending that the break between the personal and the political was inevitable, that is as reasonable an interpretation as any that he implied. He did not say that the personalistic impulse had primacy over the political in the New Left enterprise, but he offered an observation which is most amenable to that interpretation: "My impression is that many people who once found the universe of political action and ideology meaningful and enlivening, now find it empty and boring—and on top of that, they feel guilty for being bored."[37] Why so, unless politics, rather than being their primary motive force, was a secondary factor, an outworking of something more fundamental?

Kopkind listed former Movement friends who have become New Mystics. "Rennie Davis, once the New Leftist *par excellence*, has become a devoted organizer for the aggressive religion of the Satguru Maharaj Ji, the teenage Avatar (that is, God)."[38] He quoted Davis as effusing, "I think the combination of a politics and a spirit led by God Itself is a very far-out vision."[39] Kopkind also reported that "Greg Calvert . . . has been seriously into Sufism and Gestalt Therapy."[40] He also listed Sally Kempton, Jerry Rubin, and others as New Mystics.

His article concluded with a discussion of what happens when prophecy fails. Each believer must then readjust his beliefs somehow to take into account the unexpected reality. That so many have converted to one form of religion or another is surely, as Kopkind suggested, a fact pregnant with significance.

The most important application of this religious analysis to the academic radicals has to do with their drive to develop a comprehensive world view which will provide a criterion to apply in their perspectival criticism. Edward Shils has written illuminatingly on this point:

> What are the articles of faith of ideological politics? First and above all, the assumption that politics should be conducted from the standpoint of a coherent, comprehensive set of beliefs which must override every other consideration. . . . The centrality of this belief has required that it radiate into every sphere of life—that it replace religion, that it provide aesthetic criteria, that it rule over scientific research and philosophic thought, that it regulate sexual and family life.
>
> It has been the belief of those who practice politics ideologically that they alone have the truth about the right ordering of life—of life as a whole, and not just of political life.[41]

Radicals have declared that everything is politics. But to affirm this, one must first posit certain assumptions about the nature of reality. Everything is everything—undifferentiated and incomprehensible, until one places an interpretation upon it; and this interpretation can grow only out of the assumptions one first adopts. To encompass in one coherent viewpoint that "everything" which constitutes reality is precisely what it means to construct a world view. Any comprehensive world view must deal with ultimate issues of the meaning of life and reality; these ultimate issues are of paramount importance to world-view builders. Answers to ultimate questions can never, by their very nature, be proven beyond a shadow of a doubt. Even though they may be based on experience with reality, observation of reality, and reflection about reality and therefore need not be totally irrational, they inevitably entail a faith commitment. The radicals' declaration that everything is politics is a position which can be grounded ultimately only on faith. It belongs to the category of presuppositions, not empirically or rationally verifiable facts.

The typical academic posture toward such matters is to ignore them, to stay safely within the cocoon of relativism, which breeds agnosticism about ultimate issues, since these are not amenable to the kind of proof which satisfies the scientific mind. Nevertheless, those perennial questions of ultimate concern continue to haunt the minds of men. If the academy ignores them, it will have drastically foreshortened the range of reality allowed within its purview.

The radicals have sought to draw the larger issues back into the academic discussion. If they are finally adjudged to have failed in this attempt, it is altogether plausible that their failure can be explained in terms of the intrinsic incoherence in the world view which they have chosen as the basis for their work, not necessarily in terms of their desire to locate a world view by which to guide their work. The most beneficial legacy of the new academic radicals would be to drive the academy back to a consideration of the question of truth. Does reality have resident within it some coherent form which is worth an attempt to search out? If it has—if, even, it might have—scholars are unforgivably remiss if they do not investigate the question.

Notes

1: The Early Phase

1. Richard Flacks, *Youth and Social Change* (Chicago: Markham Publishing Company, 1971), p. 76.

2. Ibid., p. 78.

3. Richard Flacks, "Is the Great Society Just a Barbecue?", *Thoughts of the Young Radicals* (New Republic, 1966), p. 53.

4. Todd Gitlin, "Power and the Myth of Progress," *Thoughts of the Young Radicals* (New Republic, 1966), pp. 22–23.

5. See, e.g., Kenneth Keniston regarding interviews with radical leaders. *Young Radicals: Notes on Committed Youth* (New York: Harcourt, Brace & World, 1968), p. 180.

6. Joan Wallach, "Chapter Programming," SDS National Council Meeting Working Papers (1963), p. 1.

7. Loren Baritz, ed., *The American Left: Radical Political Thought in the Twentieth Century* (New York: Basic Books, 1971), p. 386.

8. See Paul Jacobs and Saul Landau, eds., *The New Radicals: A Report with Documents* (New York: Vintage Books, 1966), pp. 28–29.

9. E.g., Staughton Lynd, important in the New Left but with life-long Old Left ties, took issue with fellow New Leftists in 1963 for their "taboo on socialism" and considered it "the obstacle to intellectual coherence" for the Movement. He defined the term with a precision avoided by most New Leftists: "What I mean by socialism is comprehensive planning, involving maximum popular participation, based on public ownership of all major industries." "Socialism, the Forbidden Word," *Studies on the Left* 3 (Summer 1963): 14.

10. Paul Potter, "The 'Incredible' War," *National Guardian* 17 (April 24, 1965): 5.

11. Dale L. Johnson, "On the Ideology of Campus Revolution," *Studies on the Left* 1 (1961): 75. See also Kenneth Keniston, who asked radical leaders what kind of new society they envisioned to replace the old; they spoke vaguely of "a society that has never existed," "new values," a "more humane world," "liberation" in some psychological, cultural, and historical sense. *Youth and Dissent: The Rise of a New Opposition* (New York: Harcourt Brace Jovanovich, 1971), p. 314.

12. Thomas Hayden, "A Letter to the New (Young) Left," in *The New Student Left: An Anthology*, ed. Mitchell Cohen and Dennis Hale (Boston: Beacon Press, 1966), p. 8.

13. Greg Calvert and Carol Neiman, *A Disrupted History: The New Left and the New Capitalism* (New York: Random House, 1971), p. 16.

14. Richard Flacks, "Some Problems, Issues, Proposals," in *The New Radicals*, ed. Jacobs and Landau, p. 163.

15. *Port Huron Statement* (New York: Students for a Democratic Society, 1964), pp. 6–7.

16. Flacks, *Youth and Social Change*, p. 6.

17. Keniston, *Young Radicals*, p. 26.

18. Flacks, "Some Problems, Issues, Proposals," in *The New Radicals*, ed. Jacobs and Landau, p. 163.

19. Ibid., p. 164.

20. *Port Huron Statement*, p. 62.

21. Flacks, "Some Problems, Issues, Proposals," in *The New Radicals*, ed. Jacobs and Landau, p. 164.

22. Ronald Aronson, "Dear Herbert," *Radical America* 4 (April 1970): 9.

23. Greg Calvert and Carol Neiman, "The New Left" (Ann Arbor: Radical Education Project, n.d.), p. 12.

24. Keniston, *Youth and Dissent*, p. 303.

25. Carl Wittman and Thomas Hayden, "An Interracial Movement of the Poor?", in *The New Student Left*, ed. Cohen and Hale, p. 218.

26. Gitlin explained that the young radicals "have had good reason to be tentative and skeptical about blueprints" because "blueprints tend to freeze. . . . But rigid agnosticism too can be and is being transcended. Values and experience generate certain guidelines." "Power and the Myth of Progress," *Thoughts of the Young Radicals*, p. 22.

27. *Port Huron Statement*, p. 6.

28. Keniston, *Young Radicals*, p. 176.

29. Flacks, *Youth and Social Change*, p. 130.

30. *Port Huron Statement*, p. 6.

31. Ibid., p. 4.

32. Ibid.

33. Flacks, *Youth and Social Change*, p. 101.

34. For further discussion of this point, see Keniston, *Young Radicals*, p. 181.

35. Todd Gitlin, "The Politics and Vision of the New Left" (San Francisco: Clergy and Laymen Radical Education Project, n.d.), p. 2.

36. Hayden, "Letter to the New (Young) Left," in *The New Student Left*, ed. Cohen and Hale, p. 7.

37. Massimo Teodori, ed., *The New Left: A Documentary History* (Indian-

apolis: Bobbs–Merrill, 1969), p. 38.

38. Robert A. Haber, "From Protest to Radicalism: An Appraisal of the Student Movement 1960," in *The New Student Left*, ed. Cohen and Hale, pp. 46–47.

39. Paul Potter and Hal Benenson, "A Critique of Radical Perspectives on the Campus," *New Left Notes* 2 (May 29, 1967): 4.

40. "Radical Education Project" (Ann Arbor: Radical Education Project, 1966), p. 2. See also columnist Michael Munk: "The fact is that most New Left youths have been brought to their radical stance largely through a moral reaction to poverty, discrimination and unemployment at home and counterrevolutionary wars abroad." "Perspectives on the New Left," *National Guardian* 17 (October 2, 1965): 6. Ronald Aronson listed the Movement's attitudes which were "most disconcerting to non-movement radicals" as the "intense concern for human principles and values among the organizers, their refusal to compromise these values at any point, their preoccupation with personal relationships." "The Movement and Its Critics," *Studies on the Left* 6 (January–February 1966): 11. In Keniston's words: "Formal statements of rationalized philosophy, articulated interpretations of history and political life, and concrete visions of political objectives were almost completely absent in the interviews (and in this respect, as in many others, this is a typically American group). But what did emerge was a strong, if largely implicit, belief in a set of basic moral principles: justice, decency, equality, responsibility, non-violence, and fairness. . . . Convinced that the personal and the political were linked, and emphatically anti-ideological in their ideologies, these young men and women usually emphasized the personal satisfaction they derived from Movement activities." *Young Radicals*, p. 28.

41. "Radical Education Project," p. 2.

42. *Port Huron Statement*, p. 3.

43. Paul Lauter and Florence Howe, *The Conspiracy of the Young* (New York: Meridian Books, 1971), p. 15.

44. Staughton Lynd, *Intellectual Origins of American Radicalism* (New York: Pantheon Books, 1968), p. 161.

45. Edward Schwartz analyzed the Movement as "a last, desperate attempt to revive the American democratic tradition." *Will the Revolution Succeed? Rebirth of the Radical Democrat* (New York: Criterion Books, 1972), p. 110.

46. Aronson, "The Movement and Its Critics," *Studies on the Left*, p. 13. See also Keniston: "Although the changes in institutions and policies proposed by the New Left are often revolutionary, and the means proposed to attain them are sometimes disruptive, the essential values of the New Left are, after all, the traditional values of American democracy: peace, justice, freedom, participation, equality." *Young Radicals*, p. 227.

47. See "From the Haight," in *The New Left: A Documentary History*, ed. Teodori, p. 362.

48. See, e.g., Flacks, *Youth and Social Change*, p. 59.

49. Lauter and Howe, *The Conspiracy of the Young*, pp. 14–19.

50. Flacks, *Youth and Social Change*, p. 59.

51. Paul Goodman, "The Black Flag of Anarchism," in *Anarchism*, ed. Robert Hoffman (New York: Atherton Press, 1970), p. 158.

52. Quoted in Malinda Berry, "Hayden Advocates Unity to Push Student Ideals," in *Student Power, Participation and Revolution*, ed. John and Susan Erlich (New York: Association Press, 1970), p. 23.

53. Thomas Hayden, "Student Social Action: From Liberation to Community," in *The New Student Left*, ed. Cohen and Hale, pp. 287–288. See also Staughton Lynd, more consistently political than most New Leftists, who considered the original impulse of the New Left to be "neither the implementation of a preconceived theory nor a response to material deprivation, but an improvised act of will." "Introduction," in *The New Left: A Collection of Essays*, ed. Priscilla Long (Boston: Porter Sargent, 1969), p. 6. He labeled this "existential radicalism," despite being somewhat critical of it. "Lynd Bids Left Take Direct Action on Concrete Programs," *National Guardian* 17 (December 5, 1964): 7–8.

54. *Port Huron Statement*, p. 7. The minutes of the SDS National Executive Committee meeting on May 6–7, 1962, record an argument over the content of the Port Huron Statement. Tom Hayden, its principal author, wanted to emphasize values. Steve Max led a minority wanting to stress politics, arguing that an organization could not develop around a value-oriented manifesto. Most leaders resisted turning SDS into "an organization with a political 'line.' " As a concession, a section on politics, authored by Max and two others, was appended to Hayden's manuscript on values. Had the majority won, the Statement's relatively mild and reformist political section would have been even more moderate.

55. Howard Zinn, "The Old Left and the New: Emancipation from Dogma," *Nation* 202 (April 4, 1966): 387.

56. Jack Newfield, *A Prophetic Minority* (New York: New American Library, 1966), pp. 120–121.

57. Lewis S. Feuer, *The Conflict of Generations: The Character and Significance of Student Movements* (New York: Basic Books, 1969), p. 477.

58. Carl Oglesby, "The Revolted," in *The American Left: Radical Political Thought in the Twentieth Century* (New York: Basic Books, 1971), pp. 438, 442.

59. Rudolf Rocker, "Anarcho-Syndicalism," in *The New Left: A Collection of Essays*, ed. Long, p. 50.

60. Gil Green, *The New Radicalism: Anarchist or Marxist?* (New York: International Publishers, 1971), p. 19.

61. David T. Wieck, "Preface," in *Social Anarchism*, ed. Giovanni Baldelli (Chicago: Aldine–Atherton, 1971), p. ix.

62. Gitlin, "The Politics and Vision of the New Left," p. 3.

63. Robert Hoffman, ed., *Anarchism*, p. 4.

64. Ibid., pp. 1–2.

65. Ibid., p. 9.

66. Joel Whitebrook, *Liberation* 16 (January 1972): 20–27; Todd Gitlin,

Nation 214 (March 6, 1972): 309–311.

67. Murray Bookchin, *Post-Scarcity Anarchism* (Berkeley: Ramparts Press, 1971), p. 19.

68. Ibid.

69. Ibid., p. 44.

70. Ibid., p. 70.

71. Goodman, "Black Flag," in *Anarchism*, ed. Robert Hoffman, p. 157.

72. Ibid., pp. 149–150.

73. Paul Goodman, *New Reformation: Notes of a Neolithic Conservative* (New York: Random House, 1970), pp. 161–162.

74. Richard Flacks, "On the Uses of Participatory Democracy," *Dissent* 13 (November–December 1966): 708.

75. Aronson, "The Movement and Its Critics," *Studies on the Left*, p. 15.

76. Hoffman, ed., *Anarchism*, p. 4.

77. Johnson, "On the Ideology of Campus Revolution," *Studies on the Left*, p. 75.

78. Hayden, "Letter to the New (Young) Left," in *The New Student Left*, ed. Cohen and Hale, p. 3.

79. Flacks, "On the Uses of Participatory Democracy," *Dissent*, p. 708.

80. Lynd, "Socialism, the Forbidden Word," *Studies on the Left*, pp. 14–20. See also Michael Munk, in the *National Guardian's* first serious look at the New Left, who described SDS as "the non-socialist radicals of the New Left." "New Left: The Ideological Bases," *National Guardian* 17 (September 25, 1965): 3.

81. John and Barbara Ehrenreich, "From Resistance to Revolution," in *The New Left: A Documentary History*, ed. Teodori, p. 465.

82. Goodman, *New Reformation*, p. 125.

83. Seymour Martin Lipset, *Revolution and Counterrevolution: Change and Persistence in Social Structures* (New York: Basic Books, 1968), p. 129.

84. Lewis S. Feuer, *Marx and the Intellectuals: A Set of Post-Ideological Essays* (Garden City, New York: Anchor Books, 1969), p. 96.

85. Paul Breines, "From Guru to Spectre: Marcuse and the Implosion of the Movement," in *Critical Interruptions: New Left Perspectives on Herbert Marcuse*, ed. Paul Breines (New York: Herder and Herder, 1970), p. 18.

86. Carl Oglesby, "Trapped in a System," in *The New Left: A Documentary History*, ed. Teodori, pp. 182–183.

87. C. Clark Kissinger, "The S.D.S. Chapter Organizer's Handbook" (n.p.: n.d.), p. 4.

88. Calvert and Neiman, "The New Left," p. 12. See also Lauter and Howe: "In U. S. society, the thrust of the old liberalism is centrifugal, toward order, organization, centralization, productivity, toward molding individuals through the schools or the military to fit the determined needs of society. But the thrust of increasing numbers of young people is centripetal, toward self-determination,

decentralization, spontaneity, toward using the resources of society to improve the quality of all human life." *The Conspiracy of the Young,* p. 346.

89. Staughton Lynd, "Prospects for the New Left," *Liberation* 15 (January 1971): 17.

90. Calvert and Neiman, *Disrupted History,* p. 130.

91. James P. O'Brien, "The New Left's Early Years," *Radical America* 2 (May–June 1968): 25.

92. Richie Rothstein, "E.R.A.P. and How It Grew," in *SDS Goes to Work Again* (Ann Arbor: Radical Education Project, n.d.), p. 34. "America and the New Era" was written in 1963 and reprinted in *New Left Notes* 1 (December 9, 1966): 10, 12; (December 16, 1966): 3–6, 8. It provides a critique of "managerial politics" and interacts with the politics of the New Frontier; its general tone is decidedly reformist.

93. Rothstein, "E.R.A.P. and How It Grew," in *SDS Goes to Work Again,* p. 34.

94. Ibid., p. 36.

95. Richard Flacks, "Organizing the Unemployed: the Chicago Project," in *The New Student Left,* ed. Cohen and Hale, pp. 132–147.

96. Wittman and Hayden, "An Interracial Movement of the Poor?", in *The New Student Left,* ed. Cohen and Hale, pp. 190, 203.

97. Todd Gitlin, "The Battlefields and the War," in *The New Student Left,* ed. Cohen and Hale, p. 126.

98. Ibid., p. 131.

99. Rennie Davis, "The War on Poverty: Notes on Insurgent Response," in *The New Student Left,* ed. Cohen and Hale, p. 158.

100. Kirkpatrick Sale, *SDS* (New York: Random House, 1973), p. 100.

101. Quoted in Carol Stevens, "SDS Convention Charts Projects for the Year," *National Guardian* 18 (January 15, 1966): 5.

2: The Middle Phase

1. See, e.g., the title of the article by Carl Davidson, "Where Are We Heading? The New Left in Transition, 1967–68," *Guardian,* March 23, 1968, p. 16.

2. Carl Oglesby, "Notes on a Decade Ready for the Dustbin," *Liberation* 14 (August–September 1969): 7. In this article 1968 is given as the date when SDS officially embraced Marxism–Leninism.

3. Robert Wolfe, "Beyond Protest," *Studies on the Left* 7 (January–February 1967): 10.

4. Tom Good, "Ideology and SDS," *New Left Notes* 1 (August 5, 1966): 5.

5. Steve Weissman, "Beyond the Moral Imperative," *Liberation* 11 (August 1966): 46.

6. Staughton Lynd, "Prospects for the New Left," *Liberation* 15 (January 1971): 16.

7. Staughton Lynd, "The Movement: A New Beginning," *Liberation* 14 (May 1969): 19.

8. Richard Flacks, "The New Left and American Politics after Ten Years," *Journal of Social Issues* 27 (1971): 30.

9. Michael Miles, *The Radical Probe: The Logic of Student Rebellion* (New York: Atheneum, 1971), p. 264.

10. Flacks, "New Left and American Politics," *Journal of Social Issues*, pp. 30–31.

11. Richard Flacks, *Youth and Social Change* (Chicago: Markham Publishing Company, 1971), p. 84.

12. Lee Baxandall, ed., *Radical Perspectives in the Arts* (Baltimore: Penguin Books, 1972), p. 33.

13. Flacks, "New Left and American Politics," *Journal of Social Issues*, p. 30.

14. Paul Booth and Lee Webb, "The Anti-War Movement: From Protest to Radical Politics," *Our Generation* 3, 4 (May 1966): 88.

15. Paul Jacobs and Saul Landau, *The New Radicals: A Report with Documents* (New York: Vintage Books, 1966), p. 81.

16. Eugene Genovese, "Genovese Looks at American Left—New and Old," *National Guardian* 18 (February 19, 1966): 6–7.

17. "Radical Education Project" (Ann Arbor: Radical Education Project, 1966), p. 18.

18. Ibid., p. 5.

19. "Education Proposal: Calls for Radical Reconstruction," *New Left Notes* 1 (April 22, 1966): 5.

20. "Radical Education Project," p. 2.

21. Ibid., p. 4.

22. Todd Gitlin, "The Politics and Vision of the New Left" (San Francisco: Clergy and Laymen Radical Education Project, n.d.), p. 4.

23. Jack A. Smith, "SDS Aim: To Build a Revolutionary Consciousness," *National Guardian* 19 (April 15, 1967): 5.

24. Peter Berger, quoted in Seymour Martin Lipset and Gerald M. Schaflander, *Passion and Politics: Student Activism in America* (Boston: Little, Brown and Company, 1971), p. 119.

25. Paul Potter and Hal Benenson, "A Critique of Radical Perspectives on the Campus," *New Left Notes* 2 (May 29, 1967): 3.

26. Eric Mann, "Appraisal and Perspectives," *New Left Notes* 3 (March 18, 1968): 6.

27. Paul Goodman, "The Black Flag of Anarchism," in *Anarchism*, ed. Robert Hoffman (New York: Atherton Press, 1970), p. 153.

28. Ronald Aronson, "The Movement and Its Critics," *Studies on the Left* 6 (January–February 1966): 4.

29. Loren Baritz, ed., *The American Left: Radical Political Thought in the*

Twentieth Century (New York: Basic Books, 1971), p. 387.

30. Martin J. Sklar and James Weinstein, "Socialism and the New Left," *Studies on the Left* 6 (March–April 1966): 68, 70. See also Steve Baum and Bernard Faber: "At this point [1966], we in SDS must begin to write about and talk about socialist theory, so that we will be prepared to play a major role in developments, creating larger numbers of socialists, and developing socialist consciousness in all institutions in which we organize." "From Protest to Politics," *New Left Notes* 1 (September 2, 1966): 12.

31. George Graham, "Unite the International Proletariat," *Something Else!* 2 (November–December 1969): 7.

32. Staughton Lynd, "Factionalism the New Left Can't Afford," *Liberation* 14 (March–April 1969): 6.

33. Miles, *The Radical Probe*, p. 262.

34. Sidney Lens, "The Road to Power and Beyond," *Liberation* 13 (November 1968): 9.

35. Miles, *The Radical Probe*, p. 266.

36. William Pfaff, *Condemned to Freedom* (New York: Random House, 1971), p. 120.

37. Kenneth A. Megill, *The New Democratic Theory* (New York: Free Press, 1970), pp. 33–34.

38. Gabriel Kolko, "The Decline of American Radicalism in the Twentieth Century," *Studies on the Left* 6 (September–October 1966): 10–11.

39. Julius Lester, "Lester on the Movement," *Guardian*, April 27, 1968, p. 4.

40. Richard Flacks, "Revolt of the Young Intelligentsia: Revolutionary Class-Consciousness in Post-Scarcity America," in *The New American Revolution*, ed. Roderick Aya and Norman Miller (New York: Free Press, 1971), pp. 231, 252.

41. David Horowitz, "Hand-Me-Down Marxism in the New Left," in *Weatherman*, ed. Harold Jacobs (Berkeley: Ramparts Press, 1970), p. 99.

42. Howard Zinn, "Marxism and the New Left," in *The New Left: A Collection of Essays*, ed. Priscilla Long (Boston: Porter Sargent, 1969), p. 56.

43. Ibid., pp. 62, 66.

44. Ibid., p. 63.

45. Flacks, "New Left and American Politics," *Journal of Social Issues*, p. 31.

46. Tom Hayden, "The Ability to Face Whatever Comes," in *Thoughts of the Young Radicals* (New York: New Republic, 1966), p. 40.

47. Herbert Marcuse, *Counterrevolution and Revolt* (Boston: Beacon Press, 1972), pp. 5–6. See also Zinn: "Certainly, in the United States, the traditional idea that the agent of social change will be the proletariat needs re-examination, when the best-organized of the workers are bribed into silence with suburban houses and automobiles, and drugged into compliance with mass entertainment." "Marxism and the New Left," in *The New Left: A Collection of Essays*, ed. Long, p. 66.

48. Zinn, "Marxism and the New Left," in *The New Left: A Collection of*

Essays, ed. Long, p. 66. See also Nick Egleson, 1967 SDS president: *"For the immediate future* we might specify the poor, and almost as a separate group the poor Negro population, unorganized poor labor, and students (chiefly as catalysts) as the chief agents of change in the immediate future." "National President's Report," *New Left Notes* 2 (January 13, 1967): 4.

49. Lee Baxandall, "Issues and Constituencies of the New Left," *Liberation* 11 (April 1966): 21.

50. C. Wright Mills, "On the New Left," *Studies on the Left* 1 (1961): 70–72. See also John and Margaret Rowntree: "The essential exploited class for the perpetuation of the existing economic system is now the young. . . . As happens when a class is exploited, young people are beginning to become aware of their exploitation. Many have taken the essential first step to consciousness, the rejection of the present system and are available to develop a consciousness of themselves as a class." "Youth as a Social Class," in *The New Left: A Documentary History,* ed. Massimo Teodori (Indianapolis: Bobbs–Merrill, 1969), p. 418.

51. Bob Gottlieb, Gerry Tenney, and Dave Gilbert, "Praxis and the New Left," *New Left Notes* 2 (February 13, 1967): 5–6, 9–10.

52. Greg Calvert, "In White America: Radical Consciousness and Social Change," *Guardian* 19 (March 25, 1967): 4.

53. See Greg Calvert and Carol Neiman, "Socialist Consciousness and the New Left," *Guardian,* August 24, 1968, p. 13.

54. Flacks, "New Left and American Politics," *Journal of Social Issues,* p. 31.

55. Flacks, *Youth and Social Change,* p. 116.

56. Flacks, "Revolt of the Young Intelligentsia," *The New American Revolution,* p. 225.

57. See, e.g., Marcuse, *Counterrevolution and Revolt,* p. 46.

58. Stanley Aronowitz, "SDSer's Views Criticized," *National Guardian* 20 (November 25, 1967): 5.

59. Bob Pardun, "On the Cadre in Mass Organization," *New Left Notes* 3 (June 10, 1968): 7.

60. Miles, *The Radical Probe,* p. 13.

61. See, e.g., Megill, *The New Democratic Theory,* p. 40.

62. Carl Davidson, "Beyond the Campus: Resistance Federations," *Guardian,* April 6, 1968, p. 16.

63. Noam Chomsky, "Some Tasks for the Left," *Liberation* 14 (August–September 1969): 43.

64. Paul Breines, "From Guru to Spectre: Marcuse and the Implosion of the Movement," in *Critical Interruptions: New Left Perspectives on Herbert Marcuse,* ed. Paul Breines (New York: Herder and Herder, 1970), pp. 11–12.

65. Editors of *Studies on the Left,* "Up from Irrelevance," *Studies on the Left* 5 (Spring 1965): 3.

66. Greg Calvert, "Participatory Democracy, Collective Leadership and Political Responsibility," *New Left Notes* 2 (December 18, 1967): 1.

67. Richard Flacks, "Some Roles for Radicals in America," *Liberation* 12 (May–June 1967): 45.

68. Todd Gitlin, "Theses for the Radical Movement," *Liberation* 12 (May–June 1967): 34–35.

69. Tom Hayden, "Two, Three, Many Columbias," in *The University Crisis Reader*, ed. Immanuel Wallerstein and Paul Starr, vol. 2 (New York: Random House, 1971), p. 164.

70. Calvert, "Participatory Democracy," *New Left Notes*, p. 7.

71. Staughton Lynd, "A Good Society," *Guardian*, February 17, 1968, p. 2.

72. Richard Rothstein, "Representative Democracy in SDS," *Liberation* 16 (February 1972): 12–13. See also Staughton Lynd, in whose view the weakness of participatory democracy was that it worked only in small groups; in large meetings it led to elitism. "After the inconclusive discussion, a few people went back to the office and decided." "Prospects for the New Left," *Liberation*, p. 22.

73. Marvin Garson, "The Movement: It's Theory Time," in *The New Left: A Documentary History*, ed. Teodori, p. 380.

74. Lynd, "Prospects for the New Left," *Liberation*, p. 28.

75. Aronson, "The Movement and Its Critics," *Studies on the Left*, p. 16. See Nathan Glazer for a particularly egregious example of manipulation: "By the time the movement got to Harvard, the issue hardly mattered, the revolutionizing of potential cadres was everything. So for example, on the Harvard campus when students urged that the issue of ROTC be determined by majority vote of the students, this was denounced by the radicals as 'counterrevolutionary' in just those terms. Following the antiparliamentary position in Marxism (which all the major leaders of the movement fully avow), they naturally consider elections purely tactical maneuvers; if they advance the revolution, you are for them, and if they do not you are against them." *Remembering the Answers: Essays on the American Student Revolt* (New York: Basic Books, 1970), pp. 263–264.

76. Herbert Marcuse, "On the New Left," in *The New Left: A Documentary History*, ed. Teodori, p. 469. See also Steve Halliwell, "Personal Liberation and Social Change," a title accurately reflecting his concern to perpetuate the original SDS desire to fuse the personal and the political. *New Left Notes* 2 (September 4, 1967): 1.

77. Quoted in Jack A. Smith, "Report on SDS: Students Now Stressing 'Resistance,'" *National Guardian* 19 (April 8, 1967): 8. See also Carl Davidson, who continued SDS's vision that the emphasis on the personal was a primary item separating the New Left from the Old: "Only by initially focusing on subjectivity, by talking with people about their lives, their deepest longings and aspirations, can individuals come to discover that their supposedly personal problems and frustrations are widely held. Only out of that discovery of their common humanity can the decision be shaped that men must unite in the struggle to destroy their common oppression. Adherence to that principle, at all costs, is the essential difference between the old left and the new." "Where Are We Heading?", *Guardian*, p. 16.

78. Les Coleman, "False Factionalism and Ideological Clarity," *New Left Notes* 3 (December 18, 1968): 3.

79. Mike Klonsky, "Toward a Revolutionary Youth Movement," *New Left Notes* 3 (December 23, 1968): 3.

80. Lens, "The Road to Power," *Liberation,* p. 14. See also Megill, who saw the Movement "going beyond disruption" and "organizing as a force which can seize power." He added, "For now, we can sum up: A new era of history has begun, and a new movement to radically change the world is a reality. The new democratic theory is an articulation of this force. The theory is only beginning to be worked out, but it is already a reality." *The New Democratic Theory,* pp. 151, 163–164.

81. Chomsky, "Some Tasks for the Left," *Liberation,* p. 40.

82. Lynd, "Prospects for the New Left," *Liberation,* p. 27.

83. Oglesby, "Notes on a Decade," *Liberation,* p. 19.

84. Ibid., p. 13.

3: The Late Phase

1. Greg Calvert, "Participatory Democracy, Collective Leadership and Political Responsibility," *New Left Notes* 2 (December 18, 1967): 7.

2. C. Clark Kissinger, "SLID to Resistance: Part I," *New Left Notes,* June 10, 1968, p. 18.

3. See Richard Flacks, "The New Left and American Politics after Ten Years," *Journal of Social Issues* 27 (1971): 21.

4. Greg Calvert and Carol Neiman, "Socialist Consciousness and the New Left," *Guardian,* August 24, 1968, p. 13.

5. Carl Davidson, "Where Are We Heading? Building a Base," *Guardian,* March 30, 1968, p. 16.

6. Quoted in Jack A. Smith, "Where the Revolution Is At," *Guardian,* June 22, 1968, p. 4. Smith adds: "SDS, which in the last 12 months has evolved from an anti-imperialist to an anticapitalist perspective, is on the precipice of embracing socialism or, in the terminology of a considerable number of SDS members, revolutionary communism."

7. David Horowitz, "Hand-Me-Down Marxism in the New Left," in *Weatherman,* ed. Harold Jacobs (Berkeley: Ramparts Press, 1970), p. 99. See also Richard Rothstein: "The New Left today is beset with the kind of factionalism that the 1930's Left produced. Much of the openness and experimentalism that the New Left attempted in the early 1960's is now hidden." "Evolution of the ERAP Organizers," *The New Left: A Collection of Essays,* ed. Priscilla Long (Boston: Porter Sargent, 1969), p. 273.

8. Greg Calvert and Carol Neiman, *A Disrupted History: The New Left and the New Capitalism* (New York: Random House, 1971), p. 27.

9. Les Coleman, "False Factionalism and Ideological Clarity," *New Left*

Notes 3 (December 18, 1968): 3.

10. Ibid.

11. Michael Miles, *The Radical Probe: The Logic of Student Rebellion* (New York: Atheneum, 1971), p. 264.

12. Staughton Lynd, "Factionalism the New Left Can't Afford," *Liberation* 14 (March–April 1969): 5–6.

13. For a discussion of the controversy over PLP in SDS, see the following: "PLP: A Critique" (Detroit: Radical Education Project, 1969); *Debate Within SDS: RYM II vs. Weatherman* (Detroit: Radical Education Project, 1969); and Kirkpatrick Sale, *SDS* (New York: Random House, 1973).

14. Jim Mellen, "More on Youth Movement," in *Debate Within SDS*, p. 4.

15. Les Coleman, "Notes on Class Analysis: Some Implications for a Revolutionary Youth Movement," in *Debate Within SDS*, p. 6.

16. Carl Oglesby, "1969," in *Weatherman*, ed. Jacobs, p. 129.

17. Karin Ashley *et al.*, "You Don't Need a Weatherman to Know Which Way the Wind Blows," in *Debate Within SDS*, pp. 23, 27–29.

18. Ibid., p. 23.

19. Ibid., p. 30.

20. Mike Klonsky *et al.*, "Revolutionary Youth Movement II," in *Debate Within SDS*, p. 15.

21. Noel Ignatin, "Without a Science of Navigation We Cannot Sail in Stormy Seas," in *Debate Within SDS*, pp. 41, 43, 36.

22. *Debate Within SDS*, p. iii.

23. Alan Haber, "Nonexclusionism: The New Left and the Democratic Left," in *The New Left: A Documentary History*, ed. Massimo Teodori (Indianapolis: Bobbs–Merrill, 1969), pp. 218–228.

24. Carl Oglesby, "Notes on a Decade Ready for the Dustbin," *Liberation* 14 (August–September 1969): 6.

25. Ibid., p. 15.

26. Tom Hayden, *Trial* (New York: Holt, Rinehart and Winston, 1970), p. 9.

27. Ibid., p. 93.

28. Ibid., p. 112.

29. Ibid., p. 167.

30. Flacks, "New Left and American Politics," *Journal of Social Issues*, p. 21. Cf. Calvert and Neiman: "We have not achieved one single radical reform which transferred power from the corporate elite to the people. . . . We who tried most desperately to turn America-the-Obscene into America-the-Beautiful failed miserably" (*Disrupted History*, p. x); Todd Gitlin, after recounting the failures of the Movement, bemoaned: "None of the reforms that we have embodied in ourselves . . . have lasted" ("The Politics and Vision of the New Left" [San Francisco: Clergy and Laymen Radical Education Project, n.d.], pp. 4–5); Paul Buhle: "A century since the first wide-scale attempts at working-class self-organization and

the introduction of the Marxian critique in the United States, there is today no radical social movement of any importance" ("Marxism in the U. S.: 39 Propositions," *Radical America* 5 [November–December 1971]: 63).

31. Rothstein, "Evolution of the ERAP Organizers," *The New Left: A Collection of Essays,* ed. Long, p. 272.

32. Todd Gitlin, "Toward a New New Left," *Partisan Review* 39 (Summer 1972): 454–455. Cf. Richard Flacks, who lamented that the New Left had "transformed itself from a non-ideological movement for social criticism, finally into a movement spearheaded by revolutionaries tending to look more and more to classical revolutionary doctrine for guiding principles for their own action." He contended that the "tendency to return to the dogmatisms of the old left . . . may have enhanced the revolutionary purity of adherents but seems incapable of encompassing the radical aspirations that have been the motivating force of the youth movement and the intelligentsia" ("Revolt of the Young Intelligensia: Revolutionary Class-Consciousness in Post-Scarcity America," in *The New American Revolution,* ed. Roderick Aya and Norman Miller [New York: Free Press, 1971], p. 251); Oglesby also considered SDS's embrace of Marxism a liability, since, while it temporarily solved some intellectual problems, it did not do so as an outgrowth of experience, which the early SDS had always insisted be the touchstone for any development of theory. In his judgment " . . . the attempt to reduce the New Left's inchoate vision to the Old Left's perfected remembrance has produced a layer of bewilderment and demoralization which no cop with his club or senator with his committee could ever have induced" ("Notes on a Decade," *Liberation,* p. 15); Calvert and Neiman, who had been among the initiators of the revolutionary rhetoric, grieved: "But both [of us] have seen the disintegration of the organization (SDS) which we helped to build and the repression of our former friends and comrades. . . . SDS . . . was thwarted and stifled by a dogmatic rigidity which killed debate before it had ever gotten off the ground" (*Disrupted History,* pp. ix–x); Paul Breines considered the New Left's "re-Marxifying" of itself to have been regressive and repressive, "a suppression and flight from its own most basic impulses and implications" ("From Guru to Spectre: Marcuse and the Implosion of the Movement," in *Critical Interruptions: New Left Perspectives on Herbert Marcuse,* ed. Paul Breines [New York: Herder and Herder, 1970], pp. 13–14).

33. Calvert and Neiman, *Disrupted History,* pp. 141–142.

34. Gitlin, "Politics and Vision," pp. 1–3.

35. See Jerry Avorn *et al., Up Against the Ivy Wall: A History of the Columbia Crisis* (New York: Atheneum, 1969), pp. 63, 182–183. The black role in the uprising at Columbia University was a good example of this process. While black militants did not denounce white radicals, they chose to occupy a building by themselves and to cut to a minimum their communications with whites occupying other buildings.

36. Roberta Salper, "Introduction," in *Female Liberation: History and Current Politics,* ed. Roberta Salper (New York: Alfred A. Knopf, 1972), pp. 14–22.

37. Barbara Burris et al., "Fourth World Manifesto," in Female Liberation, ed. Salper, p. 241.

38. Naomi Jaffe and Bernardine Dohrn, "The Look Is You," New Left Notes 3 (March 18, 1968): 5.

39. Quoted in Roberta Salper, "The Development of the American Women's Liberation Movement, 1967–71," in Female Liberation, ed. Salper, p. 173.

40. Kathy McAfee and Myrna Wood, "Bread and Roses," in Female Liberation, ed. Salper, p. 164.

41. See Buhle, "Marxism in the U. S.," Radical America, p. 80.

42. Shulamith Firestone, The Dialectic of Sex: The Case for Feminist Revolution (New York: Bantam Books, 1970), p. 38.

43. Melanie Kaye, in Female Studies VI: Closer to the Ground: Women's Classes, Criticisms, Programs–1972, ed. Nancy Hoffman, Cynthia Secor, and Adrian Tinsley (Old Westbury, N. Y.: Feminist Press, 1972), p. 233.

44. Burris et al., "Fourth World Manifesto," in Female Liberation, ed. Salper, p. 236.

45. Lillian S. Robinson, "Who's Afraid of a Room of One's Own?", in The Politics of Literature: Dissenting Essays on the Teaching of English, ed. Louis Kampf and Paul Lauter (New York: Pantheon Books, 1970), p. 363. See also Salper for the usual radical litany which blamed oppression on forces outside the oppressed: "the problem is not inside of us, . . . it is not our fault." In Female Liberation, ed. Salper, p. 200. Jaffe and Dohrn wrote that the fault is society's— the realization of which "is an exhilarating and expressive breakthrough." "The Look Is You," New Left Notes, p. 5.

46. Quoted in Salper, "Development of the American Women's Liberation Movement," in Female Liberation, ed. Salper, p. 174.

47. McAfee and Wood, "Bread and Roses," in Female Liberation, ed. Salper, p. 165.

48. See, e.g., McAfee and Wood, "Bread and Roses," in Female Liberation, ed. Salper, pp. 154–155; Salper, "Development of the American Women's Liberation Movement," in Female Liberation, ed. Salper, p. 176.

49. McAfee and Wood, "Bread and Roses," in Female Liberation, ed. Salper, p. 154.

50. Salper, "Development of the American Women's Liberation Movement," in Female Liberation, ed. Salper, p. 184. See also Marlene Dixon, who noted as a symptom of its subjectiveness that the women's movement spoke more about oppression than about exploitation. This analysis fitted the early SDS. She called for an emphasis on fighting exploitation, because "Fighting against exploitation is revolutionary." "Why Women's Liberation–2?", in Female Liberation, ed. Salper, pp. 196–197.

51. Jane Alpert, "Mother Right: A New Feminist Theory," Ms. 2 (August 1973): 53.

52. Ibid.

53. Ibid., p. 55.

54. Quoted in Kirkpatrick Sale, *SDS*, p. 187. Gitlin's comment on Potter continued: "Pure SDS. . . . he doesn't get it out of books—he has a remarkable ability to think for himself and not pay attention to all the rhetorical shit whether academic or political."

55. Paul Potter, *A Name for Ourselves* (Boston: Little, Brown and Company, 1971), pp. 6–7.

56. Ibid., pp. 4–5.

57. Ibid., p. 132.

58. Ibid.

59. Ibid., pp. 149–150.

60. Ibid., p. 42.

61. Ibid., pp. 44–45.

62. Ibid., p. 46.

63. Ibid., p. 52.

64. Ibid., pp. 56–57.

65. Ibid., p. 63.

66. Ibid., p. 66.

67. Ibid., pp. 174–175.

68. Ibid., p. 101.

69. Ibid., p. 120.

70. Ibid., p. 219.

71. Ibid., pp. 219–220.

72. Calvert and Neiman, *Disrupted History*, p. xii.

73. Ronald Aronson, "The Movement and Its Critics," *Studies on the Left* 6 (January–February 1966): 11.

74. Ronald Aronson, "Dear Herbert," *Radical America* 4 (April 1970): 15.

75. Ibid., p. 17.

76. Ibid., pp. 14–15.

77. Herbert Marcuse, *Counterrevolution and Revolt* (Boston: Beacon Press, 1972), p. 126.

78. Ibid., p. 48.

79. Ibid., pp. 130–131.

80. Ibid., pp. 133–134.

81. "Why?—An Analysis," *New American Movement* 1 (n.d.): 4.

82. "The New American Movement: A Way to Overcome the Mistakes of the Past," *Socialist Revolution* 2 (January–February 1971): 39.

83. "Why?—An Analysis," *New American Movement*, p. 4.

84. Ibid.

85. "New American Movement," *Socialist Revolution*, p. 37; Michael Lerner,

"Why This Is the Right Time," *New American Movement* 1 (November–December 1971): 3.

86. Michael Seliger, "Editorial: The New American Movement," *Liberation* 16 (January 1972): 4.

87. "New American Movement," *Socialist Revolution,* p. 39.

88. Michael Lerner, "May Day: Anatomy of the Movement," *Ramparts* 10 (July 1971): 42.

89. "Our Vision," *New American Movement* 1 (November–December 1971): 2.

90. Richard Flacks, *Youth and Social Change* (Chicago: Markham Publishing Company, 1971), p. 93.

91. Flacks, "New Left and American Politics," *Journal of Social Issues,* p. 33.

92. Ibid., p. 22.

93. Ibid., pp. 32–33.

94. Flacks, *Youth and Social Change,* p. 101.

4:   Organizing of Academicians

1. Richard Flacks, "Revolt of the Young Intelligentsia: Revolutionary Class-Consciousness in Post-Scarcity America," in *The New American Revolution,* ed. Roderick Aya and Norman Miller (New York: Free Press, 1971), p. 242. Flacks observed, "the Port Huron Statement and other early New Left writing viewed the university as a kind of resource (or potential resource) for movements for change."

2. Thomas Hayden, "Student Social Action: From Liberation to Community," in *The New Student Left: An Anthology,* ed. Mitchell Cohen and Dennis Hale (Boston: Beacon Press, 1966), p. 284.

3. Carl Davidson, "Toward a Student Syndicalist Movement," *New Left Notes* 1 (September 9, 1966): 11.

4. Ibid.

5. Carl Davidson, "The New Radicals and the Multiversity," in *The New Left: A Documentary History,* ed. Massimo Teodori (Indianapolis: Bobbs–Merrill Company, 1969), p. 324.

6. *The Port Huron Statement* (New York: Students for a Democratic Society, 1964), p. 10.

7. Paul Jacobs and Saul Landau, *The New Radicals: A Report with Documents* (New York: Vintage Books, 1966), p. 59.

8. Paul Potter, "The New Radical Encounters the University" (Students for a Democratic Society, n.d.), p. 2.

9. Paul Potter, "The Intellectual as an Agent of Social Change" (Students for a Democratic Society, 1963), p. 1.

10. Hayden, "Student Social Action," in *The New Student Left,* ed. Cohen and Hale, p. 282.

11. Ibid., p. 281.

12. Paul Booth, "A Basis for University Reform" (Students for a Democratic Society, 1964), p. 3.

13. "Radical Education Project" (Ann Arbor: Radical Education Project, 1966), p. 16.

14. Ibid.

15. Ibid.

16. Richard Flacks, *Youth and Social Change* (Chicago: Markham Publishing Company, 1971), p. 82.

17. Davidson, "New Radicals and the Multiversity," in *The New Left: A Documentary History*, ed. Teodori, p. 324.

18. Ibid.

19. Ibid.

20. Flacks, *Youth and Social Change.* p. 88.

21. Quoted in Sidney Hook, "The Prospects of the Academy," in *The Radical Left: The Abuse of Discontent*, ed. William P. Gerberding and Duane E. Smith (Boston: Houghton Mifflin Company, 1970), p. 206.

22. Bob Davis, "Editorial," *This Magazine is About Schools* 2 (Autumn 1968): 1.

23. Ibid., p. 2.

24. Ted Steege, "Introduction," *Radicals in Professions: Selected Papers* (Ann Arbor: Radical Education Project, 1967), p. 4.

25. Rudi Dutschke's term, cited in Herbert Marcuse, *Counterrevolution and Revolt* (Boston: Beacon Press, 1972), p. 55.

26. Announcement in *Radical America* 4 (April 1970): 1.

27. Brochure, Socialist Scholars Conference (April 8, 1970). Announcement of forthcoming annual meeting of SSC.

28. *Radical America* 4 (April 1970): 1.

29. Kathy Ellis, "A Body of Socialist Scholarship," *NUC Newsletter* 3 (October 1, 1969): 11.

30. *NUC Newsletter* 3 (August 15, 1969): 1.

31. Ibid. (October 20, 1969), p. 1.

32. "The Student Rebellion" (Chicago: New University Conference, February 1969), p. 2.

33. Tom Hecht, "Where From Here?", *NUC Newsletter* 5 (January 1972): 10.

34. Cited in almost all NUC material, including the issues of the *Newsletter*.

35. Chuck Kleinhans, "1 + 1 Is More Than 2: A Radical Proposal for Financing NUC," *NUC Newsletter* 4 (May 15, 1971): 2.

36. Robert Baker, "Some Reflections," *NUC Newsletter* 3 (August 15, 1969): 5.

37. Ibid., pp. 5–6.

38. Everett C. Frost, "Can Anyone Here Dump the Dean at FSC? or What Am

I Doing in Baltimore When There Are Barricades Back Home?", *NUC Newsletter* 3 (January 20, 1960): 2.

39. Mel Rothenberg, "In Defense of Ideology," *NUC Newsletter* 3 (September 15, 1969): 5.

40. Moe Levitt, "Thoughts on NUC," *NUC Newsletter* 5 (January 1972): 3.

41. "Let's Get Together: A Report from the Commission on Campus Organization," *NUC Newsletter* 1 (May 24, 1968): 3.

42. *NUC Newsletter* 5 (November 1971): 14.

43. "Whence Cometh the Axe? An Editorial," *NUC Newsletter* 2 (January 1969): 21.

44. Bob Ross, "Perspectives for the NUC," *NUC Newsletter* 1 (November 1968): 1, 3.

45. Howard J. Ehrlich, "The Sense of Community," *NUC Newsletter* 3 (August 15, 1969): 5–6.

46. Tom Hecht and Barbara Kessel: "NUC must not act as house source for the development of theory and research into the political economy while remaining relatively safe behind academic privilege. We are not scholars who happen to be radicals, but rather political co-belligerents in a broad struggle who happen to work at universities and colleges." "Spring Program," *NUC Newsletter* 3 (April 1, 1970): 1–3.

47. Michele Russell, "A Future Direction for NUC?", *NUC Newsletter* 3 (April 1, 1970): 7.

48. John McDermott, "NUC as Cadre," *NUC Newsletter* 3 (January 20, 1970): 7.

49. Ibid., p. 8.

50. See Will Watson, "Transforming the University," *NUC Newsletter* 3 (January 20, 1970): 10; also Roberta Salper, "The Long March," *NUC Newsletter* 4 (September 15, 1970): 5–6.

51. Ross, "Perspectives for the NUC," *NUC Newsletter*, p. 8.

52. McDermott, "NUC as Cadre," *NUC Newsletter*, p. 8.

53. Mel Rothenberg, "SDS' Political Problems," *NUC Newsletter* 4 (May 15, 1971): 21.

54. Rosario Levins, "Letter of Resignation," *NUC Newsletter* 4 (January 21, 1971): 9.

55. *NUC Newsletter* 5 (November 1971): 1.

56. Elizabeth Diggs, *NUC Newsletter* 3 (September 15, 1969): 1–2.

57. Russell, "A Future Direction for NUC?", *NUC Newsletter*, p. 8.

58. Referred to in Rosario Levins, "Letter of Resignation," *NUC Newsletter*, p. 9.

59. "Understanding Revolutionary Violence," *NUC Newsletter* 4 (October 1, 1970): 13.

60. The main volume representing radicals in the literary profession was dedi-

cated to George Jackson, Jonathan's brother: Louis Kampf and Paul Lauter, eds., *The Politics of Literature: Dissenting Essays on the Teaching of English* (New York: Pantheon Books, 1970).

61. "Crisis Paper: Violence, Non-Violence, and Change" (Chicago: New University Conference, May 15, 1970), p. 4.

62. Ibid., p. 3.

63. Staughton Lynd, *NUC Newsletter* 3 (December 15, 1969): 9.

64. See, e.g., Wells Keddie, "Socialist Academics and Unions," *NUC Newsletter* 5, 7 (n.d.): 6–12.

65. Tom Hecht, "An Overview for the Coming Months," *NUC Newsletter* 5 (November 1971): 5.

66. Hecht, "Where From Here?", *NUC Newsletter*, pp. 12–13.

67. "New University Conference Folds," *Guardian*, July 5, 1972, p. 3.

68. See, e.g., *NUC Newsletter* 5 (December 20, 1970): 2.

69. Barbara Andrews, "Problems of NUC" (Chicago: New University Conference, n.d.), p. 2.

70. "Anti-Imperialist Work and NUC," *NUC Newsletter* 5 (December 1971): 12.

71. Len Radinsky, "How Men Discuss Sexism," *NUC Newsletter* 4 (July 4, 1971): 15.

72. Ruth Mahaney, "Women's Caucus," *NUC Newsletter* 4 (July 4, 1971): 15.

73. Kathy Ellis, Lucy Gadlin, and Terry Radinsky, "Why a Women's Caucus," *NUC Newsletter* 3 (December 1, 1969): 1.

74. Andrews, "Problems of NUC," p. 1.

75. Hecht, "An Overview for the Coming Months," *NUC Newsletter*, p. 2.

76. Andrews, "Problems of NUC," p. 2.

77. Ibid.

78. Ibid., p. 1.

79. Quoted in "New University Conference Folds," *Guardian*, p. 3.

5: Academic Radical Self-Definition

1. Carol Sheehan, open letter to Chandler Davis, in *On Radicals and Research* (Chicago: New University Conference, 1970), pp. 16–17.

2. Ellen Cantarow, "Why Teach Literature? An Account of How I Came to Ask That Question," in *The Politics of Literature: Dissenting Essays on the Teaching of English*, ed. Louis Kampf and Paul Lauter (New York: Pantheon Books, 1970), p. 94.

3. Barbara Haber and Al Haber, "Getting By with a Little Help from Our Friends," in *Radicals in Professions: Selected Papers* (Ann Arbor: Radical Education Project, 1967), p. 50.

4. Ibid., pp. 50–51.

5. Quoted in Hamish Sinclair, "Diggers Jog SDS 'Grads,' " *National Guardian* 19 (July 1, 1967): 4.

6. Haber and Haber, "Getting By with a Little Help," *Radicals in Professions,* p. 44.

7. Ibid., p. 49.

8. Ibid.

9. Bob Gottlieb and Marge Piercy, "Movement for Democratic Society," in *The New Left: A Documentary History,* ed. Massimo Teodori (Indianapolis: Bobbs–Merrill Company, 1969), p. 409.

10. Haber and Haber, "Getting By with a Little Help," *Radicals in Professions,* p. 60.

11. Ibid., pp. 60–61.

12. Ibid., p. 60.

13. Mike Goldfield, "A Report on the Conference," in *Radicals in Professions,* p. 8.

14. Carl Davidson, "New Radicals and the Multiversity," in *The New Left: A Documentary History,* ed. Teodori, p. 326.

15. Ted Steege, "Introduction," in *Radicals in Professions,* p. 5.

16. Haber and Haber, "Getting By with a Little Help," *Radicals in Professions,* pp. 56–57.

17. Ibid., p. 58.

18. Ibid.

19. Ibid., p. 51.

20. Ibid., p. 59.

21. Tom Hecht, "An Overview for the Coming Months," *NUC Newsletter* 5 (November 1971): 4.

22. Steege, "Introduction," in *Radicals in Professions,* p. 7.

23. Robert Meredith, "Subverting Culture," *Radical Teacher,* no. 2 (December 30, 1969): 5.

24. "New University Conference Organized," *NUC Newsletter* 1 (May 24, 1968): 1.

25. A representative statement showing an attempted coalescence of the three views as well as implicit favoritism toward Lynd's view is found in "The Radical Teacher at Work: A Report from the Commission on Education and the University II," *NUC Newsletter* 1 (May 24, 1968): 7.

26. Jesse Lemisch, "What's Your Evidence? Radical Scholarship and Scientific Method and Anti-Authoritarianism, Not 'Relevance,' " in *On Radicals and Research,* p. 12.

27. Ibid., pp. 9–10.

28. Ibid., p. 11.

29. Jesse Lemisch, "Who Will Write a Left History of Art While We Are All Putting Our Balls on the Line?", *NUC Newsletter* 1 (May 24, 1968): 6.

30. "Radical Teacher at Work," *NUC Newsletter*, p. 7.

31. Noam Chomsky, "Knowledge and Power: Intellectuals and the Welfare/Warfare State," in *The New Left: A Collection of Essays*, ed. Priscilla Long (Boston: Porter Sargent, 1969), pp. 175–176.

32. Ibid., p. 177.

33. Ibid., p. 193.

34. Chandler Davis, "Sticking Up for Theory," in *On Radicals and Research*, p. 15.

35. Ibid., p. 14.

36. Ibid., p. 13.

37. Ibid., p. 15.

38. Ibid., p. 16.

39. Richard Levins, open letter to Chandler Davis, in *On Radicals and Research*, p. 19.

40. Richard Flacks, *Youth and Social Change* (Chicago: Markham Publishing Company, 1971), pp. 3–4.

41. Ibid., p. 5.

42. Robert Paul Wolff, *The Ideal of the University* (Boston: Beacon Press, 1969), p. 129.

43. Ibid.

44. Staughton Lynd, "Academic Freedom and the First Amendment," *Radical Teacher*, no. 1 (April–May 1969): 25.

45. Ibid., pp. 25–26.

46. Theodore Roszak, "On Academic Delinquency," in *The Dissenting Academy*, ed. Theodore Roszak (New York: Pantheon Books, 1967), p. 37.

47. Ibid., pp. 32–33.

48. Lynd, "Academic Freedom and the First Amendment," *Radical Teacher*, p. 26.

49. Staughton Lynd, "The Responsibility of Radical Intellectuals," *NUC Newsletter* 1 (May 24, 1968): 5–6.

50. Herbert Marcuse, *Counterrevolution and Revolt* (Boston: Beacon Press, 1972), p. 55.

51. Louis Kampf, "The Scandal of Literary Scholarship," in *The Dissenting Academy*, ed. Roszak, p. 51.

52. See, e.g., Martin Nicolaus: "It's possible for us within the university to write book critiques—papers against Lipset and Hoffer, for example; this is excellent and really must be done. But it's still not entirely possible for very many of us to look at the world through the eyes of people who aren't even in the university. This is one of the things that the university has done to us, for in

'inducating' us into the knowledge industry it has 'exducted' us out of the people." "The Iceberg Strategy: Universities and the Military-Industrial Complex" (Ann Arbor: Radical Education Project, 1967), p. 5.

53. Lynd, "Responsibility of Radical Intellectuals," *NUC Newsletter*, p. 5.

54. Noam Chomsky, *Problems of Knowledge and Freedom* (New York: Vintage Books, 1971), p. 78.

55. See, e.g., Paul Lauter and Florence Howe, who praised the free universities for providing an alternative to the established educational pattern, but complained of co-optation when some of the ideas originating in the free universities were picked up by established universities. This infiltration of approved ideas might have been seen as a victory of sorts; but they could not take that view because their outlook had to be adopted wholesale rather than piecemeal. *The Conspiracy of the Young* (New York: Meridian Books, 1971), p. 112.

56. Mike Zweig, "Stony Brook: A Model," *NUC Newsletter* 3 (January 20, 1970): 12.

57. Peter Irons, "Prison Notes," in *The New Left: A Collection of Essays*, ed. Long, p. 121.

58. See, e.g., Tom Hecht, "The Spring National Committee Meeting: An Overview" (Chicago: New University Conference, 1972), p. 1.

59. Barbara Andrews, "Women's Caucus NC Report," *NUC Newsletter* 5 (November 1971): 8.

60. "Analysis: Open Up the Schools—Political Perspective," *NUC Papers 3: Open Up the Schools* (Chicago: New University Conference, 1971), p. 8.

6:    Proposals for the University

1. Paul Lauter and Florence Howe, *The Conspiracy of the Young* (New York: Meridian Books, 1971), p. 248.

2. "The Student Rebellion" (Chicago: New University Conference, n.d.), p. 2.

3. Richard Flacks, "Radicals in the Universities," *NUC Newsletter* 1 (May 24, 1968): 4.

4. Martin Nicolaus, "The Iceberg Strategy: Universities and the Military-Industrial Complex" (Ann Arbor: Radical Education Project, 1967), p. 3.

5. John McDermott, "The Laying On of Culture," *Nation* 208 (March 10, 1969): 297.

6. Ibid., p. 298.

7. Ibid.

8. Ibid., p. 297.

9. Ibid.

10. "Analysis: Open Up the Schools—Political Perspective," *NUC Papers 3: Open Up the Schools* (Chicago: New University Conference, 1971), p. 5.

11. Lauter and Howe, *The Conspiracy of the Young*, p. 217.

12. Ibid., p. 121.

13. Ibid., pp. 214–215.

14. Ibid., pp. 220–221.

15. Ibid., p. 210.

16. Ibid.

17. Ibid., pp. 223–224.

18. William Labov, "The Logic of Nonstandard English," in *The Politics of Literature: Dissenting Essays on the Teaching of English*, ed. Louis Kampf and Paul Lauter (New York: Pantheon Books, 1970), p. 228.

19. Wayne O'Neil, "The Politics of Bidialectalism," in *The Politics of Literature*, ed. Kampf and Lauter, p. 245.

20. Ibid., p. 254.

21. Ibid., p. 253.

22. Ibid.

23. Ibid.

24. Ibid., p. 245.

25. Flacks, "Radicals in the Universities," *NUC Newsletter*, p. 4.

26. Richard Rothstein, "Socialization in the High Schools," *NUC–MLC* [Modern Language Caucus] *Newsletter* 1 (October 1969): 4.

27. Michael W. Miles, *The Radical Probe: The Logic of Student Rebellion* (New York: Atheneum, 1971), p. 180.

28. Louis Kampf, *On Modernism: The Prospects for Literature and Freedom* (Cambridge, Massachusetts: M.I.T. Press, 1967), p. 153. See also Flacks: "Vastly overshadowing the tradition of disinterested scolarship [*sic*] is the emergence of the knowledge industry, a system of research and training, housed in the university, which services the needs of the state and the corporations, especially their planning and development functions. . . . Thus the universities no longer serve only the somewhat luxurious function of socializing elites and invigorating the going value system; they are now far more closely integrated into the political economy." "Radicals in the Universities," *NUC Newsletter*, p. 4.

29. Miles, *The Radical Probe*, p. 77.

30. Kampf, *On Modernism*, p. 156.

31. Alan Wolfe, "On Higher Education," *NUC Newsletter* 4 (October 15, 1970): 9.

32. Hal Draper, "The Mind of Clark Kerr" (Ann Arbor: Radical Education Project, n.d.), pp. 3–4, i.

33. Ibid., pp. ii–iii.

34. John A. Howard and H. Bruce Franklin, *Who Should Run the Universities* [a debate] (Washington: American Enterprise Institute, 1969), pp. 41, 68.

35. Ibid., p. 69.

36. Ibid., pp. 69–70.

37. Robert Paul Wolff, *The Ideal of the University* (Boston: Beacon Press, 1969), pp. 44–45.

38. Ibid., p. 47. See also Kenneth Keniston: The allegation that "higher education indoctrinates students with a military-industrial, racist-imperialist mentality," he contended, "suffers before the facts. Studies of the effects of higher education show that it lessens rather than increases students' unquestioning acceptance of the status quo. When students who go to college are compared with youths of equal ability and motivation who do not, we find that the college students become less authoritarian, more open to new ideas, less dogmatic, and more inquiring and open-minded." He dismissed the accusation that universities are unduly tied to political and corporate interests: "Yet it is ironic that leftists, who once bitterly assailed Senator McCarthy's tactic of 'guilt by association,' today use this same tainted brush against all trustees with business associations, arguing that their business contacts prove they are mere tools of the military-industrial complex." *Youth and Dissent: The Rise of a New Opposition* (New York: Harcourt Brace Jovanovich, 1971), pp. 359, 361.

39. Noam Chomsky, "Some Tasks for the Left," *Liberation* 14 (August–September 1969): 42.

40. Wolff, *The Ideal of the University*, p. 30.

41. Robert Nisbet, *The Degradation of the Academic Dogma: The University in America, 1945–1970* (New York: Basic Books, 1971), pp. 72–73.

42. Seymour Martin Lipset and Gerald M. Schaflander, *Passion and Politics: Student Activism in America* (Boston: Little, Brown and Company, 1971), p. 227.

43. Ibid., p. 219.

44. "Whence Cometh the Axe? An Editorial," *NUC Newsletter* 2 (January 1969): 2.

45. Michael Ducey, "Comments on the NUC Research Group," *NUC Newsletter* 5 (December 1971): 20.

46. Tom Hecht, "The Spring National Committee Meeting: An Overview" (Chicago: New University Conference, 1972), p. 3.

47. "Analysis: Open Up the Schools," *NUC Papers* 3, p. 7.

48. Chomsky, "Some Tasks for the Left," *Liberation*, p. 42.

49. Noam Chomsky, *Problems of Knowledge and Freedom* (New York: Vintage Books, 1971), p. 72.

50. Ibid.

51. Cited in Roger Rapaport and Laurence J. Kirshbaum, *Is the Library Burning?* (New York: Random House, 1969), pp. 45–46.

52. See Lipset and Schaflander, *Passion and Politics*, p. 209.

53. Wolff, *The Ideal of the University*, pp. 74–75.

54. "The Open Up the Schools Program," *NUC Papers* 3, p. 1.

55. "Analysis: Open Up the Schools," *NUC Papers* 3, p. 5.

56. Ibid.

57. "The Open Up the Schools Program," *NUC Papers 3*, pp. 2–3.

58. "Analysis: Open Up the Schools," *NUC Papers 3*, p. 6.

59. Lauter and Howe, *The Conspiracy of the Young*, p. 89.

60. "The Open Up the Schools Program," *NUC Papers 3*, p. 1.

61. For a defense of the present grading system, see Nathan Glazer, *Remembering the Answers: Essays on the American Student Revolt* (New York: Basic Books, 1970), pp. 245–249.

62. Bill Zimmerman, "Radical Practice in the Classroom," *NUC Newsletter* 5:7 (n.d. [1972]): 14.

63. Ibid.

64. Tom Hecht, "An Overview for the Coming Months," *NUC Newsletter* 5 (November 1971): 3–4.

65. "Education for the People: Smash the Hegemony of Bourgeois Ideology," *NUC Newsletter* 5 (November 1971): 18.

66. Ibid.

67. Ibid., p. 19.

68. Ibid., p. 20.

69. Ibid.

70. Ibid.

71. Ibid.

72. Ibid., p. 23.

73. "Proposal on Colleges and Universities" [pamphlet] (New American Movement, n.d.), pp. 1–2.

7:    Politicization and the University

1. Richard Ohmann, "Teaching and Studying Literature at the End of Ideology," in *The Politics of Literature: Dissenting Essays on the Teaching of English*, ed. Louis Kampf and Paul Lauter (New York: Pantheon Books, 1970), pp. 154–155. Cf. Ellen Cantarow: "The conclusion, a gut one, was that indeed 'politics' meant all actions and activities taken in pursuit of a social goal. 'Politics' as defined by capitalism was a single, sterile, and compartmentalized act in which one was literally boxed in, isolated from others, rendered individual in the ultimate sense of the word. Such a definition was as mechanical and asocial as similar definitions of knowledge and education." "Why Teach Literature? An Account of How I Came to Ask That Question," in *The Politics of Literature*, ed. Kampf and Lauter, pp. 74–75.

2. Paul Lauter and Florence Howe, *The Conspiracy of the Young* (New York: Meridian Books, 1971), p. 89.

3. Robert Meredith, "Subverting Culture," *Radical Teacher*, no. 2 (December 30, 1969): 6.

4. Ibid., p. 7.

5. John A. Howard and H. Bruce Franklin, *Who Should Run the Universities* (Washington: American Enterprise Institute, 1969), p. 78.

6. Ibid., p. 239.

7. Jesse Lemisch, "What's Your Evidence? Radical Scholarship and Scientific Method and Anti-Authoritarianism, not 'Relevance,' " in *On Radicals and Research* (Chicago: New University Conference, 1970), p. 12.

8. "The Radicalism of Disclosure: A Statement by the Editors," *Studies on the Left* 1 (Fall 1959): 2–4.

9. Theodore Roszak, *The Making of a Counter Culture: Reflections on the Technocratic Society and Its Youthful Opposition* (Garden City, New York: Anchor Books, 1969), pp. 208–209.

10. Louis Kampf, "The Scandal of Literary Scholarship," in *The Dissenting Academy,* ed. Theodore Roszak (New York: Pantheon Books, 1967), p. 58.

11. David Eakins, "Objectivity and Commitment," *Studies on the Left* 1 (Fall 1959): 44.

12. Sheila Delany, ed., *Counter-Tradition: A Reader in the Literature of Dissent and Alternatives* (New York: Basic Books, 1971), p. 6.

13. Michael Novak, "God in the Colleges: The Dehumanization of the University," in *The New Student Left: An Anthology,* ed. Mitchell Cohen and Dennis Hale (Boston: Beacon Press, 1966), pp. 260–261.

14. Lemisch, "What's Your Evidence?", in *On Radicals and Research,* p. 9.

15. Ibid.

16. Lauter and Howe, *The Conspiracy of the Young,* p. 277. For another example, see David Hakken, who praises the *Critical Anthropologist,* a radical journal, for propounding the argument that "anthropology is inherently radical, that the problems within the discipline would be solved if the anthropologists were to act truly professional—i.e., be objective." "Organizing in Professional Associations," *NUC Newsletter* 5 (December 1971): 16.

17. Louis Kampf, *On Modernism: The Prospects for Literature and Freedom* (Cambridge, Massachusetts: M.I.T. Press, 1967), p. 197.

18. Herbert Marcuse, "Repressive Tolerance," in Robert Paul Wolff, Barrington Moore, Jr., and Herbert Marcuse, *A Critique of Pure Tolerance* (Boston: Beacon Press, 1965), pp. 82–83.

19. Ibid., p. 97.

20. Ibid.

21. Ibid., p. 85.

22. Ibid., p. 89.

23. Ibid., p. 94.

24. Ibid., p. 100.

25. Ibid., pp. 100–101.

26. Ibid., p. 101.

27. Ibid., pp. 105–106.

28. Ibid., p. 106.

29. Ibid., p. 109.

30. Ibid., pp. 112–113.

31. Eliseo Vivas, *Contra Marcuse* (New Rochelle, New York: Arlington House, 1971), p. 86.

32. Seymour Martin Lipset and Gerald M. Schaflander, *Passion and Politics: Student Activism in America* (Boston: Little, Brown and Company, 1971), pp. 207–208.

33. Stuart Hampshire, "Commitment and Imagination," in Northrop Frye, Stuart Hampshire, and Conor Cruise O'Brien, *The Morality of Scholarship*, ed. Max Black (Ithaca, New York: Cornell University Press, 1967), p. 40.

34. Howard and Franklin, *Who Should Run the Universities*, p. 227.

35. Robert Paul Wolff, *The Ideal of the University* (Boston: Beacon Press, 1969), p. 73.

36. Ibid., p. 123.

8: Professional Literary Organizations

1. Lionel Trilling, *The Liberal Imagination: Essays on Literature and Society* (Garden City, New York: Doubleday and Company, 1954), p. 5.

2. Ibid.

3. Ibid., p. 6.

4. "Radical Education Project" (Ann Arbor: Radical Education Project, 1966), p. 12.

5. Ibid.

6. Ibid.

7. Ibid., pp. 17, 12.

8. Ibid., p. 15.

9. Sheila Delany, "Up Against the Great Tradition," in *The Politics of Literature: Dissenting Essays on the Teaching of English*, ed. Louis Kampf and Paul Lauter (New York: Pantheon Books, 1970), p. 321.

10. Louis Kampf and Paul Lauter, "Introduction," in *The Politics of Literature*, ed. Kampf and Lauter, p. 34.

11. Louis Kampf, "The Scandal of Literary Scholarship," in *The Dissenting Academy*, ed. Theodore Roszak (New York: Pantheon Books, 1967), pp. 48–49.

12. Ibid.

13. Richard Ohmann, "An Informal and Perhaps Unreliable Account of the

Modern Language Association of America," *Antioch Review* 29 (Fall 1969): 333.

14. Ibid., pp. 336–337.

15. Ibid., pp. 339–340.

16. Kampf and Lauter, "Introduction," in *The Politics of Literature*, ed. Kampf and Lauter, pp. 32–40; Ohmann, "Informal and Perhaps Unreliable Account," *Antioch Review*, pp. 329–347; Florence Howe and Ellen Cantarow, "What Happened at MLA: The Radical Perspective," *College English* 30 (March 1969): 484–487; Florence Howe, "What Success at MLA?", *NUC Newsletter* 2 (January 1969): 1, 18–20.

17. Kampf and Lauter, "Introduction," in *The Politics of Literature*, ed. Kampf and Lauter, p. 34.

18. Howe, "What Success at MLA?", *NUC Newsletter*, p. 19.

19. Ibid.

20. Paul Lauter, "The Imperial Scholar," *College English* 30 (March 1969): 504–507.

21. Ohmann, "Informal and Perhaps Unreliable Account," *Antioch Review*, p. 330.

22. Howe, "What Success at MLA?", *NUC Newsletter*, p. 19.

23. Ibid.

24. Howe and Cantarow, "What Happened at MLA," *College English*, p. 486.

25. Ibid.

26. Howe, "What Success at MLA?", *NUC Newsletter*, p. 19.

27. Ibid.

28. Howe and Cantarow, "What Happened at MLA," *College English*, p. 486.

29. Howe, "What Success at MLA?", *NUC Newsletter*, p. 1.

30. Kampf and Lauter, "Introduction," in *The Politics of Literature*, ed. Kampf and Lauter, p. 39.

31. Howe and Cantarow, "What Happened at MLA," *College English*, p. 484.

32. Ibid.

33. Ibid., pp. 486–487.

34. Howe, "What Success at MLA?", *NUC Newsletter*, p. 20.

35. Ibid.

36. Ibid.

37. John Hurt Fisher, "Memorandum 1969–3: 2 January 1969," *College English* 30 (March 1969): 487.

38. Ibid., p. 488.

39. Ibid.

40. Ibid., p. 487.

41. Ibid.

42. Ibid., p. 488.

43. "Duke–North Carolina Petition," *College English* 30 (March 1969): 491.

44. Ohmann, "Informal and Perhaps Unreliable Account," *Antioch Review*, p. 338.

45. Ibid., p. 333.

46. Bruce Harkness, Letter to Richard Ohmann, *College English* 30 (March 1969): 493.

47. Ibid., p. 494.

48. G. H. Fleming, Memorandum, *College English* 30 (March 1969): 492.

49. Clare Goldfarb, "The 1968 MLA Convention," *College English* 30 (March 1969): 501.

50. Ibid., p. 503.

51. Ibid., p. 501.

52. Ibid., p. 504.

53. Maynard Mack, "To See It Feelingly," *PMLA* 86 (May 1971): 363–374.

54. Henry Nash Smith, "Something Is Happening but You Don't Know What It Is, Do You, Mr. Jones?", *PMLA* 85 (May 1970): 417.

55. Ibid., pp. 419–420. See also Rima Drell Reck, who did not agree with the radicals' critique but approved of their operations: "I did not feel that a vocal minority had the right to countermand the wishes of the tongue-tied or absent majority. I have come to modify my position in the last twelve months. There is no reason why the intense awareness of the few should not override the vast unconsciousness of the many." "The Politics of Literature," *PMLA* 85 (May 1970): 429.

56. Ruth Misheloff, "Modern Language Caucus News," *NUC Newsletter* 4 (September 15, 1970): 7.

57. *NUC Newsletter* 3 (December 1, 1969): 5–7.

58. "Resolutions Passed by the National Council of Teachers of English at the Fifty-ninth Annual Meeting, 1969," *College English* 31 (February 1970): 528–529.

59. *NUC Newsletter* 3 (October 1, 1969): 9.

60. William A. Jenkins, "Counciletter: Charting Our Course," *College English* 31 (April 1970): 758.

61. James E. Miller, Jr., "Counciletter: The NCTE and Politics," *College English* 32 (April 1971): 815–816.

62. Ibid., p. 816.

63. Kampf and Lauter, "Introduction," in *The Politics of Literature*, ed. Kampf and Lauter, p. 39.

64. "Affirmative Action for Women in 1971: A Report of the Modern Language Association Commission on the Status of Women in the Profession," *PMLA* 87 (May 1972): 530–540.

65. Louis Kampf, " 'It's Alright, Ma (I'm Only Bleeding)': Literature and Language in the Academy," *PMLA* 87 (May 1972): 382.

9:    Critique of Literature and Culture

1. Louis Kampf and Paul Lauter, "Introduction," in *The Politics of Literature: Dissenting Essays on the Teaching of Literature,* ed. Louis Kampf and Paul Lauter (New York: Pantheon Books, 1970), p. 40.

2. Ibid., p. 39.

3. Ruth Misheloff, "Modern Language Caucus News," *NUC Newsletter* 4 (September 15, 1970): 7.

4. Sheila Delany, "At Odds with the Curriculum," *Radical Teacher*, no. 1 (April–May 1969): 4.

5. Louis Kampf, "The Scandal of Literary Scholarship," in *The Dissenting Academy*, ed. Theodore Roszak (New York: Pantheon Books, 1967), p. 60.

6. Kampf and Lauter, "Introduction," in *The Politics of Literature*, ed. Kampf and Lauter, p. 14.

7. Ellen Cantarow, "Why Teach Literature? An Account of How I Came to Ask That Question," in *The Politics of Literature*, ed. Kampf and Lauter, p. 58.

8. Ibid., p. 63.

9. Ibid., p. 68.

10. Ibid., p. 71.

11. Ibid., p. 72.

12. Ibid., p. 83.

13. Ibid., p. 86.

14. Ibid., pp. 92–93.

15. Ibid., p. 95.

16. Ibid., p. 96.

17. Louis Kampf, " 'It's Alright, Ma (I'm Only Bleeding)': Literature and Language in the Academy," *PMLA* 87 (May 1972): 378.

18. Ibid., p. 380.

19. Robert Meredith, "A Paradigmatic Case," *NUC–MLC Newsletter* 1 (December 1969): 18.

20. Ibid.

21. Gaylord LeRoy, "The Radical Teacher in Our Discipline," *College English* 33 (April 1972): 764.

22. Louis Kampf, "Culture Without Criticism," *Massachusetts Review* 11 (Autumn 1970): 644.

23. Sheila Delany, "Up Against the Great Tradition," in *The Politics of Literature*, ed. Kampf and Lauter, p. 321.

24. Carl Oglesby, "The Deserters: The Contemporary Defeat of Fiction," in *Radical Perspectives in the Arts*, ed. Lee Baxandall (Baltimore: Penguin Books, 1972), pp. 33–34.

25. Kampf and Lauter, "Introduction," in *The Politics of Literature*, ed. Kampf and Lauter, pp. 37–38.

26. Donald Lazere, "Down with Culture?", *NUC–MLC Newsletter* 1 (December 1969): 19.

27. Ibid.

28. Richard Ohmann, *Shaw: The Style and the Man* (Middletown, Connecticut: Wesleyan University Press, 1962).

29. H. Bruce Franklin, *The Wake of the Gods: Melville's Mythology* (Stanford: Stanford University Press, 1963).

30. Sheila Delany, *Chaucer's House of Fame: The Poetics of Skeptical Fideism* (Chicago: University of Chicago Press, 1972).

31. Louis Kampf, *On Modernism: The Prospects for Literature and Freedom* (Cambridge: M.I.T. Press, 1967).

32. One Kampf article which conveys a low-key radicalism similar in tone to *On Modernism* is "The Humanist Tradition in Eighteenth-Century England—and Today," *New Literary History* 3 (Autumn 1971): 157–170.

33. Barbara Kessel, "The English Teacher as Civilizer," *NUC–MLC Newsletter* 1 (October 1969): 20.

34. Kampf, "Culture Without Criticism," *Massachusetts Review,* p. 624. Cf. Lillian S. Robinson and Lise Vogel, who asserted that the ideas conveyed in literature "have a class origin and a class function. What we mean when we say that an idea is bourgeois is that it arises out of the circumstances of the present ruling class and that it helps in some way to justify or perpetuate the hegemony of that class." "Modernism and History," *New Literary History* 3 (Autumn 1971): 195.

35. Kampf, "Culture Without Criticism," *Massachusetts Review,* p. 624.

36. Richard Wasson, review of Theodore Roszak, *The Making of a Counter Culture, College English* 31 (March 1970): 628.

37. Meredith Tax, "Introductory: Culture Is Not Neutral, Whom Does It Serve?", in *Radical Perspectives in the Arts,* ed. Baxandall, p. 15.

38. Louis Kampf, "Cultural Elitism and the Study of Literature," *Papers of the Midwest Modern Language Association,* no. 2 (1972): 23.

39. Frederick Crews, "Do Literary Studies Have an Ideology?", *PMLA* 85 (May 1970): 427.

40. Kampf, " 'It's Alright, Ma,' " *PMLA,* p. 379.

41. Kampf, "The Scandal of Literary Scholarship," in *The Dissenting Academy,* ed. Roszak, p. 56.

42. Bruce Franklin, "The Teaching of Literature in the Highest Academies of the Empire," in *The Politics of Literature,* ed. Kampf and Lauter, p. 103.

43. Barbara Kessel, "Free, Classless, and Urbane?", in *The Politics of Literature,* ed. Kampf and Lauter, p. 177.

44. Paul Lauter, "The Imperial Scholar," *College English* 30 (March 1969): 506.

45. Kampf, "The Scandal of Literary Scholarship," in *The Dissenting Acad-*

emy, ed. Roszak, p. 55.

46. Ibid., p. 49.

47. Louis Kampf, "The Humanities and Inhumanities," *Nation* 207 (September 30, 1968): 311.

48. Robinson and Vogel, "Modernism and History," *New Literary History,* p. 183.

49. Katherine Ellis, "Arnold's Other Axiom," in *The Politics of Literature,* ed. Kampf and Lauter, p. 162.

50. Lazere, "Down with Culture?", *NUC–MLC Newsletter,* p. 19.

51. Ibid.

52. Louis Kampf, "Notes Toward a Radical Culture," in *The New Left: A Collection of Essays,* ed. Priscilla Long (Boston: Porter Sargent, 1969), p. 432.

53. Lazere, "Down with Culture?", *NUC–MLC Newsletter,* p. 1.

54. See Kampf: "Cultural critics are part of the society's intellectual workforce, and as producers of ideologies they play an important role. Intellectuals and their ideologies, as the C.I.A. let us know a few years ago, are important instruments in waging the Cold War, and in developing the domestic social controls requisite to the maintenance of America's empire." "Culture Without Criticism," *Massachusetts Review,* p. 633.

55. Kampf and Lauter, "Introduction," in *The Politics of Literature,* ed. Kampf and Lauter, p. 13.

56. Ibid., pp. 8–9.

57. See ibid., p. 41.

58. Ibid., p. 22.

59. Kampf, " 'It's Alright, Ma,' " *PMLA,* p. 383.

60. Franklin, "Teaching of Literature in the Highest Academies," in *The Politics of Literature,* ed. Kampf and Lauter, p. 126.

61. Ibid., p. 118.

62. Ibid., p. 103.

63. R. G. Davis, "Radical, Independent, Chaotic, Anarchic Theatre vs. Institutional, University, Little, Commercial, Ford and Stock Theatres," *Studies on the Left* 4 (Spring 1964): 31.

64. Ibid., p. 35.

65. Kampf, "The Scandal of Literary Scholarship," in *The Dissenting Academy,* ed. Roszak, p. 58.

66. Lazere, "Down with Culture?", *NUC–MLC Newsletter,* p. 19.

67. Kampf, "Notes Toward a Radical Culture," in *The New Left,* ed. Long, p. 420.

68. Ibid., p. 424.

69. Kampf, "Culture Without Criticism," *Massachusetts Review,* p. 640.

70. Kampf, "Notes Toward a Radical Culture," in *The New Left,* ed. Long, p. 426.

71. Kampf, "The Scandal of Literary Scholarship," in *The Dissenting Academy*, ed. Roszak, p. 57.

72. Kampf, "Culture Without Criticism," *Masschusetts Review*, p. 628.

73. Kampf, *On Modernism*, p. 140.

74. Robert Brustein, *Revolution as Theatre: Notes on the New Style* (New York: Liveright, 1971).

75. Jonah Raskin, *The Mythology of Imperialism* (New York: Random House, 1971), p. 5. Cf. Allen Grossman, who found ours a "discredited civilization," one which is "not worth having"; he even specified that our discredited civilization is "almost indiscriminable from civilization itself." "Teaching Literature in a Discredited Civilization," *Massachusetts Review* 10 (Summer 1969): 420, 431.

76. Kampf, "Notes Toward a Radical Culture," in *The New Left*, ed. Long, p. 426.

77. Delany, "Up Against the Great Tradition," in *The Politics of Literature*, ed. Kampf and Lauter, p. 310.

78. Delany, "At Odds with the Curriculum," *Radical Teacher*, p. 3.

79. Ibid., p. 4.

80. Ibid.

81. Sheila Delany, ed., *Counter-Tradition: A Reader in the Literature of Dissent and Alternatives* (New York: Basic Books, 1971), p. 3.

82. Ibid., p. 6.

83. Ibid.

84. Ibid., p. 7.

85. Ibid., p. 3.

86. Raskin, *The Mythology of Imperialism*, p. 10.

87. Delany, "At Odds with the Curriculum," *Radical Teacher*, p. 4.

88. Robinson and Vogel, "Modernism and History," *New Literary History*, p. 195.

89. Delany, "At Odds with the Curriculum," *Radical Teacher*, p. 4.

90. Ibid.

91. Herbert Marcuse, *Counterrevolution and Revolt* (Boston: Beacon Press, 1972), p. 88.

92. Cantarow, "Why Teach Literature?", in *The Politics of Literature*, ed. Kampf and Lauter, p. 79. Western literature presented the view that history is shaped by "the discoveries, the productions, the acts of heroism, of individual men who, giantlike, all-powerful, masterfully stride forth to change whole epochs, whole civilizations." Ibid., p. 88.

93. Kampf, "The Scandal of Literary Scholarship," in *The Dissenting Academy*, ed. Roszak, pp. 56–57.

94. Kampf, "Notes Toward a Radical Culture," in *The New Left*, ed. Long, p. 432.

95. James G. Kennedy, "The Two European Cultures and the Necessary New Sense of Literature," *College English* 31 (March 1970): 576.

96. Franklin, "Teaching of Literature in the Highest Academies," in *The Politics of Literature,* ed. Kampf and Lauter, p. 104.

97. Kampf, "Notes Toward a Radical Culture," in *The New Left,* ed. Long, p. 434.

98. Ibid., p. 433.

99. Kampf, "Cultural Elitism and the Study of Literature," *Papers of the Midwest Modern Language Association,* p. 27.

100. Kampf, "Culture Without Criticism," *Massachusetts Review,* p. 637.

101. Ibid.

102. Kampf, "Notes Toward a Radical Culture," in *The New Left,* ed. Long, p. 427.

103. Ibid.

104. Kampf and Lauter, "Introduction," in *The Politics of Literature,* ed. Kampf and Lauter, p. 10.

105. See Homer Hogan, "English Studies and the Dialectics of Consumerism," *College English* 32 (December 1970): 267; Delany, "Up Against the Great Tradition," in *The Politics of Literature,* ed. Kampf and Lauter, p. 317.

106. Martha Vicinus, "The Study of Nineteenth-Century British Working-Class Poetry," in *The Politics of Literature,* ed. Kampf and Lauter, p. 323.

107. Ibid., pp. 341–342.

108. Kampf and Lauter, "Introduction," in *The Politics of Literature,* ed. Kampf and Lauter, p. 47.

109. Nick Aaron Ford, "Black Literature and the Problem of Evaluation," *College English* 32 (February 1971): 537.

110. Michele Russell, "Erased, Debased, and Encased: The Dynamics of African Educational Colonization in America," *College English* 31 (April 1970): 673.

111. Ibid., p. 674.

112. Kessel, "Free, Classless, and Urbane?", in *The Politics of Literature,* ed. Kampf and Lauter, pp. 177–178.

113. Kampf and Lauter, "Introduction," in *The Politics of Literature,* ed. Kampf and Lauter, pp. 41–42.

114. "For Members Only—Vignette CX," *PMLA* 84 (October 1969): 1662.

115. *Guide to College of Old Westbury* (1972), p. 22.

116. Kampf and Lauter, "Introduction," in *The Politics of Literature,* ed. Kampf and Lauter, p. 41.

117. John Moore, "Radical Academic Guide: Perspective for a Partisan Anthropology," *Liberation* 16 (November 1971): 34.

118. LeRoy, "The Radical Teacher in Our Discipline," *College English,* p. 757.

119. H. R. Wolf, "The Classroom as Microcosm," *College English* 33 (December 1971): 259–267.

120. James E. Miller, Jr., "Counciletter: Notes for an Anti-Curriculum in English," *College English* 33 (May 1972): 964-965.

121. Brent Harold, "Beyond Student-Centered Teaching: The Dialectical Materialist Form of a Literature Course" (Radical Caucus of the MLA, n.d.), p. 1.

122. Ibid., p. 7.

123. Ibid., pp. 8–9.

124. Grossman, "Teaching Literature in a Discredited Civilization," *Massachusetts Review*, p. 419.

125. Kampf, "The Scandal of Literary Scholarship," in *The Dissenting Academy*, ed. Roszak, p. 61.

126. For a critical treatment of Marcuse's views on art, see Eliseo Vivas, *Contra Marcuse* (New Rochelle, N. Y.: Arlington House, 1971), pp. 61–67.

127. See, e.g., Marcuse, *Counterrevolution and Revolt*, p. 129.

128. Ibid., p. 98.

129. Herbert Marcuse, "Repressive Tolerance," in Robert Paul Wolff, Barrington Moore, Jr., and Herbert Marcuse, *A Critique of Pure Tolerance* (Boston: Beacon Press, 1965), p. 89.

130. Marcuse, *Counterrevolution and Revolt*, p. 105.

131. Herbert Marcuse, "Art in a One-Dimensional Society," in *Radical Perspectives in the Arts*, ed. Baxandall, p. 55. See also Herbert Marcuse, *An Essay on Liberation* (Boston: Beacon Press, 1969), p. 57.

132. Oglesby, "The Deserters," in *Radical Perspectives in the Arts*, ed. Baxandall, pp. 34–35.

133. Marcuse, "Art in a One-Dimensional Society," in *Radical Perspectives in the Arts*, ed. Baxandall, p. 54.

134. C. S. Lewis, "Learning in War-Time," in *The Weight of Glory* (Grand Rapids: Wm. B. Eerdmans Publishing Co., 1965), pp. 43–46.

135. David Daiches, "Politics and the Literary Imagination," in *Liberations: New Essays on the Humanities in Revolution*, ed. Ihab Hassan (Middletown, Connecticut: Wesleyan University Press, 1971), pp. 114–115.

10: Critique of the Literary Profession

1. For the most vitriolic portrayal of the style of literature professors, see Bruce Franklin, "The Teaching of Literature in the Highest Academies of the Empire," in *The Politics of Literature: Dissenting Essays on the Teaching of English*, ed. Louis Kampf and Paul Lauter (New York: Pantheon Books, 1970), pp. 101–102.

2. Ellen Cantarow, "Why Teach Literature? An Account of How I Came

to Ask That Question," in *The Politics of Literature*, ed. Kampf and Lauter, pp. 72–73.

3. Barbara Kessel, "Free, Classless, and Urbane?", in *The Politics of Literature*, ed. Kampf and Lauter, p. 185.

4. Katherine Ellis, "Arnold's Other Axiom," in *The Politics of Literature*, ed. Kampf and Lauter, p. 166.

5. Cantarow, "Why Teach Literature?", in *The Politics of Literature*, ed. Kampf and Lauter, p. 59.

6. Louis Kampf and Paul Lauter, "Introduction," in *The Politics of Literature*, ed. Kampf and Lauter, p. 18.

7. Kampf, " 'It's Alright, Ma (I'm Only Bleeding)': Literature and Language in the Academy," *PMLA* 87 (May 1972): 380.

8. Katherine Ellis, "The Function of Northrop Frye at the Present Time," *College English* 31 (March 1970): 546.

9. Louis Kampf, "The Scandal of Literary Scholarship," in *The Dissenting Academy*, ed. Theodore Roszak (New York: Pantheon Books, 1967), pp. 46, 53.

10. Kampf and Lauter, "Introduction," in *The Politics of Literature*, ed. Kampf and Lauter, p. 28.

11. Kampf, "The Scandal of Literary Scholarship," in *The Dissenting Academy*, ed. Roszak, p. 54.

12. Kampf and Lauter, "Introduction," in *The Politics of Literature*, ed. Kampf and Lauter, p. 22. Also, John Moore: " 'Publish or perish' becomes simply the academic variant of the general cultural slogan, 'Sell, sell, sell.' " "Radical Academic Guide: Perspective for a Partisan Anthropology," *Liberation* 16 (November 1971): 38.

13. Franklin, "The Teaching of Literature in the Highest Academies," in *The Politics of Literature*, ed. Kampf and Lauter, p. 113.

14. Ibid., pp. 113–114. The crudity of Franklin's attack on the New Criticism was paralleled by Jonah Raskin's attack in the same vein on Lionel Trilling, a crudity fully reflected in his diction:

> The final Wanted poster is for an Amerikan, a cold warrior: Lionel Trilling. He is the prototype of the liberal anticommunist academician. . . . But when we tear aside his liberal garments we see the uniform of a prison guard. Trilling is the jailer. He is repressive; he wants to lock us up. . . .
>
> Trilling is the mid-twentieth-century Matthew Arnold. He votes for the state. For three decades he acted as a free agent for the Amerikan power elite. Like the State Department officials and the generals in the Pentagon, he designated communism as the "new imperialism." In that way he tried to hide from our eyes the repression in our society; to cover up the fact that our greatest writers have been held in prison, forced to become outlaws or fugitives because of their resistance to the state.

The Mythology of Imperialism (New York: Random House, 1971), pp. 8–10.

15. Jackie Di Salvo, "This Murder . . . Literary Criticism and Literary Scholarship," *NUC–MLC Newsletter* 1:3 (1969): 11.

16. Kampf, "The Scandal of Literary Scholarship," in *The Dissenting Academy*, ed. Roszak, p. 51.

17. Di Salvo, "This Murder," *NUC–MLC Newsletter*, p. 11.

18. Richard Ohmann, "Teaching and Studying Literature at the End of Ideology," in *The Politics of Literature*, ed. Kampf and Lauter, p. 154.

19. Ibid., p. 142.

20. Ibid., pp. 143–144.

21. Ibid., p. 146.

22. Mary L. Briscoe and Martha Vicinus, "Lawrence among the Radicals: MMLA, 1969: An Exchange," *D. H. Lawrence Review* 3 (Spring 1970): 64.

23. Ellis, "Arnold's Other Axiom," in *The Politics of Literature*, ed. Kampf and Lauter, p. 163.

24. Ibid.

25. Meredith Tax, "Introductory: Culture Is Not Neutral, Whom Does It Serve?", in *Radical Perspectives in the Arts*, ed. Lee Baxandall (Baltimore: Penguin Books, 1972), p. 18.

26. Di Salvo, "This Murder," *NUC–MLC Newsletter*, p. 11.

27. Franklin, "The Teaching of Literature in the Highest Academies," in *The Politics of Literature*, ed. Kampf and Lauter, p. 122.

28. Ellis, "Arnold's Other Axiom," in *The Politics of Literature*, ed. Kampf and Lauter, p. 160.

29. Franklin, "The Teaching of Literature in the Highest Academies," in *The Politics of Literature*, p. 102.

30. Northrop Frye, *Anatomy of Criticism: Four Essays* (Princeton: Princeton University Press, 1971), p. 347.

31. Ellis, "The Function of Northrop Frye," *College English*, p. 543.

32. Ibid.

33. Ellis, "Arnold's Other Axiom," in *The Politics of Literature*, ed. Kampf and Lauter, p. 171.

34. Kampf, "The Scandal of Literary Scholarship," in *The Dissenting Academy*, ed. Roszak, p. 57.

35. Louis Kampf, "Culture Without Criticism," *Massachusetts Review* 11 (Autumn 1970): 632.

36. Kampf, " 'It's Alright, Ma,' " *PMLA*, p. 378.

37. Franklin, "The Teaching of Literature in the Highest Academies," in *The Politics of Literature*, ed. Kampf and Lauter, p. 103.

38. Ibid., p. 127.

39. Ira Shor, "Questions Marxists Ask about Literature," *College English* 34 (November 1972): 179.

40. Lillian S. Robinson, "Dwelling in Decencies: Radical Criticism and the Feminist Perspective," *College English* 32 (May 1971): 889.

41. Michael Novak, "God in the Colleges: The Dehumanization of the University," in *The New Student Left: An Anthology,* ed. Mitchell Cohen and Dennis Hale (Boston: Beacon Press, 1966), p. 266.

42. Sheila Delany, "Up Against the Great Tradition," in *The Politics of Literature,* ed. Kampf and Lauter, p. 316.

43. Kampf and Lauter, "Introduction," in *The Politics of Literature,* ed. Kampf and Lauter, p. 45.

44. Carl Oglesby, "The Deserters: The Contemporary Defeat of Fiction," in *Radical Perspectives in the Arts,* ed. Baxandall, p. 35.

45. Robert Meredith, "A Paradigmatic Case," *NUC–MLC Newsletter* 1 (December 1969): 11.

46. Ellis, "The Function of Northrop Frye," *College English,* p. 544.

47. Raskin, *The Mythology of Imperialism,* p. 7.

48. Sheila Delany, "At Odds with the Curriculum," *Radical Teacher,* no. 1 (April–May 1969): 4–5.

49. Cantarow, "Why Teach Literature?", in *The Politics of Literature,* ed. Kampf and Lauter, p. 95.

50. Kampf and Lauter, "Introduction," in *The Politics of Literature,* ed. Kampf and Lauter, p. 32.

51. Di Salvo, "This Murder," *NUC–MLC Newsletter,* p. 11.

52. Oglesby, "The Deserters," in *Radical Perspectives in the Arts,* ed. Baxandall, p. 35.

53. Ibid., pp. 35–36.

54. Louis Kampf, *On Modernism: The Prospects for Literature and Freedom* (Cambridge: M.I.T. Press, 1967), p. vii.

55. Kampf, "Culture Without Criticism," *Massachusetts Review,* p. 639.

56. Kampf, "The Scandal of Literary Scholarship," in *The Dissenting Academy,* ed. Roszak, pp. 60–61.

57. Ibid.

58. Lauter, "The Imperial Scholar," *College English,* p. 507.

59. Kampf, "Humanities and Inhumanities," *Nation,* p. 311.

60. Kampf, "Culture Without Criticism," *Massachusetts Review,* p. 640. Cf. Lauter: "[Culture] provides answers to the eager, youthful and central questions: what shall I do? which side am I on? why should that be good? Culture, so understood, is the inlet to action. And action, I would argue after Emerson and Mao, is the fulfillment of thought and experience. Indeed, it is finally only in practice that we discover the meaning of our lives." "The Imperial Scholar," *College English,* p. 506.

61. Louis Kampf, "Cultural Elitism and the Study of Literature," *Papers of the Midwest Modern Language Association,* no. 2 (1972): 31.

62. Kampf, " 'It's Alright, Ma,' " *PMLA*, p. 381.

63. Gaylord LeRoy, "Radical Criticism of Radical Literature," *NUC–MLC Newsletter* 1 (October 1969): 9.

64. Ibid.

65. Ibid., p. 18.

66. Franklin, "The Teaching of Literature in the Highest Academies," in *The Politics of Literature*, ed. Kampf and Lauter, p. 128.

67. Delany, "At Odds with the Curriculum," *Radical Teacher*, p. 6.

68. Kampf and Lauter, "Introduction," in *The Politics of Literature*, ed. Kampf and Lauter, p. 47.

69. Ibid., p. 45.

70. Ibid., p. 51.

71. Lillian S. Robinson, "Cultural Criticism and the Horror Vacui: Response to Sonja Wieta," *College English* 33 (March 1972): 735.

72. Louis Kampf, "Notes Toward a Radical Culture," in *The New Left: A Collection of Essays*, ed. Priscilla Long (Boston: Porter Sargent, 1969), p. 420.

73. Ibid., p. 422.

74. Ibid., p. 423.

75. Ibid., p. 434.

76. Cantarow, "Why Teach Literature?", in *The Politics of Literature*, ed. Kampf and Lauter, p. 81.

77. Kampf, "Culture Without Criticism," *Massachusetts Review*, pp. 643–644.

78. Cf. Gaylord LeRoy, *Marxism and Modern Literature* (New York: American Institute for Marxist Studies, 1967), p. 10.

79. See Carl Boggs, "Toward a New Consciousness," *Liberation* 16 (January 1972): 38–39.

80. See Tax, "Introductory," in *Radical Perspectives in the Arts*, ed. Baxandall, pp. 26–27.

81. See Kampf and Lauter, "Introduction," in *The Politics of Literature*, ed. Kampf and Lauter, p. 47.

82. Todd Gitlin: "Too little of our history survives already; we can't afford to be cavalier about the rest, and I think the poems say much of what is worth remembering about the long march through the Sixties." Ed., *Campfires of the Resistance: Poetry from the Movement* (Indianapolis: Bobbs–Merrill Co., 1971), p. xvi.

83. "Eight Steps from Paradise: A Talk with Judith Malina and Julian Beck," *Liberation* 13 (November 1968): 36.

84. Herbert Marcuse, *Counterrevolution and Revolt* (Boston: Beacon Press, 1972), p. 113.

85. John Weber, "Murals as Peoples Art," *Liberation* 16 (September 1971): 45, 47, 48.

86. Leah Fritz, "Art and the Movement," *Liberation* 13 (December 1968): 34.

87. Marcuse, *Counterrevolution and Revolt*, p. 127.

88. Franklin, "The Teaching of Literature in the Highest Academies," in *The Politics of Literature*, ed. Kampf and Lauter, p. 105.

89. John A. Howard and H. Bruce Franklin, *Who Should Run the Universities* (Washington: American Enterprise Institute, 1969), p. 68.

90. Delany, "Up Against the Great Tradition," in *The Politics of Literature*, ed. Kampf and Lauter, pp. 309–310.

91. Cantarow, "Why Teach Literature?", in *The Politics of Literature*, ed. Kampf and Lauter, p. 93.

92. Ibid., pp. 93–94.

93. J. P. O'Flinn, "Orwell on Literature and Society," *College English* 31 (March 1970): 603–612.

94. James E. Miller, Jr., "The 'Classic' American Writers and the Radicalized Curriculum," *College English* 31 (March 1970): 569.

95. Briscoe and Vicinus, "Lawrence among the Radicals," *D. H. Lawrence Review*, p. 66.

96. Ibid.

97. Ibid., p. 68.

98. Ibid., pp. 68–69.

99. Bruce Franklin, "Chic Bleak in Fantasy Fiction," *Saturday Review of the Arts* 55 (July 15, 1972): 42, 44.

100. Ibid., p. 44.

101. Ibid., p. 45.

102. Ibid.

103. Raskin, *The Mythology of Imperialism*, p. 11.

104. Ibid., p. 140.

105. Ibid., p. 26.

106. Ibid., p. 29.

107. Ibid., p. 149.

108. Ibid., p. 154.

109. Ibid., pp. 159–160.

110. Ibid., p. 160.

111. James G. Kennedy, "The Two European Cultures and the Necessary New Sense of Literature," *College English* 31 (March 1970): 593.

112. Ibid., p. 594.

113. Ibid.

11: Diverging Paths

1. Richard Wasson, "New Marxist Criticism: Introduction," *College English* 34 (November 1972): 169.

2. Ibid.

3. "MLA Commission," *NUC–MLC Newsletter* 1:3 (1969): 9.

4. Wasson, "New Marxist Criticism," *College English*, pp. 169–170.

5. Ibid., p. 170.

6. Ibid.

7. Ibid., p. 172.

8. Frederic Jameson, "The Great American Hunter, or, Ideological Content in the Novel," *College English* 34 (November 1972): 197.

9. Ira Shor, "Notes on Marxism and Method," *College English* 34 (November 1972): 174.

10. Ibid., p. 177.

11. Ira Shor, "Questions Marxists Ask about Literature," *College English* 34 (November 1972): 179.

12. Ibid.

13. Gaylord LeRoy, "Comment," *College English* 34 (November 1972): 266.

14. Annette Conn, "Comment," *College English* 34 (November 1972): 284.

15. Ibid.

16. M. L. Raina, "Marxism and Literature—A Select Bibliography," *College English* 34 (November 1972): 308–314.

17. Elaine Hedges, "Women in the Colleges: One Year Later," *College English* 34 (October 1972): 2.

18. Florence Howe, "A Report on Women and the Profession," *College English* 32 (May 1971): 849.

19. Elaine Showalter, "Women and the Literary Curriculum," *College English* 32 (May 1971): 860.

20. Lillian S. Robinson, "Dwelling in Decencies: Radical Criticism and the Feminist Perspective," *College English* 32 (May 1971): 879.

21. Ibid., p. 889.

22. Ibid., p. 879.

23. Ibid., p. 882.

24. Ibid., p. 879.

25. Ibid., p. 880.

26. Ibid., pp. 880–881.

27. Ibid., p. 884.

28. Ibid., p. 889.

Concluding Essay

1. Nathan Glazer, *Remembering the Answers: Essays on the American Student Revolt* (New York: Basic Books, 1970), p. 158.

2. Ibid., p. 159.

3. Ibid., pp. 159–60.

4. Philip Altbach, "The Student and Religious Commitment," in *The New Student Left: An Anthology,* ed. Mitchell Cohen and Dennis Hale (Boston: Beacon Press, 1966), p. 26.

5. Paul Goodman, *New Reformation: Notes of a Neolithic Conservative* (New York: Random House, 1970), p. 162.

6. Ibid., p. xi.

7. Arthur Waskow, "The Religious Upswelling of the New Left," *Liberation* 14 (July 1969): 36.

8. Arthur Waskow, "Business, Religion and the Left," *Liberation* 14 (August–September 1969): 48.

9. Ibid., pp. 47–48.

10. Kenneth Keniston, *Young Radicals: Notes on Committed Youth* (New York: Harcourt, Brace & World, 1968), p. 65.

11. Ibid., p. 80.

12. Ibid., p. 31.

13. Ibid.

14. Edward Schwartz, *Will the Revolution Succeed? Rebirth of the Radical Democrat* (New York: Criterion Books, 1972), p. 67.

15. Ibid.

16. Ibid., p. 70.

17. Staughton Lynd, "Restructuring the University" (Chicago: New University Conference, 1969), pp. 31–32.

18. Paul Potter, *A Name for Ourselves* (Boston: Little, Brown and Co., 1971), p. 185.

19. Ibid., p. 184.

20. Ibid., p. 183.

21. Quoted in Kirkpatrick Sale, *SDS* (New York: Random House, 1973), p. 87.

22. Carl Oglesby, "The Revolted," in *The American Left: Radical Political Thought in the Twentieth Century,* ed. Loren Baritz (New York: Basic Books, 1971), p. 437.

23. Bob Gottlieb and Marge Piercy, "Movement for a Democratic Society, Beginning to Begin to Begin," in *The New Left: A Documentary History,* ed. Massimo Teodori (Indianapolis: Bobbs–Merrill Co., 1969), p. 409.

24. Greg Calvert and Carol Neiman, *A Disrupted History: The New Left and the New Capitalism* (New York: Random House, 1971), p. xi.

25. *Vocations for Social Change,* no. 22 (March–April 1971): 5.

26. Barbara Haber and Al Haber, "Getting By with a Little Help from Our Friends," in *Radicals in Professions: Selected Papers* (Ann Arbor: Radical Education Project, 1967), p. 51.

27. Keniston, *Young Radicals,* p. 125.

28. Herbert J. Gans, "The New Radicalism: Sect or Action Movement?", *Studies on the Left* 5 (Summer 1965): 126.

29. Calvert and Neiman, *A Disrupted History,* pp. 140–141.

30. David Doggett, letter, *New Left Notes* 4 (May 20, 1969): 2. Reprinted as "Parasites of the Youth Revolution" in *The University Crisis Reader,* ed. Immanuel Wallerstein and Paul Starr, vol. 2 (New York: Random House, 1971), pp. 230–231.

31. Quoted in Howard Zinn, *SNCC: The New Abolitionists* (Boston: Beacon Press, 1964), p. 34.

32. Keniston, *Young Radicals,* pp. 111–120; Richard Flacks, "The Liberated Generation: An Exploration of the Roots of Student Protest," *Journal of Social Issues* 23 (July 1967): 52–75.

33. Glazer, *Remembering the Answers,* p. 164.

34. Andrew Kopkind, "Mystic Politics: Refugees from the New Left," *Ramparts* 12 (July 1973): 26.

35. Ibid., p. 28.

36. Ibid.

37. Ibid.

38. Ibid., p. 26.

39. Ibid., p. 47.

40. Ibid., p. 48.

41. Edward Shils, "Ideology and Civility: On the Politics of the Intellectual," in *The Radical Left: The Abuse of Discontent,* ed. William P. Gerberding and Duane E. Smith (Boston: Houghton Mifflin Co., 1970), pp. 104–105.

Bibliography

Books

Avorn, Jerry, et al. *Up Against the Ivy Wall: A History of the Columbia Crisis*. New York: Atheneum, 1969.

Aya, Roderick, and Miller, Norman, eds. *The New American Revolution*. New York: Free Press, 1971.

Baldelli, Giovanni, ed. *Social Anarchism*. Chicago: Aldine-Atherton, 1971.

Baritz, Loren, ed. *The American Left: Radical Political Thought in the Twentieth Century*. New York: Basic Books, 1971.

Baxandall, Lee, ed. *Radical Perspectives in the Arts*. Baltimore: Penguin Books, 1971.

Bookchin, Murray. *Post-Scarcity Anarchism*. Berkeley: Ramparts Press, 1971.

Breines, Paul, ed. *Critical Interruptions: New Left Perspectives on Herbert Marcuse*. New York: Herder and Herder, 1970.

Brustein, Robert. *Revolution as Theatre: Notes on the New Style*. New York: Liveright, 1971.

Calvert, Greg, and Neiman, Carol. *A Disrupted History: The New Left and the New Capitalism*. New York: Random House, 1971.

Chomsky, Noam. *Problems of Knowledge and Freedom*. New York: Vintage Books, 1971.

Cohen, Mitchell, and Hale, Dennis, eds. *The New Student Left: An Anthology*. Boston: Beacon Press, 1966.

Delany, Sheila. *Chaucer's House of Fame: The Poetics of Skeptical Fideism*. Chicago: University of Chicago Press, 1972.

Delany, Sheila, ed. *Counter-Tradition: A Reader in the Literature of Dissent and Alternatives*. New York: Basic Books, 1971.

Erlich, John and Susan, eds. *Student Power, Participation and Revolution*. New York: Association Press, 1970.

Feuer, Lewis S. *The Conflict of Generations: The Character and Significance of Student Movements*. New York: Basic Books, 1969.

Feuer, Lewis S. *Marx and the Intellectuals: A Set of Post-Ideological Essays*. Garden City, N.Y.: Anchor Books, 1969.

Firestone, Shulamith. *The Dialectic of Sex: The Case for Feminist Revolution.* New York: Bantam Books, 1970.

Flacks, Richard. *Youth and Social Change.* Chicago: Markham Publishing Co., 1971.

Franklin, Bruce. *From the Movement/Toward Revolution.* New York: Van Nostrand Reinhold Co., 1971.

Franklin, H. Bruce. *The Wake of the Gods: Melville's Mythology.* Stanford: Stanford University Press, 1963.

Frye, Northrop. *Anatomy of Criticism: Four Essays.* Princeton: Princeton University Press, 1971.

Frye, Northrop; Hampshire, Stuart; and O'Brien, Conor Cruise. *The Morality of Scholarship,* edited by Max Black. Ithaca: Cornell University Press, 1967.

Gerberding, William F., and Smith, Duane E., eds. *The Radical Left: The Abuse of Discontent.* Boston: Houghton Mifflin Co., 1970.

Gitlin, Todd, ed. *Campfires of the Resistance: Poetry from the Movement.* Indianapolis: Bobbs-Merrill Co., 1971.

Glazer, Nathan. *Remembering the Answers: Essays on the American Student Revolt.* New York: Basic Books, 1970.

Goodman, Paul. *New Reformation: Notes of a Neolithic Conservative.* New York: Random House, 1970.

Green, Gil. *The New Radicalism: Anarchist or Marxist?* New York: International Publishers, 1971.

Hassan, Ihab, ed. *Liberations: New Essays on the Humanities in Revolution.* Middletown, Conn.: Wesleyan University Press, 1971.

Hayden, Tom. *Trial.* New York: Holt, Rinehart and Winston, 1970.

Hoffman, Robert, ed. *Anarchism.* New York: Artherton Press, 1970.

Howard, John A., and Franklin, H. Bruce. *Who Should Run the Universities.* Washington: American Enterprise Institute, 1969.

Jacobs, Harold, ed. *Weatherman.* Berkeley: Ramparts Press, 1970.

Jacobs, Paul, and Landau, Saul. *The New Radicals: A Report with Documents.* New York: Vintage Books, 1966.

Kampf, Louis. *On Modernism: The Prospects for Literature and Freedom.* Cambridge: M.I.T. Press, 1967.

Kampf, Louis, and Lauter, Paul, eds. *The Politics of Literature: Dissenting Essays on the Teaching of English.* New York: Pantheon Books, 1970.

Keniston, Kenneth. *Young Radicals: Notes on Committed Youth.* New York: Harcourt, Brace & World, 1968.

Keniston, Kenneth. *Youth and Dissent: The Rise of a New Opposition.* New York: Harcourt Brace Jovanovich, 1971.

Lauter, Paul, and Howe, Florence. *The Conspiracy of the Young.* New York: Meridian Books, 1971.

LeRoy, Gaylord. *Marxism and Modern Literature.* New York: American Institute for Marxist Studies, 1967.

Lewis, C. S. *The Weight of Glory.* Grand Rapids: Wm. B. Eerdmans Co., 1965.

Lipset, Seymour Martin. *Revolution and Counterrevolution: Change and Persistence in Social Structures.* New York: Basic Books, 1968.

Lipset, Seymour Martin, and Schaflander, Gerald M. *Passion and Politics: Student Activism in America.* Boston: Little, Brown and Co., 1971.

Long, Priscilla, ed. *The New Left: A Collection of Essays.* Boston: Porter Sargent, 1969.

Lynd, Staughton. *Intellectual Origins of American Radicalism.* New York: Pantheon Books, 1968.

Marcuse, Herbert. *Counterrevolution and Revolt.* Boston: Beacon Press, 1972.

Marcuse, Herbert. *An Essay on Liberation.* Boston: Beacon Press, 1969.

Megill, Kenneth A. *The New Democratic Theory.* New York: Free Press, 1970.

Miles, Michael. *The Radical Probe: The Logic of Student Rebellion.* New York: Atheneum, 1971.

Newfield, Jack. *A Prophetic Minority.* New York: New American Library, 1966.

Nisbet, Robert. *The Degradation of the Academic Dogma: The University in America, 1945–1970.* New York: Basic Books, 1971.

Ohmann, Richard. *Shaw: The Style and the Man.* Middletown, Conn.: Wesleyan University Press, 1962.

Pfaff, William. *Condemned to Freedom.* New York: Random House, 1971.

Potter, Paul. *A Name for Ourselves.* Boston: Little, Brown and Co., 1971.

Raskin, Jonah. *The Mythology of Imperialism.* New York: Random House, 1971.

Rapaport, Roger, and Kirshbaum, Laurence J. *Is the Library Burning?* New York: Random House, 1969.

Roszak, Theodore, ed. *The Dissenting Academy.* New York: Pantheon Books, 1967.

Roszak, Theodore. *The Making of a Counter Culture: Reflections on the Technocratic Society and Its Youthful Opposition.* Garden City, N.Y.: Anchor Books, 1969.

Runkle, Gerald. *Anarchism Old and New.* New York: Delacorte Press, 1972.

Sale, Kirkpatrick. *SDS.* New York: Random House, 1973.

Salper, Roberta, ed. *Female Liberation: History and Current Politics.* New York: Alfred A. Knopf, 1972.

Schwartz, Edward. *Will the Revolution Succeed? Rebirth of the Radical Democrat.* New York: Criterion Books, 1972.

Teodori, Massimo, ed. *The New Left: A Documentary History.* Indianapolis: Bobbs–Merrill, 1969.

Thoughts of the Young Radicals. New Republic, 1966.

Trilling, Lionel. *The Liberal Imagination: Essays on Literature and Society.* Garden City, N.Y.: Doubleday and Co., 1954.

Vivas, Eliseo. *Contra Marcuse.* New Rochelle, N.Y.: Arlington House, 1971.

Wallerstein, Immanuel, and Starr, Paul, eds. *The University Crisis Reader,* 2 vols. New York: Random House, 1971.

Wolff, Robert Paul. *The Ideal of the University.* Boston: Beacon Press, 1969.

Wolff, Robert Paul; Moore, Barrington, Jr.; and Marcuse, Herbert. *A Critique of Pure Tolerance.* Boston: Beacon Press, 1965.

Zinn, Howard. *SNCC: The New Abolitionists.* Boston: Beacon Press, 1964.

Articles

"Affirmative Action for Women in 1971: A Report of the Modern Language Association Commission on the Status of Women in the Profession." *PMLA* 87 (May 1972): 530–40.

Altbach, Philip. "The Student and Religious Commitment." In *The New Student Left: An Anthology,* edited by Mitchell Cohen and Dennis Hale, pp. 22–26. Boston: Beacon Press, 1966.

Alpert, Jane. "Mother Right: A New Feminist Theory." *Ms.* 2 (August 1973): 52–55, 88–94.

"America and the New Era." Reprinted in *New Left Notes* 1 (December 9, 1966): 10, 12; (December 16, 1966): 3–6, 8.

"Analysis: Open Up the Schools—Political Perspective." *NUC Papers* 3: *Open Up the Schools,* pp. 5–10. Chicago: New University Conference, 1971.

Andrews, Barbara. "NUC and Education Schools." *NUC Women's Caucus Newsletter,* 1971, 3–5.

Andrews, Barbara. "Women's Caucus NC Report." *NUC Newsletter* 5 (November 1971): 7–9.

"Anti-Imperialist Work and NUC." *NUC Newsletter* 5 (December 1971): 12–13.

Aronowitz, Stanley. "Aronowitz Replies." *National Guardian* 19 (February 4, 1967): 12.

Aronowitz, Stanley. "SDSer's Views Criticized." *National Guardian* 20 (November 25, 1967): 5.

Aronson, Ronald. "Dear Herbert." *Radical America* 4 (April 1970): 3–18.

Aronson, Ronald. "The Movement and Its Critics." *Studies on the Left* 6 (January–February 1966): 3–19.

Ashley, Karin, et al. "You Don't Need a Weatherman to Know Which Way the Wind Blows." In *Debate Within SDS: RYM II vs. Weatherman,* pp. 19–30. Detroit: Radical Education Project, 1969.

Baker, Robert. "Some Reflections." *NUC Newsletter* 3 (August 15, 1969): 5–6.

Baum, Steve, and Faber, Bernard. "From Protest to Politics." *New Left Notes* 1 (September 2, 1966): 9–12.

Baxandall, Lee. "Issues and Constituencies of the New Left." *Liberation* 11 (April 1966): 21–25, 39.

Berry, Malinda. "Hayden Advocates Unity to Push Student Ideals." In *Student Power, Participation and Revolution,* edited by John and Susan Erlich, pp. 23–24. New York: Association Press, 1970.

Boggs, Carl. "Toward a New Consciousness." *Liberation* 16 (January 1972): 30–41.

Booth, Paul. "Facing the American Leviathan." *New Left Notes* 1 (July 29, 1966): 4.

Booth, Paul, and Webb, Lee. "The Anti-War Movement: From Protest to Radical Politics." *Our Generation* 3, 4 (May 1966): 78–90.

Breines, Paul. "From Guru to Spectre: Marcuse and the Implosion of the Movement." In *Critical Interruptions: New Left Perspectives on Herbert Marcuse,* edited by Paul Breines, pp. 1–21. New York: Herder and Herder, 1970.

Briscoe, Mary L., and Vicinus, Martha. "Lawrence among the Radicals: MMLA, 1969: An Exchange." *D. H. Lawrence Review* 3 (Spring 1970): 63–69.

Buhle, Paul. "Marxism in the U. S.: 39 Propositions." *Radical America* 5 (November–December 1971): 62–88.

Burris, Barbara, et al. "Fourth World Manifesto." In *Female Liberation: History and Current Politics,* edited by Roberta Salper, pp. 233–42. New York: Alfred A. Knopf, 1972.

Calvert, Greg. "In White America: Radical Consciousness and the New Left." *Guardian* 19 (March 25, 1967): 3–4.

Calvert, Greg. "Participatory Democracy, Collective Leadership and Political Responsibility." *New Left Notes* 2 (December 18, 1967): 1, 7.

Calvert, Greg, and Neiman, Carol. "Socialist Consciousness and the New Left." *Guardian* (August 24, 1968): 13.

Cantarow, Ellen. "Why Teach Literature? An Account of How I Came to Ask That Question." In *The Politics of Literature: Dissenting Essays on the Teaching of English,* edited by Louis Kampf and Paul Lauter, pp. 57–100. New York: Pantheon Books, 1970.

Chomsky, Noam. "Knowledge and Power: Intellectuals and the Welfare/Warfare State." In *The New Left: A Collection of Essays,* edited by Priscilla Long, pp. 172–99. Boston: Porter Sargent, 1969.

Chomsky, Noam. "Some Tasks for the Left." *Liberation* 14 (August-September 1969): 38–43.

Coleman, Les. "False Factionalism and Ideological Clarity." *New Left Notes* 3 (December 18, 1968): 3.

Coleman, Les. "Notes on Class Analysis: Some Implications for the Revolutionary Youth Movement." In *Debate Within SDS: RYM II vs. Weatherman,* pp. 6–12. Detroit: Radical Education Project, 1969.

Conn, Annette. "Comment." *College English* 34 (November 1972): 284–86.

Crews, Frederick. "Do Literary Studies Have an Ideology?" *PMLA* 85 (May 1970): 423–28.

Daiches, David. "Politics and the Literary Imagination." In *Liberations: New Essays on the Humanities in Revolution,* edited by Ihab Hassan, pp. 100–16. Middletown, Conn.: Wesleyan University Press, 1971.

Davidson, Carl. "Beyond the Campus: Resistance Federations." *Guardian* (April 6, 1968): 16.

Davidson, Carl. "The New Radicals and the Multiversity." In *The New Left: A Documentary History,* edited by Massimo Teodori, pp. 323–35. Indianapolis: Bobbs-Merrill Co., 1969.

Davidson, Carl. "Toward a Student Syndicalist Movement." *New Left Notes* 1 (September 9, 1966): 2, 11.

Davidson, Carl. "Where Are We Heading? Building a Base." *Guardian,* March 30, 1968, 16.

Davidson, Carl. "Where Are We Heading? The New Left in Transition, 1967–68." *Guardian,* March 23, 1968, 16.

Davis, Bob. "Editorial." *This Magazine Is About Schools* 2 (Autumn 1968): 1–3.

Davis, Chandler. "Sticking Up for Theory." In *On Radicals and Research,* pp. 13–16. Chicago: New University Conference, 1970.

Davis, R. G. "Radical, Independent, Chaotic, Anarchic Theatre vs. Institutional, University, Little, Commercial, Ford and Stock Theatres." *Studies on the Left* 4 (April 1964): 28–38.

Davis, Rennie. "The War on Poverty: Notes on Insurgent Response." In *The New Student Left: An Anthology,* edited by Mitchell Cohen and Dennis Hale, pp. 154–69. Boston: Beacon Press, 1966.

Delany, Sheila. "At Odds with the Curriculum." *Radical Teacher,* no. 1 (April–May 1969): 3–6.

Delany, Sheila. "Up Against the Great Tradition." In *The Politics of Literature: Dissenting Essays on the Teaching of English,* edited by Louis Kampf and Paul Lauter, pp. 308–21. New York: Pantheon Books, 1970.

Diggs, Elizabeth. Untitled. *NUC Newsletter* 3 (September 15, 1969): 1–2.

Di Salvo, Jackie. "This Murder . . . Literary Criticism and Literary Scholarship." *NUC–MLC Newsletter* 1:3 (1969): 11.

Dixon, Marlene. "Why Women's Liberation—2?" In *Female Liberation: History and Current Politics,* edited by Roberta Salper, pp. 184–200. New York: Alfred A. Knopf, 1972.

Doggett, David. Letter. *New Left Notes* 4 (May 20, 1969): 2. Reprinted as "Parasites of the Youth Revolution." In *The University Crisis Reader,* vol. 2, edited by Immanuel Wallerstein and Paul Starr, pp. 230–31. New York: Random House, 1971.

Ducey, Michael. "Comments on the NUC Research Group." *NUC Newsletter* 5 (December 1971): 20–22.

"Duke–North Carolina Petition." *College English* 30 (March 1969): 490–91.

Eakins, David. "Objectivity and Commitment." *Studies on the Left* 1 (Fall 1959): 44–53.

Editors of Studies on the Left. "Up from Irrelevance." *Studies on the Left* 5 (Spring 1965): 3–12.

"Education for the People: Smash the Hegemony of Bourgeois Ideology." *NUC Newsletter* 5 (November 1971): 18–24.

"Education Proposal: Calls for Radical Reconstruction." *New Left Notes* 1 (April 22, 1966): 3, 5, 8.

Egleson, Nick. "National President's Report." *New Left Notes* 2 (January 13, 1967): 4.

Ehrenreich, John and Barbara. "From Resistance to Revolution." In *The New Left: A Documentary History,* edited by Massimo Teodori, pp. 459–65. Indianapolis: Bobbs–Merrill, 1969.

Ehrlich, Howard J. "The Sense of Community." *NUC Newsletter* 3 (August 15, 1969): 5–6.

"Eight Steps from Paradise: A Talk with Judith Malina and Julian Beck." *Liberation* 13 (November 1968): 36–38.

Ellis, Katherine. "Arnold's Other Axiom." In *The Politics of Literature: Dissenting Essays on the Teaching of English,* edited by Louis Kampf and Paul Lauter, pp. 160–73. New York: Pantheon Books, 1970.

Ellis, Kathy. "A Body of Socialist Scholarship." *NUC Newsletter* 3 (October 1, 1969): 11–12.

Ellis, Katherine. "The Function of Northrop Frye at the Present Time." *College English* 31 (March 1970): pp. 541–47.

Ellis, Katherine. "Politicizing Freshman English." *Radical Teacher,* no. 2 (December 30, 1969): 19–24.

Ellis, Kathy; Gadlin, Lucy; and Radinsky, Terry. "Why a Women's Caucus." *NUC Newsletter* 3 (December 1, 1969): 1, 7.

"Fall Offensive." *NUC Newsletter* 3 (October 1, 1969): 1–2.

Fisher, John Hurt. "Memorandum 1969–3: 2 January 1969." *College English* 30 (March 1969): 487–89.

Flacks, Richard. "Is the Great Society Just a Barbecue?" In *Thoughts of the Young Radicals,* pp. 48–56. New Republic, 1966.

Flacks, Richard. "The Liberated Generation: An Exploration of the Roots of Student Protest." *Journal of Social Issues* 23 (July 1967): 52–75.

Flacks, Richard. "The New Left and American Politics after Ten Years." *Journal of Social Issues* 27 (1971): 21–34.

Flacks, Richard. "On the Uses of Participatory Democracy." *Dissent* 13 (November–December 1966): 701–708.

Flacks, Richard. "Organizing the Unemployed: The Chicago Project." In *The New Student Left: An Anthology,* edited by Mitchell Cohen and Dennis Hale, pp. 132–47. Boston: Beacon Press, 1966.

Flacks, Richard. "Radicals in the Universities." *NUC Newsletter* 1 (May 24, 1968): 4.

Flacks, Richard. "Revolt of the Young Intelligentsia: Revolutionary Class-Consciousness in Post-Scarcity America." In *The New American Revolution,* edited by Roderick Aya and Norman Miller, pp. 223–59. New York: Free Press, 1971.

Flacks, Richard. "Some Problems, Issues, Proposals." In *The New Radicals: A Report with Documents,* edited by Paul Jacobs and Saul Landau, pp. 162–65. New York: Vintage Books, 1966.

Flacks, Richard. "Some Roles for Radicals in America." *Liberation* 12 (May–June 1967): 42–45.

Fleming, G. H. Memorandum. *College English* 30 (March 1969): 492.

"For Members Only–Vignette CX," *PMLA* 84 (October 1969): 1662.

Ford, Nick Aaron. "Black Literature and the Problem of Evaluation." *College English* 32 (February 1971): 536–47.

Franklin, Bruce. "Chic Bleak in Fantasy Fiction." *Saturday Review of the Arts* 55 (July 15, 1972): 42–45.

Franklin, Bruce. "The Teaching of Literature in the Highest Academies of the Empire." In *The Politics of Literature: Dissenting Essays on the Teaching of English,* edited by Louis Kampf and Paul Lauter, pp. 101–29. New York: Pantheon Books, 1970.

Fritz, Leah. "Art and the Movement." *Liberation* 13 (December 1968): 32–35.

"From the Haight." In *The New Left: A Documentary History,* edited by Massimo Teodori, pp. 362–64. Indianapolis: Bobbs–Merrill, 1969.

Frost, Everett C. "Can Anyone Here Dump the Dean at FSC? or, What Am I Doing in Baltimore When There Are Barricades Back Home?" *NUC Newsletter* 3 (January 20, 1970): 2–3.

Fruchter, Norman. "A Realist Perspective." *Studies on the Left* 4 (Fall 1964): 110–34.

Fruchter, Norman. "SDS: In and Out of Context." *Liberation* 16 (February 1972): 19–32.

Gans, Herbert J. "The New Radicalism: Sect or Action Movement?" *Studies on the Left* 5 (Summer 1965): 126–31.

Garson, Marvin. "The Movement: It's Theory Time." In *The New Left: A Documentary History,* edited by Massimo Teodori, pp. 380–84. Indianapolis: Bobbs–Merrill, 1969.

Genovese, Eugene. "Genovese Looks at American Left–New and Old." *National Guardian* 18 (February 19, 1966): 6–7.

Gitlin, Todd. "The Battlefields and the War." In *The New Student Left: An Anthology,* edited by Mitchell Cohen and Dennis Hale, pp. 120–31. Boston: Beacon Press, 1966.

Gitlin, Todd. "Power and the Myth of Progress." In *Thoughts of the Young Radicals,* pp. 17–25. New Republic, 1966.

Gitlin, Todd. "Theses for the Radical Movement." *Liberation* 12 (May–June 1967): 34–36.

Gitlin, Todd. "To the Far Side of the Abyss." Review of *Post-Scarcity Anarchism,* by Murray Bookchin. *Nation* 214 (March 6, 1972): 309–11.

Gitlin, Todd. "Toward a New New Left." *Partisan Review* 39 (Summer 1972): 454–61.

Goldfarb, Clare. "The 1968 MLA Convention." *College English* 30 (March 1969): 501–504.

Goldfield, Mike. "A Report on the Conference." In *Radicals in Professions: Selected Papers,* pp. 8–10. Ann Arbor: Radical Education Project, 1967.

Good, Tom. "Ideology and SDS." *New Left Notes* 1 (August 5, 1966): 5.

Goodman, Paul. "The Black Flag of Anarchism." In *Anarchism,* edited by Robert Hoffman, pp. 147–59. New York: Atherton Press, 1970.

Gottlieb, Bob, and Piercy, Marge. "Movement for a Democratic Society, Beginning to Begin to Begin." In *The New Left: A Documentary History,* edited by Massimo Teodori, pp. 403–10. Indianapolis: Bobbs–Merrill Co., 1969.

Gottlieb, Bob; Tenney, Gerry; and Gilbert, Dave. "Praxis and the New Left." *New Left Notes* 2 (February 13, 1967): 5–6, 9–10.

Graham, George. "Unite the International Proletariat." *Something Else!* 2 (November–December 1969): 7–10.

Grossman, Allen. "Teaching Literature in a Discredited Civilization." *Massachusetts Review* 10 (Summer 1969) 419–32.

Haber, Barbara, and Haber, Al. "Getting By with a Little Help from Our Friends." In *Radicals in Professions: Selected Papers,* pp. 44–62. Ann Arbor: Radical Education Project, 1967.

Haber, Robert A. "From Protest to Radicalism: An Appraisal of the Student Movement 1960." In *The New Student Left: An Anthology,* edited by Mitchell Cohen and Dennis Hale, pp. 41–49. Boston: Beacon Press, 1966.

Hakken, David. "Organizing in Professional Associations." *NUC Newsletter* 5 (December 1971): 15–19.

Halliwell, Steve. "Personal Liberation and Social Change." *New Left Notes* 2 (September 4, 1967): 1.

Hampshire, Stuart. "Commitment and Imagination." In Northrop Frye, Stuart Hampshire, and Conor Cruise O'Brien, *The Morality of Scholarship,* edited by Max Black, pp. 29–55. Ithaca: Cornell University Press, 1967.

Harkness, Bruce. Letter to Richard Ohmann. *College English* 30 (March 1969): 493–96.

Hayden, Tom. "The Ability to Face Whatever Comes." In *Thoughts of the Young Radicals*, pp. 35–42. New Republic, 1966.

Hayden, Thomas. "A Letter to the New (Young) Left." In *The New Student Left: An Anthology*, edited by Mitchell Cohen and Dennis Hale, pp. 2–9. Boston: Beacon Press, 1966.

Hayden, Tom. "The Politics of 'The Movement.'" *Dissent* 13 (January–February 1966): 75–87.

Hayden, Thomas. "Student Social Action: From Liberation to Community." In *The New Student Left: An Anthology*, edited by Mitchell Cohen and Dennis Hale, pp. 270–88. Boston: Beacon Press, 1966.

Hayden, Tom. "Two, Three, Many Columbias." In *The University Crisis Reader*, vol. 2, edited by Immanuel Wallerstein and Paul Starr, pp. 162–65. New York: Random House, 1971.

Hecht, Tom. "An Overview for the Coming Months." *NUC Newsletter* 5 (November 1971): 2–6.

Hecht, Tom. "A Strategy for NUC." *NUC Newsletter* 4 (June 1, 1971): 2–5, 7.

Hecht, Tom. "Where From Here?" *NUC Newsletter* 5 (January 1972): 10–13.

Hecht, Tom, and Kessel, Barbara. "Spring Program." *NUC Newsletter* 3 (April 1, 1970): 1–3.

Hedges, Elaine. "Women in the Colleges: One Year Later." *College English* 34 (October 1972): 1–5.

Hogan, Homer. "English Studies and the Dialectics of Consumerism." *College English* 32 (December 1970): 261–69.

Hook, Sidney. "The Prospects of the Academy." In *The Radical Left: The Abuse of Discontent*, edited by William P. Gerberding and Duane E. Smith, pp. 201–11. Boston: Houghton Mifflin Co., 1970.

Horowitz, David. "Hand-Me-Down Marxism in the New Left." In *Weatherman*, edited by Harold Jacobs, pp. 97–103. Berkeley: Ramparts Press, 1970.

Horowitz, David. "Revolutionary Karma vs. Revolutionary Politics." *Ramparts* 9 (March 1971): 27–29, 33.

Howe, Florence. "A Report on Women and the Profession." *College English* 32 (May 1971): 847–54.

Howe, Florence. "What Success at MLA?" *NUC Newsletter* 2 (January 1969): 1, 18–20.

Howe, Florence. "Why Teach Poetry?—An Experiment." In *The Politics of Literature: Dissenting Essays on the Teaching of English*, edited by Louis Kampf and Paul Lauter, pp. 259–307. New York: Pantheon Books, 1970.

Howe, Florence, and Cantarow, Ellen. "What Happened at MLA: The Radical Perspective." *College English* 30 (March 1969): 484–87.

Ignatin, Noel. "Without a Science of Navigation We Cannot Sail in Stormy Seas." In *Debate Within SDS: RYM II vs. Weatherman*, pp. 31–44. Detroit: Radical Education Project, 1969.

Irons, Peter. "Prison Notes." In *The New Left: A Collection of Essays*, edited by Priscilla Long, pp. 114–27. Boston: Porter Sargent, 1969.

Jaffe, Naomi, and Dohrn, Bernardine. "The Look Is You." *New Left Notes* 3 (March 18, 1968): 5.

Jameson, Frederic. "The Great American Hunter, or, Ideological Content in the Novel." *College English* 34 (November 1972): 180–97.

Jenkins, William A. "Counciletter: Charting Our Course." *College English* 31 (April 1970): 757–58.

Johnson, Dale L. "On the Ideology of Campus Revolution." *Studies on the Left* 1 (1961): 73–75.

Kampf, Louis. "Cultural Elitism and the Study of Literature." *Papers of the Midwest Modern Language Association*, no. 2 (1972): 21–31.

Kampf, Louis. "Culture Without Criticism." *Massachusetts Review* 11 (Autumn 1970): 624–44.

Kampf, Louis. Foreword to *Counter-Tradition: A Reader in the Literature of Dissent and Alternatives*, edited by Sheila Delany. New York: Basic Books, 1971.

Kampf, Louis. "The Humanist Tradition in Eighteenth-Century England—And Today." *New Literary History* 3 (Autumn 1971): 157–70.

Kampf, Louis. "The Humanities and Inhumanities." *Nation* 207 (September 30, 1968): 309–15.

Kampf, Louis. " 'It's Alright, Ma (I'm Only Bleeding)': Literature and Language in the Academy." *PMLA* 87 (May 1972): 377–83.

Kampf, Louis. "Must We Have a Cultural Revolution?" *College Composition and Communication* 21 (October 1970): 245–49.

Kampf, Louis. "Notes Toward a Radical Culture." In *The New Left: A Collection of Essays*, edited by Priscilla Long, pp. 420–34. Boston: Porter Sargent, 1969.

Kampf, Louis. "The Scandal of Literary Scholarship." In *The Dissenting Academy*, edited by Theodore Roszak, pp. 43–61. New York: Pantheon Books, 1967.

Kampf, Louis, and Lauter, Paul. Introduction to *The Politics of Literature: Dissenting Essays on the Teaching of English*, edited by Louis Kampf and Paul Lauter, pp. 3–54. New York: Pantheon Books, 1970.

Kaye, Melanie. In *Female Studies VI: Closer to the Ground: Women's Classes, Criticisms, Programs–1972*, edited by Nancy Hoffman, Cynthia Secor, and Adrian Tinsley, p. 233. Old Westbury, N.Y.: Feminist Press, 1972.

Keddie, Wells. "Socialist Academics and Unions." *NUC Newsletter* 5:7 (n.d.): 6–12.

Keniston, Kenneth. "The Sources of Student Dissent." *Journal of Social Issues* 23 (July 1967): 108–37.

Kennedy, James G. "The Two European Cultures and the Necessary New Sense of Literature." *College English* 31 (March 1970): 571–602.

Kessel, Barbara. "The English Teacher as Civilizer." *NUC–MLC Newsletter* 1 (October 1969): 1, 3, 20.

Kessel, Barbara. "Free, Classless, and Urbane?" In *The Politics of Literature: Dissenting Essays on the Teaching of English*, edited by Louis Kampf and Paul Lauter, pp. 177–93. New York: Pantheon Books, 1970.

Kissinger, C. Clark. "SLID to Resistance: Part I." *New Left Notes* (June 19, 1968): 18.

Kleinhans, Chuck. "1 + 1 Is More Than 2: A Radical Proposal for Financing NUC." *NUC Newsletter* 4 (May 15, 1971): 2.

Klonsky, Mike. "Toward a Revolutionary Youth Movement." *New Left Notes* 3 (December 23, 1968): 3.

Klonsky, Mike, et. al. "Revolutionary Youth Movement II." In *Debate Within SDS: RYM II vs. Weatherman*, pp. 13–19. Detroit: Radical Education Project, 1969.

Kolko, Gabriel. "The Decline of American Radicalism in the Twentieth Century." *Studies on the Left* 6 (September–October 1966): 9–26.

Kopkind, Andrew. "Mystic Politics: Refugees from the New Left." *Ramparts* 12 (July 1973): 26–28, 47–50.

Labov, William. "The Logic of Nonstandard English." In *The Politics of Literature: Dissenting Essays on the Teaching of English*, edited by Louis Kampf and Paul Lauter, pp. 193–244. New York: Pantheon Books, 1970.

Lauter, Paul. "The Imperial Scholar." *College English* 30 (March 1969): 504–507.

Lazere, Donald. "Down with Culture?" *NUC–MLC Newsletter* 1 (December 1969): 1, 19.

Lemisch, Jesse. "What's Your Evidence? Radical Scholarship and Scientific Method and Anti-Authoritarianism, Not 'Relevance.' " In *On Radicals and Research*, pp. 9–12. Chicago: New University Conference, 1970.

Lemisch, Jesse. "Who Will Write a Left History of Art While We Are All Putting Our Balls on the Line?" *NUC Newsletter* 1 (May 24, 1968): 6.

Lens, Sidney. "The Road to Power and Beyond." *Liberation* 13 (November 1968): 8–15.

Lerner, Michael. "May Day: Anatomy of the Movement." *Ramparts* 10 (July 1971): 18–25, 40–42.

Lerner, Michael. "Why This Is the Right Time." *New American Movement* 1 (November–December 1971): 3, 14–15.

LeRoy, Gaylord. "Comment." *College English* 34 (November 1972): 266–68.

LeRoy, Gaylord. "Radical Criticism of Radical Literature." *NUC–MLC Newsletter* 1 (October 1969): 9, 18.

LeRoy, Gaylord. "The Radical Teacher in Our Discipline." *College English* 33 (April 1972): 756–64.

Lester, Julius. "Lester on the Movement." *Guardian*, April 27, 1968, 4.

"Let's Get Together: A Report from the Commission on Campus Organization." *NUC Newsletter* 1 (May 24, 1968): 3.

Levins, Richard. Open letter to Chandler Davis. In *On Radicals and Research*, p. 19. Chicago: New University Conference, 1970.

Levins, Rosario. "Letter of Resignation." *NUC Newsletter* 4 (January 21, 1971): 8–10.

Levitt, Moe. "Thoughts on NUC." *NUC Newsletter* 5 (January 1972): 2–9.

Lewis, C. S. "Learning in War-Time." In *The Weight of Glory*, pp. 43–54. Grand Rapids: Wm. B. Eerdmans Publishing Co., 1965.

Lynd, Staughton. "Academic Freedom and the First Amendment." *Radical Teacher*, no. 1 (April–May 1969): 23–28.

Lynd, Staughton. "Factionalism the New Left Can't Afford." *Liberation* 14 (March–April 1969): 5–6.

Lynd, Staughton. "A Good Society." *Guardian* (February 17, 1968): 6.

Lynd, Staughton. Introduction to *The New Left: A Collection of Essays*, edited by Priscilla Long. Boston: Porter Sargent, 1969.

Lynd, Staughton. "Lynd Bids Left Take Direct Action on Concrete Programs." *National Guardian* 17 (December 5, 1964): 7–8.

Lynd, Staughton. "The Movement: A New Beginning." *Liberation* 14 (May 1969): 6–20.

Lynd, Staughton. "Prospects for the New Left." *Liberation* 15 (January 1971): 13–28.

Lynd, Staughton. "The Responsibility of Radical Intellectuals." *NUC Newsletter* 1 (May 24, 1968): 5–6.

Lynd, Staughton. "Socialism, The Forbidden Word." *Studies on the Left* 3 (Summer 1963): 14–20.

Lynd, Staughton. Untitled. *NUC Newsletter* 3 (December 15, 1969): 9.

Mack, Maynard. "To See It Feelingly." *PMLA* 86 (May 1971): 362–74.

Mahaney, Ruth. "Women's Caucus." *NUC Newsletter* 4 (July 4, 1971): 4–5.

Mann, Eric. "Appraisal and Perspectives." *New Left Notes* 3 (March 18, 1968): 6–8.

Marcuse, Herbert. "Art in a One-Dimensional Society." In *Radical Perspectives in the Arts*, edited by Lee Baxandall, pp. 53–67. Baltimore: Penguin Books, 1972.

Marcuse, Herbert. "On the New Left." In *The New Left: A Documentary History*, edited by Massimo Teodori, pp. 468–73. Indianapolis: Bobbs–Merrill, 1969.

Marcuse, Herbert. "Repressive Tolerance." In Robert Paul Wolff, Barrington Moore, Jr., and Herbert Marcuse, *A Critique of Pure Tolerance*, pp. 81–117. Boston: Beacon Press, 1965.

McAfee, Kathy, and Wood, Myrna. "Bread and Roses." In *Female Liberation: History and Current Politics*, edited by Roberta Salper, pp. 153–69. New York: Alfred A. Knopf, 1972.

McDermott, John. "The Laying On of Culture." *Nation* 208 (March 10, 1969): 296–301.

McDermott, John. "NUC as Cadre." *NUC Newsletter* 3 (January 20, 1970): 6–8.

Mellen, Jim. "More on Youth Movement." In *Debate Within SDS: RYM II vs. Weatherman*, pp. 3–6. Detroit: Radical Education Project, 1969.

Meredith, Robert. "A Paradigmatic Case." *NUC–MLC Newsletter* 1 (December 1969): 10–11, 18.

Meredith, Robert. "Subverting Culture." *Radical Teacher*, no. 2 (December 30, 1969): 5–8.

Miller, James E., Jr. "The 'Classic' American Writers and the Radicalized Curriculum." *College English* 31 (March 1970): 565–70.

Miller, James E., Jr. "Counciletter: The NCTE and Politics." *College English* 32 (April 1971): 815–16.

Miller, James E., Jr. "Counciletter: Notes for an Anti-Curriculum in English." *College English* 33 (May 1972): 963–65.

Mills, C. Wright. "On the New Left." *Studies on the Left* 1 (1961): 63–72.

Misheloff, Ruth. "Modern Language Caucus News." *NUC Newsletter* 4 (September 15, 1970): 7–8.

"MLA Commission." *NUC–MLC Newsletter* 1:3 (1969): 9.

Moore, John. "Radical Academic Guide: Perspective for a Partisan Anthropology." *Liberation* 16 (November 1971): 34–43.

Munk, Michael. "New Left: The Ideological Bases." *National Guardian* 17 (September 25, 1965): 3–4.

Munk, Michael. "Perspectives on the New Left." *National Guardian* 17 (October 2, 1965): 6–7.

"New American Movement, The: A Way to Overcome the Mistakes of the Past." *Socialist Revolution* 2 (January–February 1971): 35–67.

"New University Conference Folds." *Guardian*, July 5, 1972, 3.

"New University Conference Organized." *NUC Newsletter* 1 (May 24, 1968): 1–2.

Novak, Michael. "God in the Colleges: The Dehumanization of the University." In *The New Student Left: An Anthology*, edited by Mitchell Cohen and Dennis Hale, pp. 258–70. Boston: Beacon Press, 1966.

O'Brien, James P. "The New Left's Early Years." *Radical America* 2 (May–June 1968): 1–25.

O'Flinn, J. P. "Orwell on Literature and Society." *College English* 31 (March 1970): 603–12.

Oglesby, Carl. "The Deserters: The Contemporary Defeat of Fiction." In *Radical Perspectives in the Arts*, edited by Lee Baxandall, pp. 33–52. Baltimore: Penguin Books, 1972.

Oglesby, Carl. "1969." In *Weatherman*, edited by Harold Jacobs, pp. 119–36. Berkeley: Ramparts Press, 1970.

Oglesby, Carl. "Notes on a Decade Ready for the Dustbin." *Liberation* 14 (August–September 1969): 5–19.

Oglesby, Carl. "The Revolted." In *The American Left: Radical Political Thought in the Twentieth Century,* edited by Loren Baritz, pp. 431–35. New York: Basic Books, 1971.

Oglesby, Carl. "Trapped in a System." In *The New Left: A Documentary History,* edited by Massimo Teodori, pp. 182–88. Indianapolis: Bobbs–Merrill, 1969.

Ohmann, Richard. "An Informal and Perhaps Unreliable Account of the Modern Language Association of America." *Antioch Review* 29 (Fall 1969): 329–47.

Ohmann, Richard. "Teaching and Studying Literature at the End of Ideology." In *The Politics of Literature: Dissenting Essays on the Teaching of English,* edited by Louis Kampf and Paul Lauter, pp. 130–59. New York: Pantheon Books, 1970.

O'Neil, Wayne. "The Politics of Bidialectalism." In *The Politics of Literature: Dissenting Essays on the Teaching of English,* edited by Louis Kampf and Paul Lauter, pp. 245–55. New York: Pantheon Books, 1970.

"Open Up the Schools Program, The." *NUC Papers 3: Open Up the Schools,* pp. 1–4. Chicago: New University Conference, 1971.

"Our Vision." *New American Movement* 1 (November–December 1971): 2.

Pardun, Bob. "On the Cadre in Mass Organization." *New Left Notes* 3 (June 10, 1968): 6–7.

Potter, Paul. "The 'Incredible' War." *National Guardian* 17 (April 24, 1965): 5.

Potter, Paul, and Benenson, Hal. "A Critique of Radical Perspectives on the Campus." *New Left Notes* 2 (May 29, 1967): 3–5.

Rader, Dotson. "Princeton Week-end with the SDS." *New Republic,* December 9, 1967, 15–16.

"Radical Teacher at Work, The: A Report from the Commission on Education and the University II." *NUC Newsletter* 1 (May 24, 1968): 7.

"Radicalism of Disclosure, The: A Statement by the Editors." *Studies on the Left* 1 (Fall 1959): 2–4.

Radinsky, Len. "How Men Discuss Sexism." *NUC Newsletter* 4 (July 4, 1971): 14–15.

Raina, M. L. "Marxism and Literature: A Select Bibliography." *College English* 34 (November 1972): 308–14.

Reck, Rima Drell. "The Politics of Literature." *PMLA* 85 (May 1970): 429–32.

"Resolutions Passed by the National Council of Teachers of English at the Fifty-ninth Annual Meeting, 1969." *College English* 31 (February 1970): 528–29.

Robinson, Lillian S. "Cultural Criticism and the Horror Vacui: Response to Sonja Wieta." *College English* 33 (March 1972): 731–35.

Robinson, Lillian S. "Dwelling in Decencies: Radical Criticism and the Feminist Perspective." *College English* 32 (May 1971): 879–89.

Robinson, Lillian S. "Who's Afraid of a Room of One's Own?" In *The Politics of Literature: Dissenting Essays on the Teaching of English*, edited by Louis Kampf and Paul Lauter, pp. 354–411. New York: Pantheon Books, 1970.

Robinson, Lillian S., and Vogel, Lise. "Modernism and History." *New Literary History* 3 (Autumn 1971): 177–99.

Rocker, Rudolf. "Anarcho-Syndicalism." In *The New Left: A Collection of Essays*, edited by Priscilla Long, pp. 43–55. Boston: Porter Sargent, 1969.

Ross, Bob. "Perspectives for the NUC." *NUC Newsletter* 1 (November 1968): 1, 3, 8–9, 18.

Roszak, Theodore. "On Academic Delinquency." In *The Dissenting Academy*, edited by Theodore Roszak, pp. 3–42. New York: Pantheon Books, 1967.

Rothenberg, Mel. "In Defense of Ideology." *NUC Newsletter* 3 (September 15, 1969): 5, 8.

Rothenberg, Mel. "SDS' Political Problems." *NUC Newsletter* 4 (May 15, 1971): 21–22.

Rothstein, Richie. "E.R.A.P. and How It Grew." In *SDS Goes to Work Again*, pp. 34–43. Ann Arbor: Radical Education Project, n.d.

Rothstein, Richard. "Evolution of the ERAP Organizers." In *The New Left: A Collection of Essays*, edited by Priscilla Long, pp. 272–88. Boston: Porter Sargent, 1969.

Rothstein, Richard. "Representative Democracy in SDS." *Liberation* 16 (February 1972): 10–17.

Rothstein, Richard. "Socialization in the High School." *NUC–MLC Newsletter* 1 (October 1969): 4, 18.

Rowntree, John and Margaret. "Youth as a Social Class." In *The New Left: A Documentary History*, edited by Massimo Teodori, pp. 418–25. Indianapolis: Bobbs–Merrill, 1969.

Rudich, Norman. Review of Peter Demetz, *Marx, Engels, and the Poets*. *College English* 31 (January 1970): 424–30.

Russell, Michele. "Erased, Debased, and Encased: The Dynamics of African Educational Colonization in America." *College English* 31 (April 1970): 671–81.

Russell, Michele. "A Future Direction for NUC?" *NUC Newsletter* 3 (April 1, 1970): 6–8, 12.

Salper, Roberta. "The Development of the American Women's Liberation Movement, 1967–71." In *Female Liberation: History and Current Politics*, edited by Roberta Salper, pp. 169–84. New York: Alfred A. Knopf, 1972.

Salper, Roberta. Introduction to *Female Liberation: History and Current Politics*, edited by Roberta Salper. New York: Alfred A. Knopf, 1972.

Salper, Roberta. "The Long March." *NUC Newsletter* 4 (September 15, 1970): 5–6.

Seliger, Michael. "Editorial: The New American Movement." *Liberation* 16 (January 1972): 4–5.

Sheehan, Carol. Open letter to Chandler Davis. In *On Radicals and Research,* pp. 16–17. Chicago: New University Conference, 1970.

Shils, Edward. "Ideology and Civility: On the Politics of the Intellectual." In *The Radical Left: The Abuse of Discontent,* edited by William P. Gerberding and Duane E. Smith, pp.104–37. Boston: Houghton Mifflin Co., 1970.

Shor, Ira. "Notes on Marxism and Method." *College English* 34 (November 1972): 173–77.

Shor, Ira. "Questions Marxists Ask about Literature." *College English* 34 (November 1972): 178–79.

Showalter, Elaine. "Women and the Literary Curriculum." *College English* 32 (May 1971): 855–62.

Sinclair, Hamish. "Diggers Jog SDS 'Grads.' " *National Guardian* 19 (July 1, 1967): 4.

Sklar, Martin J., and Weinstein, James. "Socialism and the New Left." *Studies on the Left* 6 (March–April 1966): 62–70.

Smith, Henry Nash. "Something Is Happening But You Don't Know What It Is, Do You, Mr. Jones?" *PMLA* 85 (May 1970): 417–22.

Smith, Jack A. "Report on SDS: Students Now Stressing 'Resistance.' " *National Guardian* 19 (April 8, 1967): 1, 8.

Smith, Jack A. "SDS Aim: To Build a Revolutionary Consciousness." *National Guardian* 19 (April 15, 1967): 5.

Smith, Jack A. "Where the Revolution Is At." *Guardian,* June 22, 1968, 1, 4–5.

Steege, Ted. Introduction to *Radicals in Professions: Selected Papers,* pp. 3–7. Ann Arbor: Radical Education Project, 1967.

Stevens, Carol. "SDS Convention Charts Projects for the Year." *National Guardian* 18 (January 15, 1966): 5.

Tax, Meredith. "Introductory: Culture Is Not Neutral, Whom Does It Serve?" In *Radical Perspectives in the Arts,* edited by Lee Baxandall, pp. 15–29. Baltimore: Penguin Books, 1972.

"Understanding Revolutionary Violence." *NUC Newsletter* 4 (October 1, 1970): 11–14.

Vicinus, Martha. "The Study of Nineteenth-Century British Working-Class Poetry." In *The Politics of Literature: Dissenting Essays on the Teaching of English,* edited by Louis Kampf and Paul Lauter, pp. 322–53. New York: Pantheon Books, 1970.

Vocations for Social Change, no. 22 (March–April 1971): 5.

Waskow, Arthur. "Business, Religion, and the Left." *Liberation* 14 (August–September 1968): 46–48.

Waskow, Arthur. "The Religious Upswelling of the New Left." *Liberation* 14 (July 1969): 36–37.

Wasson, Richard. "New Marxist Criticism: Introduction." *College English* 34 (November 1972): 169–72.

Wasson, Richard. Review of Theodore Roszak, *The Making of a Counter Culture*. *College English* 31 (March 1970): 624–28.

Watson, Will. "Transforming the University." *NUC Newsletter* 3 (January 20, 1970): 10–12.

Weber, John. "Murals as Peoples Art." *Liberation* 16 (September 1971): 42–48.

Weinstein, James. "Weatherman: A Lot of Thunder but a Short Reign." In *Weatherman*, edited by Harold Jacobs, pp. 379–93. Berkeley: Ramparts Press, 1970.

Weissman, Steve. "Beyond the Moral Imperative." *Liberation* 11 (August 1966): 43–48.

"Whence Cometh the Axe? An Editorial." *NUC Newsletter* 2 (January 1969): 1–2, 15, 21.

Whitebrook, Joel. "American Revolution and Socialist Tradition." Review of *Post-Scarcity Anarchism*, by Murray Bookchin. *Liberation* 16 (January 1972): 20–27.

"Why?—An Analysis." *New American Movement* 1 (n.d.): 2–4.

Wieck, David T. Preface to *Social Anarchism*, edited by Giovanni Baldelli. Chicago: Aldine–Atherton, 1971.

Wittman, Carl, and Hayden, Thomas. "An Interracial Movement of the Poor?" In *The New Student Left: An Anthology*, edited by Mitchell Cohen and Dennis Hale, pp. 180–219. Boston: Beacon Press, 1966.

Wolf, H. R. "The Classroom as Microcosm." *College English* 33 (December 1971): 259–67.

Wolfe, Alan. "On Higher Education." *NUC Newsletter* 4 (October 15, 1970): 9–10.

Wolfe, Robert. "Beyond Protest: Editorial Statement." *Studies on the Left* 7 (January–February 1967): 3–21.

Zimmerman, Bill. "Radical Practice in the Classroom." *NUC Newsletter* 5:7 (n.d.), 13–17.

Zinn, Howard. "Marxism and the New Left." In *The New Left: A Collection of Essays*, edited by Priscilla Long, pp. 56–68. Boston: Porter Sargent, 1969.

Zinn, Howard. "The Old Left and the New: Emancipation from Dogma." *Nation* 202 (April 4, 1966): 385–89.

Zweig, Mike. "Stony Brook: A Model." *NUC Newsletter* 3 (January 20, 1970): 12–13.

Pamphlets

Andrews, Barbara. "Problems of NUC." Chicago: New University Conference, n.d.

Booth, Paul. "A Basis for University Reform." Students for a Democratic Society, 1964.

Brochure. Socialist Scholars Conference, April 8, 1970.

Calvert, Greg, and Neiman, Carol. "The New Left." Ann Arbor: Radical Education Project, n.d.

"Crisis Paper: Violence, Non-Violence, and Change." Chicago: New University Conference, May 15, 1970.

Debate Within SDS: RYM II vs. Weatherman. Detroit: Radical Education Project, 1969.

Draper, Hal. "The Mind of Clark Kerr." Ann Arbor: Radical Education Project, n.d.

Gitlin, Todd. "The Politics and Vision of the New Left." San Francisco: Clergy and Laymen Radical Education Project, n.d.

Guide to College of Old Westbury, 1972.

Harold, Brent. "Beyond Student-Centered Teaching: The Dialectical Materialist Form of a Literature Course." Radical Caucus of the MLA, n.d.

Hecht, Tom. "The Spring National Committee Meeting: An Overview." Chicago: New University Conference, 1972.

Kissinger, C. Clark. "The S.D.S. Chapter Organizer's Handbook." N.p., n.d.

Lynd, Staughton. "Restructuring the University." Chicago: New University Conference, 1969.

Nicolaus, Martin. "The Iceberg Strategy: Universities and the Military-Industrial Complex." Ann Arbor: Radical Education Project, 1967.

NUC Papers 3: Open Up the Schools. Chicago: New University Conference, 1971.

On Radicals and Research. Chicago: New University Conference, 1970

"PLP: A Critique." Detroit: Radical Education Project, 1969.

Port Huron Statement. New York: Students for a Democratic Society, 1964.

Potter, Paul. "The Intellectual as an Agent of Social Change." Students for a Democratic Society, 1963.

Potter, Paul. "The New Radical Encounters the University." Students for a Democratic Society, n.d.

"Proposal on Colleges and Universities." New American Movement, n.d.

"Radical Education Project." Ann Arbor: Radical Education Project, 1966.

Radicals in Professions: Selected Papers. Ann Arbor: Radical Education Project, 1967.

SDS Goes to Work Again. Ann Arbor: Radical Education Project, n.d.

"Student Rebellion, The." Chicago: New University Conference, February 1969.

Wallach, Joan. "Chapter Programming." SDS National Council Meeting Working Papers, 1963.

Index